GOD
SPEAKS

GOD SPEAKS AGAIN

An Introduction to the Bahá'í Faith

Kenneth E. Bowers

Bahá'í
PUBLISHING

Wilmette, Illinois

Bahá'í Publishing, 415 Linden Avenue, Wilmette, IL 60091-2886
Copyright © 2004 by Kenneth E. Bowers
All rights reserved. Published 2004
Printed in the United States of America on acid-free paper ∞

09   08   07   5   4   3

Library of Congress Cataloging-in-Publication Data
Bowers, Kenneth E.
    God speaks again : an introduction to the Bahá'í Faith / by Kenneth E. Bowers.
        p. cm.
    Includes bibliographical references and index.
    ISBN 978-1-931847-12-4 (alk. paper)
        1. Bahai Faith. I. Title.

BP365.B64 2004
297.9'3—dc22
                                                                    2003062595

Cover design by Robert A. Reddy
Book design by Patrick J. Falso

IN LOVING MEMORY OF MY GRANDMOTHER,
DOROTHY DANIEL FORD

CONTENTS

Acknowledgments xi
A Note to the Reader 2
Introduction 3

Part 1: The Birth of the Bahá'í Faith

Chapter 1:   The Dawn 9
              The Search for the Promised One 13
              The Gate of God 15
Chapter 2:   "He Whom God Shall Make Manifest" 17
Chapter 3:   The Ministry of the Báb 21
Chapter 4:   The New Revelation 27
Chapter 5:   Exile 35
              Bahá'u'lláh's Arrival in Baghdad 39
              Revival of the Bábí Community 43
Chapter 6:   God and History................................... 47
              Mankind Has Always Rejected
              the Manifestations of God 48
              The People Blindly Follow the Clergy 49
              The True Standard for Judgment 51
Chapter 7:   Renewal of Opposition 53
Chapter 8:   The Declaration of Bahá'u'lláh 57
              Further Exile 58
              Crisis from Within 59
Chapter 9:   Proclamation to the Kings and Rulers 63
Chapter 10:   Further Banishment 71
              Arrival in 'Akká 72
              The Reason for Bahá'u'lláh's Imprisonment ... 75

Chapter 11:   Years of Confinement 77
              The Most Holy Book 80
              Departure from 'Akká 82

Part 2: Some Basic Teachings of Bahá'u'lláh

Chapter 12:   The Ocean of His Words 89
Chapter 13:   Spiritual Truths 93
              Progressive Revelation 96
              What Distinguishes the Prophets 99
              The Word of God 100
              The Significance of Bahá'u'lláh's Revelation 102
              God's Call to Humanity 105
Chapter 14:   The Reality of the Soul 107
              Heaven and Hell 109
Chapter 15:   The Path of Spiritual Progress 111
              True Freedom 113
              Self-Knowledge and Mastery of Self 114
              Detachment 115
              Purity and Uprightness of Conduct 116
              Justice 117
              Future Manifestations of God 119
Chapter 16:   Final Years 121
Chapter 17:   The Life of a Prophet 127

Part 3: Foundations of Unity

Chapter 18:   The Covenant 133
              The Center of the Covenant 139
Chapter 19:   The Ministry of 'Abdu'l-Bahá Begins 141
Chapter 20:   'Abdu'l-Bahá in the West 145
Chapter 21:   Some Other Basic Teachings 149
              The True Meaning of Life 150
              Prayer 151
              Fasting 152
              Reading the Sacred Writings 153
Chapter 22   The Principle of Oneness 157
              The Oneness of God and the Oneness of Religion 157
              The Oneness of Humanity 158
              The Equality of Women and Men 162
Chapter 23:   The Harmony of Religion and Science 169
Chapter 24:   More Principles for World Peace 175

The Independent Investigation of Truth 175
Universal Education 176
Elimination of Extremes of Wealth and Poverty 178
Universal Language 179
Other International Measures for Peace 180
Chapter 25:   Leading a More Meaningful Life 187
True Wealth 187
The Principle of Moderation 189
The Law of God 190
Work and Service 191
Marriage and Family 193
Health and Healing 195
Music and the Arts 196
Chapter 26:   Understanding Tests and Afflictions 199
Chapter 27:   'Abdu'l-Bahá's Final Years 203
Return to the Holy Land 204

Part 4: God's Promises Fulfilled
Chapter 28:   Building a New World 213
The Plan of God 215
The Bahá'í Administrative Order 218
Consultation 220
Duties of the Elected 222
Private Balloting/No Campaigning 222
The Duties of the Spiritual Assemblies 223
A New System of Governance 224
Unity in Diversity 225
Chapter 29:   The New Jerusalem 231
The Ministry of Christ 233
The Advent of God's Kingdom 236
Christ's Triumph 238
How Bahá'u'lláh Fulfilled Prophecy 238
Jesus as a Manifestation of God 239
Miracles 242
The Nature of Evil 242
Divine Forgiveness 243
The Unity of Religions 245
The Day of Judgment 246
The Kingdom of God 247
A Challenge for Further Study 249

Chapter 30:   The Call of the Promised One 251
              The Day of World Unity 253
              Being a Bahá'í 254
              Transformation as a Process 255
              The Spread of the Bahá'í Faith 256
              The Individual's Response to Bahá'u'lláh 259
Notes 261
Glossary 272
Bibliography 281
Suggested Reading 285
Index 287

ACKNOWLEDGMENTS

Most achievements of real value are the result of successful collaboration. To the extent that this volume has any merit, it is due to the outstanding contributions of scholars of the Bahá'í Faith past and present, whose works provided invaluable information and perspective, and to the encouragement and assistance of friends and colleagues. Its deficiencies, however, are entirely of my own making.

I am deeply grateful to learned and experienced friends who agreed to read and comment on the manuscript. First and foremost is Dr. David S. Ruhe, who offered detailed comments as well as access to unpublished manuscripts of his own that cover the early history of the Bahá'í Faith. His loving encouragement throughout the process meant more than I can say. I am also indebted to the following individuals for their encouragement and their helpful comments on the concept and the manuscript: Stephen Birkland, Alan Ford Bowers, Robert C. Henderson, Jack McCants, and Erica Toussaint. My thanks also to Juana C. Conrad, Caswell and Gwen Ellis, Rebecca Ellison, William Geissler, Jena Khodadad, Paul Lample, Shelley Rastall, and Tim Tyson for their loving encouragement.

This project was blessed with an extraordinary editorial team, led by Terry Cassiday. I wish to thank her for her encouragement and the high standards she maintained throughout the process. I am also grateful to the other members: Christopher Martin, Ladan Cockshut-Miller, and Martha Villagomez-Morrison. Thanks to you, it was a wonderful and educational experience. Thanks also to Lee Minnerly, general manager of Bahá'í Publishing, for his unfailing support and collegial spirit.

Lastly, I thank my parents for their love and encouragement for all my efforts; and my dear wife Mojgan and our beautiful children, Mojdeh and Ford, for their love, patience, and moral support. I love you all very much.

KENNETH E. BOWERS
Vernon Hills, Illinois
September 2003

GOD
SPEAKS
AGAIN

A NOTE TO THE READER

The system of transliterating Persian and Arabic terms that is followed in this book is one of several that are currently in use. It has been chosen because Shoghi Effendi, Guardian of the Bahá'í Faith, advocated its use for the sake of consistency.

However, place names that have well-established English equivalents (e.g., Baghdad, Tehran) are not transliterated unless they occur as part of a quotation that employs the Bahá'í system (Baghdád, Ṭihrán). The same is true for names of titles (sultan, shah, mulla), which are not transliterated unless they occur as part of a quotation or part of a transliterated name (Sulṭán 'Abdu'l-'Azíz, Mullá Ḥusayn).

INTRODUCTION

Human beings have always longed for a sense of purpose. We have ever been in search of the meaning of existence. We have always wanted to love and to be loved. We have always dreamed of peace. This is no less true today than in ancient times.

The twentieth century was born at a time when the forces of modernism were swiftly gaining momentum. Scientific, political, and cultural advances of that day contributed to an overwhelming sense that humanity was entering a new era. With these discoveries came not only hope for dramatic and uninterrupted progress, but also new philosophies, at the center of which stood man himself. Humanity was now, according to emerging thought, unloosed from the shackles of past traditions and dogmas, free to discover truth, and firmly in control of its destiny. In the conviction that happiness and prosperity were at long last within the reach of every individual, the pioneers of that age, especially in Europe and America, poised themselves to spread the benefits of enlightened civilization across the earth.

The present perspective, however, shows that the Modern Age has been a mixed blessing. In spite of humanity's many marvelous achievements, the fundamental goal of a peaceful and just society still seems to lie beyond our reach. Although conditions have certainly improved for many people, the vast majority of the world still languishes in desperate poverty while a few enjoy luxuries such as the Caesars could not have imagined. The very advances that have transformed the planet into a "global village" have also exacerbated age-old tensions between nations, religions, and ethnic groups and have provided the means for rivals to deal with each other on a scale so vast and by means so brutal as could scarcely have been imagined in a previous age. To these tensions can be added a steadily rising environmental destruction whose ultimate consequences, if the trend is not reversed, are dreadful to contemplate.

The ironies of modern life are present also in the nations that have gained the most. In the United States, for example, the top strata of society enjoy a standard of living and a level of personal freedom unparalleled in history. Yet a large proportion of the country's citizens seem perpetually excluded from this prosperity. There is hardly a household that has not been touched by the crimes and abuses that abound in that society, and the prevalence of mental and emotional disorders demonstrates that material well-being alone is no guarantor of happiness.

As we enter the new millennium, an increasing number of thoughtful people are realizing that the Modern Age might just as aptly be labeled the Age of Frustration. History has shown that the moral aspects of civilization do not automatically progress hand-in-hand with the material ones. More and more thinkers admit that science does not, after all, address inner spiritual needs. It has been learned that even the most advanced and progressive political systems can go only so far in ensuring justice—in other words, that morality cannot be legislated. And education, for all its value, does not equal wisdom if it does not include the moral dimension. Moreover, we are presented with a chaos of choices in the form of countless religions, creeds, political movements, and other belief systems, each laying claim to solutions to the issues of human happiness. In many respects we seem no closer than we ever were to the ideal of universal human prosperity.

Yet it is clear that the world needs a common ethical center. Humanity must have a frame of reference that ministers to practical and spiritual needs and that balances individual freedom with social responsibility. There must be a unifying moral force that provides the collective will necessary to address, once and for all, the problems that threaten not only our well-being but also our very existence.

Not long ago it was generally assumed among Western leaders of thought that religion was destined to die out as society advanced. For them religion was a relic of an ignorant and superstitious age, neither compatible with scientific reality nor in keeping with the needs of the times. In addition, there were and still are abundant examples of the destructive influence of religion carried to extremes. The idea of religion is now being reexamined. It has become increasingly acknowledged that, religious fanaticism notwithstanding, religion is a powerful force for good. Many have observed that most religions have certain essential aspects in common. All cultivate a sense of the transcendent, offer meaning and value to human life, and uphold an essentially universal set of moral and ethical values.

Yet no particular creed seems capable, in and of itself, of reconciling the vast diversity of humanity into the kind of moral system of which the world is now in dire need. The world needs a universal spiritual vision, with practical effects, that can provide both the continuity and the adaptability required for an age of transition.

The Bahá'í Faith offers just such a vision. It provides the answer to the hopes and expectations of countless philosophers, teachers, and religious leaders of the past and the present. It demonstrates that the promises in the sacred scriptures of the great religions of the world—promises of a day when justice and righteousness would be firmly established—are true and are now being fulfilled. It reaffirms that humanity has a destiny, that there is a God Who cares about us and has provided a way to achieve universal peace and salvation.

The history and teachings of the Bahá'í Faith center around the inspiring person of its Founder, Bahá'u'lláh. The traits of character that He displayed throughout the course of a long and turbulent life, His voluminous and comprehensive body of written works, and the impact that He has already had in the world qualify Him for a place in the firmament of history's greatest religious luminaries.

Bahá'u'lláh, Whose name in Arabic means "The Glory of God," claimed to be none other than the Promised One foretold in the sacred scriptures of all of the world's great religions. Bahá'u'lláh's spiritual and ethical teachings embrace all aspects of the human condition and offer the means to achieve the age-old dream of world peace.

Bahá'u'lláh taught that all humanity are the children of a loving God, Who has guided our spiritual and social evolution in progressive stages until the present era, which is destined to witness the unification of the world, universal justice, and the permanent establishment of peace. This is the age when God's promise of peace, as foretold in the scriptures of the world's great religions, will be fulfilled.

Bahá'u'lláh taught that each human being is endowed with an immortal soul. The purpose of this physical life is to develop the spiritual qualities necessary for the life hereafter. Yet this does not mean that we are to disdain this world. On the contrary, the means to spiritual life is through loving service to all of humanity as well as through cultivation of personal faith and virtues.

The teachings of Bahá'u'lláh affirm the eternal truths taught by all of the great religions of the past. His teachings uphold the validity and divine inspiration of the great Prophets and Messengers such as Moses, Jesus, and Muḥammad, all of Whom were sent by God for the purpose of guiding humanity. Bahá'u'lláh has given principles that address the needs of the present age. Among them is the oneness of humanity, a principle that, in and of itself, has vast moral and social implications. This principle of the oneness of humanity implies the equality of men and women as well as the equality of all races.

The harmony of science and religion is another essential teaching of Bahá'u'lláh, as is the principle of independent investigation of truth. Among others are the need for the elimination of all forms of prejudice, the elimination of the extremes of wealth and poverty, and the principle of compulsory education for all.

Yet another teaching of Bahá'u'lláh is that the time has come to establish a system of world order. Bahá'u'lláh designed a new system of governance, based upon the principles described above, that addresses the material and spiritual needs of humanity. This system is the nucleus and pattern for a new world civilization that will emerge in the fullness of time and will mark the establishment of God's Kingdom on earth.

At its heart, the Bahá'í Faith addresses the innermost longings of the human spirit. It proclaims God's continued presence in human affairs and the joyous news that the prophecies of ancient days are to be fulfilled. It tells of God's infinite and abiding love for each one of us, His assurance that divine justice will indeed reign, and His open call to a purposeful life in this world and eternal happiness in the world to come.

Today the Bahá'í Faith counts millions of followers in virtually every nation and territory on earth, firmly establishing it as a great new world religion. The achievements of this united global community, comprising the whole diversity of the human race, already portend the realization of mankind's ancient hopes for world peace and universal happiness.

This volume focuses on several essential themes. First and foremost, it chronicles the life of Bahá'u'lláh and other central figures in the history of the religion so that the reader may better appreciate their extraordinary lives and their historical context. Interspersed with this history are sections dealing with basic Bahá'í beliefs and teachings. Other chapters deal with the specific relationship of the Bahá'í Faith to Christianity, the rise and spread of the Bahá'í Faith throughout the world, the Bahá'í vision for world peace, and what being a Bahá'í means for the individual. The aim here is simply to offer an overview that can serve as a starting point for further study.

This is the story of the Bahá'í Faith. It is unique in the annals of religious history for the circumstances of its birth, the dramatic episodes that accompanied its rise and development, and the world-embracing character of its vision. The story begins in what might seem an unlikely time and place.

PART 1

THE BIRTH OF THE BAHÁ'Í FAITH

CHAPTER 1

THE DAWN

The Iranian plateau rises like an altar in the heart of the Asian continent, as if predestined to be the opening scene of the greatest spiritual drama in the history of the world. A crossroads of civilization since history was first recorded, its peoples have made pivotal contributions to the spiritual and cultural evolution of humanity.

This is the land where the ancient Faith of Zoroaster was founded, with its depiction of the epic struggle between the forces of good and evil that would greatly influence the thinking of Jewish and European philosophers in subsequent centuries. For a time, the prophet Daniel lived there and experienced his mysterious visions of the future deliverance of God's people. The Lord then bade him to "seal" these visions until "the time of the end." Centuries later, this region became one of the most fertile fields of Islamic thought, contributing more than its share of great scientists, poets, philosophers, and theologians, the fruits of whose efforts would eventually reach the countries of Europe and help to found the Renaissance. It was here that the S̲h̲í'ih branch of Islam gained its strongest foothold and here that certain leaders of religion anticipated the advent of God's Kingdom on earth.

In the years leading up to the Alexandrian Age (336–323 B.C.), the land now known as Iran—Persia, as it was then called—was the seat of a great civilization. This was followed in successive eras by a series of notable resurgences and declines. This pattern repeated itself until the era of the Industrial Revolution, when the fortunes of the nation took a steady and marked downfall.

By the nineteenth century of our era the glory of ancient Persia was a mere memory. Its once vast domain had shrunk to the dimensions with which we are now familiar. It was a decline all the more shocking to those who knew the splendors of her past. At a time when the countries of Europe and North America were embarking upon unprecedented technological, material, and political advancement, Persia remained tragically backward in outlook, unable to free herself from the mire of endemic political and religious corruption.

Lord Curzon, a contemporary European observer, described Persia as a "Church-State," held in the combined grip of civil and religious authorities whose rule was both tyrannical and arbitrary. Lord Curzon described a system of governance whose lubricant was simple, open bribery, affecting all transactions and rulings from the lowest village to the royal court. Ultimate authority lay in the hands of the shah, who wielded absolute power.

Another writer described the situation in this way:

> Venal, cruel, and immoral as it was, it was formally religious. Muslim orthodoxy was its basis and permeated to the core both it and the social lives of the people. But otherwise there were no laws, statutes, or charters to guide the direction of public affairs. There was no House of Lords nor Privy Council, no synod, no Parliament. The Sháh was despot, and his arbitrary rule was reflected all down the official scale through every minister and governor to the lowliest clerk or remotest headman. No civil tribunal existed to check or modify the power of the monarch or the authority which he might choose to delegate to his subordinates. If there was a law, it was his word. He could do as he pleased. It was his to appoint or to dismiss all ministers, officials, officers, and judges. He had power of life and death without appeal over all members of his household and of his court, whether civil or military. The right to take life was vested in him alone; and so were all the functions of government, legislative, executive, and judicial. His royal prerogative was limited by no written restraint whatever.
>
> Descendants of the Sháhs were thrust into the most lucrative posts throughout the country, and as the generations went by they filled innumerable minor posts too, far and wide, till the land was burdened with this race of royal drones who owed their position to nothing better than their blood and who gave rise to the Persian saying that "camels, fleas, and princes exist everywhere."[1]

This despotic rule was buttressed by a brutal penal system. Lord Curzon noted,

> "Before I quit the subject of the Persian law and its administration, let me add a few words upon the subject of penalties and prisons. Nothing is more shocking to the European reader, in pursuing his way through the crime-stained and bloody pages of Persian history during the last and, in a happily less degree, during the present century, than the record of savage punish-

ments and abominable tortures, testifying alternately to the callousness of the brute and the ingenuity of the fiend. The Persian character has ever been fertile in device and indifferent to suffering; and in the field of judicial executions it has found ample scope for the exercise of both attainments. Up till quite a recent period, well within the borders of the present reign, condemned criminals have been crucified, blown from guns, buried alive, impaled, shod like horses, torn asunder by being bound to the heads of two trees bent together and then allowed to spring back to their natural position, converted into human torches, flayed while living."[2]

On the subject of litigation he wrote,

"The ultimate court of appeal in each case is the king, of whose sovereign authority these subordinate exercises of jurisdiction are merely a delegation, although it is rare that a suppliant at any distance from the capital can make his complaint heard so far. . . . Justice, as dispensed in this fashion by the officers of government in Persia, obeys no law and follows no system. Publicity is the sole guarantee for fairness; but great is the scope, especially in the lower grades, for . . . the bribe. The dárúghis [magistrates] have the reputation of being both harsh and venal, and there are some who go so far as to say that there is not a sentence of an official in Persia, even of the higher ranks, that cannot be swayed by a pecuniary consideration."[3]

Lord Curzon summed up the thorough corruption of Persian government and society in these words:

". . . Under a twofold governing system, such as that of which I have now completed the description—namely, an administration in which every actor is, in different aspects, both the briber and the bribed; and a judicial procedure, without either a law or a law court—it will readily be understood that confidence in the Government is not likely to exist, that there is no personal sense of duty or pride of honour, no mutual trust or co-operation (except in the service of ill-doing), no disgrace in exposure, no credit in virtue, above all no national spirit or patriotism."[4]

By the mid-nineteenth century there were, to be sure, an increasing number of patriotic individuals determined that Persia should compete successfully against the rising powers of Europe and America. At this time both Russia and Great Britain were making incursions into the country and threatening to reduce it to subservience. In the light of the situation described above, however, one can easily imagine how difficult it was to meet the challenge of modernization. Almost every worthwhile project, whether in transportation, commerce, education, or other areas, eventually succumbed either to the weight of bureaucratic self-interest or to a cooling of royal support. The difficulty was exacerbated by a clergy that was determined to block any innovations that they deemed potentially detrimental to their prerogatives. Proponents of unwanted change were often dealt with mercilessly.

As bleak as conditions were, and as different as the culture appeared to be from that of the Western world, there was nevertheless an interesting parallel between their religious outlooks. In the early years of the nineteenth century peoples in all of these nations sensed that world history was entering upon a new era. Often this was linked to a sense of the impending fulfillment of ancient scriptural prophecies.

In North America and Europe many believed that the return of Christ was at hand. A number of well-known religious leaders and scholars went so far as to predict the precise year that He would come again to inaugurate the Kingdom of God on earth. A well-known example is that of the Reverend William Miller. Careful study of Biblical prophecy led him to the conclusion that the long-awaited day would come in 1843 or 1844. Tens of thousands in America believed this interpretation. Of course, Christ did not appear in the heavens, and so future generations would remember the episode as "the Great Disappointment." The Millerites were but one example of a number of millennial movements that were born and flourished in those years.

It was very much the same case in the Middle East, where new movements actively proclaimed the near advent of the Promised One of Islam.* Significant numbers of Muslims expected two Figures to appear, in rapid succession, and, in a manner similar to Christian expectations, to establish God's reign in the world. Siyyid Kázim, the leader of one of the best-known of these movements, declared that the time was very close at hand. He had come to this conclusion after careful study of the Koran and various other Islamic traditions concerning the Last Days. Around him gathered a large number of followers who undertook rigorous study and discipline to prepare themselves to recognize and follow the Promised One.

---

* Because of the complexity of Islamic prophecy, we will not deal with this subject in detail. Both Shí'ih and Sunni Islam anticipate the appearance of messianic figures who are to exercise specific functions related to the Day of Judgment. For the convenience of the reader, these are all captured by the phrase "Promised One," a designation also used in the Islamic world. For further reading, please see Moojan Momen, *Islam and the Bahá'í Faith* (Oxford: George Ronald, 2000).

The Search for the Promised One

As it happened, Siyyid Kázim passed away in the year 1843. Just before his death he called upon all of his leading disciples to scatter far and wide in search of the Promised One, Who, he asserted, was alive and preparing to announce His advent.

One of these disciples, widely regarded as the ablest of them all, was a Persian by the name of Mullá Husayn. Soon after his teacher's death he set out in his search. After a period of intense prayer and fasting, he felt inspired to go to the city of Shiraz in southern Persia. Almost immediately after arriving, a chain of remarkable events was set in motion. These were later recounted to an individual who wrote the most comprehensive history of these days. Here is that individual's account of Mullá Husayn's arrival in the city to which he had felt drawn "as if by a magnet":

> On that very day, a few hours before sunset, whilst walking outside the gate of the city, his [Mullá Husayn's] eyes fell suddenly upon a Youth of radiant countenance, who wore a green turban and who, advancing towards him, greeted him with a smile of loving welcome. He embraced Mullá Husayn with tender affection as though he had been his intimate and lifelong friend. Mullá Husayn thought Him at first to be a disciple of Siyyid Kázim who, on being informed of his approach to Shíráz, had come out to welcome him.[5]

Mullá Husayn is reported to have described what happened next as follows:

"The Youth who met me outside the gate of Shíráz overwhelmed me with expressions of affection and loving-kindness. He extended to me a warm invitation to visit His home, and there refresh myself after the fatigues of my journey. I prayed to be excused, pleading that my two companions had already arranged for my stay in that city, and were now awaiting my return. 'Commit them to the care of God,' was His reply; 'He will surely protect and watch over them.' Having spoken these words, He bade me follow Him. I was profoundly impressed by the gentle yet compelling manner in which that strange Youth spoke to me. As I followed Him, His gait, the charm of His voice, the dignity of His bearing, served to enhance my first impressions of this unexpected meeting.

"We soon found ourselves standing at the gate of a house of modest appearance. He knocked at the door, which was soon opened by an Ethiopian servant. 'Enter therein in peace, secure,' were His words as He crossed the threshold and motioned me to follow Him. His invitation, uttered with power and majesty, penetrated my soul. I thought it a good augury to be addressed in such words, standing as I did on the threshold of the first house I was entering in S̲h̲íráz, a city the very atmosphere of which had produced already an indescribable impression upon me. Might not my visit to this house, I thought to myself, enable me to draw nearer to the Object of my quest? Might it not hasten the termination of a period of intense longing, of strenuous search, of increasing anxiety, which such a quest involves? As I entered the house and followed my Host to His chamber, a feeling of unutterable joy invaded my being. Immediately we were seated, He ordered a ewer of water to be brought, and bade me wash away from my hands and feet the stains of travel. I pleaded permission to retire from His presence and perform my ablutions in an adjoining room. He refused to grant my request, and proceeded to pour the water over my hands. He then gave me to drink of a refreshing beverage, after which He asked for the samovar and Himself prepared the tea which He offered me.

". . . It was about an hour after sunset when my youthful Host began to converse with me. . . .

"I sat spellbound by His utterance, oblivious of time and of those who awaited me. Suddenly the call . . . summoning the faithful to their morning prayer, awakened me from the state of ecstasy into which I seemed to have fallen. All the delights, all the ineffable glories, which the Almighty has recounted in His Book as the priceless possessions of the people of Paradise— these I seemed to be experiencing that night. Methinks I was in a place of which it could be truly said: 'Therein no toil shall reach us, and therein no weariness shall touch us'; 'No vain discourse shall they hear therein, nor any falsehood, but only the cry, "Peace! Peace!"'; 'Their cry therein shall be, "Glory be to Thee, O God!" and their salutation therein, "Peace!" And the close of their cry, "Praise be to God, Lord of all creatures!"'

"Sleep had departed from me that night. I was enthralled by the music of that voice which rose and fell as He chanted; . . . again acquiring ethereal, subtle harmonies as He uttered the prayers He was revealing. . . .

"He then addressed me in these words: 'O thou who art the first to believe in Me! Verily I say, I am the Báb, the Gate of God.' . . .

"This Revelation, so suddenly and impetuously thrust upon me, came as a thunderbolt which, for a time, seemed to have benumbed my faculties. I was blinded by its dazzling splendour and overwhelmed by its crushing force. Excitement, joy, awe, and wonder stirred the depths of my soul. Predominant among these emotions was a sense of gladness and strength which seemed to have transfigured me. How feeble and impotent, how dejected and timid,

I had felt previously! Then I could neither write nor walk, so tremulous were my hands and feet. Now, however, the knowledge of His Revelation had galvanised my being. I felt possessed of such courage and power that were the world, all its peoples and its potentates, to rise against me, I would, alone and undaunted, withstand their onslaught. The universe seemed but a handful of dust in my grasp. I seemed to be the Voice of Gabriel personified, calling unto all mankind: 'Awake, for, lo! the morning Light has broken. Arise, for His Cause is made manifest. The portal of His grace is open wide; enter therein, O peoples of the world! For He who is your promised One is come!'

"In such a state I left His house and joined my brother and nephew. . . . Ecclesiastical dignitaries and officials of the city also came to visit me. They marvelled at the spirit which my lectures revealed, unaware that the Source whence my knowledge flowed was none other than He whose advent they, for the most part, were eagerly awaiting."[6]

The Gate of God

The Person Whom Mullá Ḥusayn met and then recognized as the Promised One was a young man by the name of 'Alí-Muḥammad. His green turban indicated He was a siyyid, a descendant of the Prophet Muḥammad. Until this point He had been relatively unknown except to friends and associates in His native city of Shiraz. A merchant by profession, He had not received extensive religious training and had never even completed elementary school.

But His knowledge and character were well known to His friends and family. He was possessed of intellectual abilities and spiritual qualities that many considered miraculous. These were evident even in His writings, in both Persian and Arabic, which in the latter case were often compared to the Koran itself in their power and eloquence. One person who made His acquaintance in the years before His declaration recounted the following:

"I was enabled to meet the Báb on several occasions. Every time I met Him, I found Him in such a state of humility and lowliness as words fail me to describe. His downcast eyes, His extreme courtesy, and the serene expression of His face made an indelible impression upon my soul. I often heard those who were closely associated with Him testify to the purity of His character, to the charm of His manners, to His self-effacement, to His high integrity, and to His extreme devotion to God."[7]

He made His mission known first to Mullá Ḥusayn and then to a small circle of individuals who had likewise sought Him out. To them He announced that He was the "Gate of God," or in Arabic, the Báb.

At the heart of the Báb's claim were two themes: first, that He was the latest Messenger of God, sent to reveal a new religion on the same order as Christianity and Islam; and second, that He was the Herald of a still greater revelation, infinitely more significant than His own, which would be the fulfillment of past prophecies concerning the establishment of the Kingdom of God on earth. The Messenger of that revelation, He said, would come swiftly, but not until after He Himself had suffered martyrdom. He referred to the second Messenger, among other titles, as "He Whom God shall make manifest."

Addressing His little band of early disciples, the Báb told them to go out into the cities and regions of Persia and Iraq to proclaim His advent. With His words ringing in their ears, the disciples set out to accomplish their mission. The entire country soon came to learn of the Báb and was shaken to its depths.

The Báb was about twenty-five years old when He began His teaching. Over the course of the next several years tens of thousands of people would accept the new faith, eagerly anticipating the appearance of the One to come after the Báb.

CHAPTER 2

"HE WHOM GOD SHALL MAKE MANIFEST"

The Báb set out in October 1844 for Mecca and Medina, the holy cities of Islam, to make a pilgrimage and to publicly proclaim His mission. Before leaving He gave special instructions to Mullá Ḥusayn. Mullá Ḥusayn was told to proceed to Tehran, in the northern part of the country, a "city," said the Báb, "which enshrines a Mystery of . . . transcendent holiness. . . ."[1] Mullá Ḥusayn immediately set out on the long journey northward, proclaiming the new religion in every city along the way.

A few people who heard the new message became believers. For the most part, they were ordinary individuals, not members of the clergy or nobility. The members of these higher classes generally treated Mullá Ḥusayn with disdain, and in the coming years, this disdain grew to a level of hostility that led to barbaric cruelties against the followers of the Báb, who were known as Bábís.

In Tehran he received similar treatment at the hands of the religious leaders. One individual, observing the rude behavior of his own religious teacher, sought out Mullá Ḥusayn privately to investigate the new religion. In the course of this interview Mullá Ḥusayn asked about the son of a prominent nobleman known throughout the region for humanitarian activity. Mullá Ḥusayn requested his new friend to present a copy of some of the Báb's writings to that distinguished person.

The moment this person read a passage from the Báb's writings, He declared Himself a believer. He arose forthwith to proclaim His newfound faith. From that moment forward, His life would be dedicated to the spread of the new Cause.

His name was Mírzá Ḥusayn-'Alí. He was from the province of Núr in northern Persia. The son of a wealthy and renowned public figure, He had a noble and ancient lineage that traced its roots to the great dynasties of Persia as well as to

Abraham. His father, now deceased, had been highly regarded by the shah and the upper echelons of Persian society for his administrative prowess and for his cultural attainments.

There is a story about Mírzá Ḥusayn-'Alí's father. One day he had a vivid dream about his son, Who at the time was a small child. In that dream he saw Him swimming in a vast ocean, His body radiating light. As the boy swam through the water, His long black hair streamed out around Him. Then a multitude of fishes approached Him, each catching hold of one of the hairs of His head. But the boy swam on as freely as before, unharmed, the combined effort of the fishes unable to slow or deter Him.

Impressed by the dream, the father sought out a local soothsayer. The man told him that the dream signified that his son was destined to arouse great turmoil among the peoples of the earth, and that many would arise and oppose Him with the intention of destroying Him. But God's unfailing protection was with the boy, Who would, singlehandedly and alone, prevail over the entire world.

That boy was Mírzá Ḥusayn-'Alí, and as time passed, He showed increasing evidence of extraordinary talents and personal qualities.

His knowledge was immense from an early age, but it was not acquired through formal schooling. In addition, He possessed a remarkable degree of wisdom and spiritual perception. This was especially noticeable in relation to religious matters, although He never received more than rudimentary training in Islam, the state religion of Persia. Throughout childhood and adolescence He had encounters with Muslim clergymen, many of which have been recorded. In those days, religious discourse and leadership were the exclusive province of the clergy, who treated all who were not similarly educated with arrogance and disdain. Witnesses to these occasions were astonished at His ability to explain satisfactorily problems of theology that men who had dedicated their entire lives to religious study had proven incapable of unraveling. These same people were awed at His eloquence and especially at His apparently effortless mastery of Arabic, the language of the Koran. Competency in that language normally required years and years of rigorous study.

The brilliant qualities of His mind were matched by genuine love and compassion for all people. He was particularly sensitive to the plight of the poor and was widely known for His philanthropic efforts to relieve their sufferings. He had a keen aversion to injustice and from early childhood expressed hopes for a transformation in society that would provide justice for all. So great was the esteem in which He was held by the local population that by the time He was a young man He was known far and wide as "The Father of the Poor."[2]

Like the Báb, the charm of His personality exerted a magnetic influence on all who came into contact with Him. He was constantly surrounded by friends and admirers from every background, high and low. This prompted envious comments from some. Others, including one Persian prime minister, commented on His outstanding character, predicting that He would rise high in the world.

But the most unusual of His traits was an utter detachment from material things and worldy interests. Possessed of wealth, lineage, and ability, He could have risen to the highest spheres of power had He so chosen. Instead, He occupied Himself with service to others. When Mírzá Ḥusayn-'Alí was twenty-two, His father passed away, and He was offered the high government post that His father had occupied. To the surprise of many, He refused the offer. The prime minister is reported to have said, "'Leave him to himself. Such a position is unworthy of him. He has some higher aim in view. I cannot understand him, but I am convinced he is destined for some lofty career. His thoughts are not like ours. Let him alone.'"[3]

No one could have imagined the extraordinary destiny that was in store for Him. In 1844, at the age of twenty-seven, He joined the ranks of the Bábís. The new movement soon grew into a religious revival that would cause unprecedented turmoil in the nation. In the turbulent years ahead, Mírzá Ḥusayn-'Alí, later to be known by the title Bahá'u'lláh (meaning "The Glory of God"), would emerge as its most outstanding supporter, forfeiting position, wealth, prestige, and every hope of worldly prosperity. He would suffer all manner of humiliating afflictions but would survive undaunted and undismayed. Exiled to another land, He would, over the course of some four decades, proclaim and establish a new religion under circumstances unparalleled in religious history.

CHAPTER 3

THE MINISTRY OF THE BÁB

The ministry of the Báb lasted for six years. After His pilgrimage the Báb remained in Shiraz until 1846. Upon hearing reports about the Báb, the shah dispatched a leading Islamic clergyman to investigate the new religion on his behalf. This individual, known to history as Vaḥíd, succeeded in meeting the Báb. He soon became a believer and reported to the shah accordingly, requesting that an interview be arranged between the Báb and the shah. But no meeting with the shah ever occurred. Vaḥíd would later die for his beliefs.

In 1846 the Báb was expelled from His native city of Shiraz by the governor, who was angered by the tumult the Báb had raised. The Báb went from there to the city of Isfahan, where He gained the allegiance of many citizens, thereby incurring the opposition of most of the clergy. The clamor stirred up by the latter group became so great that the Báb's life was threatened. The governor of this city, however, became very attached to the Báb and secretly became a believer. The governor was so powerful that nobody dared to harm the Báb while He was under his protection. The governor eventually conceived a scheme whereby the Báb would attain an audience with the shah, and he personally vowed to devote all of his wealth and resources to the advancement of the new religion.

The Báb thanked the governor for this offer but then predicted that his days on earth would end very soon. He assured the governor that God would reward his intentions but that His own destiny was to suffer martyrdom. Within a very short time the governor passed away after a sudden illness.

Before his death, the governor had made preparations for the Báb to be escorted to Tehran to meet the shah. The Báb set out on this journey under armed escort. But this attempt to have the Báb meet the shah also failed. The prime minister, deeply afraid that the Báb would convince the shah of the truth of the new religion, managed to convince the sovereign to postpone the interview. Instead of going to Tehran, the Báb was sent to the northwestern province of Azerbaijan, where He was incarcerated in a fortress known as Máh-Kú. In this way the prime minister averted what to him was a serious threat to his own power. He believed that, had the sovereign accepted the new religion, it would have meant the end of his own influence.

Meanwhile, news of the newly born faith spread to every corner of the country and into the neighboring Ottoman domains. News accounts even appeared in the journals of Europe and North America. As time passed, the Báb revealed a constant stream of sacred scripture.* His main theme was anticipation of "Him Whom God shall make manifest." But the Báb also revealed new laws and teachings designed to make a deliberate break with Islam and establish the new faith as an independent religion.

His specific teachings addressed, among other things, the high station of women, the need for social and political reform, and the anticipation of a new era in human history that would witness the establishment of universal justice and brotherhood. He also abrogated many Islamic laws, calling openly for the clergy and citizenry to submit to His authority as a Messenger of God. In such ways He sought to prepare His followers and His countrymen for the new age that was now dawning.

The Báb's extraordinary claim, complemented by a revolutionary break with past traditions, was welcomed by those who saw the need for sweeping social and religious change, and who also recognized the Báb as One sent by God to establish righteousness. To this was added the Báb's astonishing boldness combined with an almost irresistible personal magnetism. As the Báb made His way towards Azerbaijan from city to city, and later while under strict confinement, tales began to spread of His charming personality, His courage, and His phenomenal knowledge. People who had seen and met Him related overwhelming spiritual experiences. There were also stories of miraculous cures and other supernatural feats. The time came when He could not enter a city without being mobbed by citizens eager to gaze upon Him. Some went so far as to carry away the water that He used to wash Himself before prayers, believing that it contained special powers.

But this was a country in the grip of narrowness and fanaticism. Its leaders, alarmed at the Báb's rapidly rising popularity and fearing for their own positions, unleashed a fury of hatred against Him and His followers. They were easily able to do so through civil and legal means, as well as by appealing to the baser instincts of a largely ignorant and benighted populace. Before long many of the Báb's fol-

---

* The term "revealed" is used to indicate that the Báb's writings are the Word of God revealed to humanity. In this volume we will frequently use this and the term "revelation" to distinguish the writings of God's Messengers from those of ordinary human beings.

lowers were killed, mainly at the instigation of the clergy, but with the support of civil authorities. Yet the Báb's popularity only seemed to grow, notwithstanding His imprisonment in a remote outpost and His resulting inaccessibility to His followers. The time came when it was clear to the prime minister of the shah that his only recourse was to bring about the Báb's death.

The Báb was summoned to the provincial capital, Tabriz. There He was interrogated by leading members of the clergy and civil authorities. He was taken to a large assemblage that included the crown prince. The historian Nabíl relates that as He entered, "The majesty of His gait, the expression of overpowering confidence which sat upon His brow—above all, the spirit of power which shone from His whole being, appeared to have for a moment crushed the soul out of the body of those whom He had greeted. A deep, a mysterious silence, suddenly fell upon them. Not one soul in that distinguished assembly dared breathe a single word."[1]

Finally, the leading divine who was presiding over the meeting asked, "Whom do you claim to be, and what is the message which you have brought?"

The Báb answered:

"I am, I am, I am, the promised One! I am the One whose name you have for a thousand years invoked, at whose mention you have risen, whose advent you have longed to witness, and the hour of whose Revelation you have prayed God to hasten. Verily I say, it is incumbent upon the peoples of both the East and the West to obey My word and to pledge allegiance to My person."[2]

This stunning pronouncement was followed by a series of questions to which the Báb responded with courage and composure. Most of those present were deeply hostile, yet they failed to intimidate Him or to prevail in debate. Nevertheless, they pronounced sentence against Him. The Báb was forced to endure the bastinado. In this punishment a person is suspended upside down, then heavy rods are used to beat the soles of the feet. This punishment was inflicted personally by the leading clergyman of Tabriz. After this the Báb was returned to confinement.

At about this time the Báb came into contact with the only European ever known to have met and left a description of Him. This person, Dr. Cormick, was an English physician called upon by the Persian authorities to pronounce on the Báb's mental condition. He wrote a letter to another physician describing his encounters. "'You ask me,'" wrote the doctor,

"for some particulars of my interview with the founder of the sect known as Bábís. Nothing of any importance transpired in this interview, as the Báb was aware of my having been sent with two other Persian doctors to see whether he was of sane mind or merely a madman, to decide the question whether he was to be put to death or not. With this knowledge he was loth to answer any questions put to him. To all enquiries he merely regarded us with a mild look, chanting in a low melodious voice some hymns, I suppose. Two other Siyyids, his intimate friends, were also present, who subsequently were put to death with him, besides a couple of government officials. He only deigned to answer me, on my saying that I was not a Musulman and was willing to know something about his religion, as I might perhaps be inclined to adopt it. He regarded me very intently on my saying this, and replied that he had no doubt of all Europeans coming over to his religion. Our report to the Sháh at that time was of a nature to spare his life. He was put to death some time after by the order of the Amír-Niẓám, Mírzá Taqí Khán. On our report he merely got the bastinado, in which operation a farrásh, whether intentionally or not, struck him across the face with the stick destined for his feet, which produced a great wound and swelling of the face. On being asked whether a Persian surgeon should be brought to treat him, he expressed a desire that I should be sent for, and I accordingly treated him for a few days, but in the interviews consequent on this I could never get him to have a confidential chat with me, as some government people were always present, he being a prisoner. He was a very mild and delicate-looking man, rather small in stature and very fair for a Persian, with a melodious soft voice, which struck me much. Being a Siyyid [a descendant of the Prophet Muḥammad], he was dressed in the habit of that sect, as were also his two companions. In fact his whole look and deportment went far to dispose one in his favour. Of his doctrine I heard nothing from his own lips, although the idea was that there existed in his religion a certain approach to Christianity. He was seen by some Armenian carpenters, who were sent to make some repairs in his prison, reading the Bible, and he took no pains to conceal it, but on the contrary told them of it. Most assuredly the Musulman fanaticism does not exist in his religion, as applied to Christians, nor is there that restraint of females that now exists."[3]

Over the course of the next several months the persecutions of the Bábís intensified. Hundreds were killed in various corners of the country. At last, the new prime minister, serving the recently crowned Náṣiri'd-Dín Sháh, decided that the Báb must die in the interests of the state. In collusion with the religious leaders in Tabriz, the warrant was signed and the Báb was brought into a barracks inside the city to face execution by firing squad. Not only did the Báb receive this news calmly; those who were with Him later recalled that He was more joyful than ever, now that His mission was reaching its climax.

The regiment assigned to execute the Báb was Armenian. Its commander, him-self a Christian, observed the character of the Báb and was overcome with grave misgivings about the order to have Him killed. He feared that such an act would incur the wrath of God. As the dreaded moment drew near, he approached the Báb. "'I profess the Christian Faith,'" he said, "'and entertain no ill will against you. If your Cause be the Cause of Truth, enable me to free myself from the obligation to shed your blood.'"[4] "'Follow your instructions,'" the Báb replied, "'and if your intention be sincere, the Almighty is surely able to relieve you from your perplexity.'"[5]

The Báb and one of His companions were suspended on a wall in the barracks square, facing a full regiment of soldiers. Thousands of onlookers had gathered to view the execution, some perhaps waiting to see if the Báb would miraculously save Himself. The commander gave the order to fire. Three ranks of soldiers, each numbering two hundred and fifty, discharged their rifles. As the smoke cleared, the crowd was astonished to see the Báb's companion standing alone and un-harmed in front of the wall. The ropes that had suspended the two had been cut to pieces by the bullets, but the young man was uninjured. The Báb was nowhere to be seen.

A frenzy ensued, but soon the Báb was found in His cell, conversing with a few of His followers. The Christian commander left with his regiment, refusing to play any further part in the affair. A second regiment—this one under a Muslim commander—was then summoned, and the Báb and His companion were sus-pended once again.

As the order to fire was about to be given, the Báb addressed the throng of onlookers:

> "Had you believed in Me, O wayward generation, every one of you would have followed the example of this youth, who stood in rank above most of you, and willingly would have sacrificed himself in My path. The day will come when you will have recognised Me; that day I shall have ceased to be with you."[6]

This time the bullets had the intended effect. The Báb and His disciple were shattered into one mass of flesh. At the very moment of execution the entire city was engulfed in a gale that obscured the light of the sun for the rest of the day. The authorities removed the mangled bodies to a moat outside the city and placed them under heavy guard. Nevertheless, a few devoted followers were able to steal past the guards and make off with the precious remains. Because of the dangers of that time, the Báb's remains would be concealed for many years, not to be perma-nently interred until more than half a century later.

It is worth noting that the prime minister who ordered the execution soon met with a disgraceful death at the hands of his own sovereign. The clergyman who inflicted the bastinado upon the Báb was visited by a fatal illness not long after the Báb's death. Even the regiment that killed Him met a grim fate. Five hundred of them were themselves executed after an attempted mutiny. The other two hundred and fifty were killed when a wall suddenly collapsed on them, leaving not one survivor. Some observers could not help but note the connection that all of them had played a role in the martyrdom of the Báb.

CHAPTER 4

THE NEW REVELATION

The Báb was executed on July 9, 1850. By this time many of His most devoted followers had also been killed, including Mullá Ḥusayn, the first to believe in Him. Those who still survived anticipated the fulfillment of the Báb's prophecies concerning the appearance of still another Messenger, Who was destined to bring about God's Kingdom on earth. One reference is the following:

"Of all the tributes I have paid to Him Who is to come after Me, the greatest is this, My written confession, that no words of Mine can adequately describe Him, nor can any reference to Him in my Book . . . do justice to His Cause."[1]

Elsewhere the Báb had alluded to the imminent appearance of "Him Whom God will make manifest":

"Wait thou until nine [years] will have elapsed. . . . Then exclaim: 'Blessed, therefore, be God, the most excellent of Makers!'"[2]

Yet another instance is this:

"Well is it with him who fixeth his gaze upon the Order of Bahá'u'lláh, and rendereth thanks unto his Lord. For He will assuredly be made manifest. God hath indeed irrevocably ordained it. . . ."[3]

Over the course of the eventful years leading up to this point, Mírzá Ḥusayn-'Alí had risen to high prominence among the Bábís. He had taught the new Faith with exemplary courage, facing many dangers without softening His resolve. Twice

He was imprisoned and once suffered the bastinado at the hands of the clergy. By 1848 He had become known as Jináb-i-Bahá ("His Honor Bahá," the latter word meaning "glory" or "splendor"), a title that had been approved by the Báb. Later, and forever after, He would be known as Bahá'u'lláh, meaning "The Glory of God." He had received many messages of praise from the Báb and had been entrusted by Him to undertake various important matters. Because of His outstanding qualities of leadership, His wisdom and courage, He enjoyed an esteem among the Bábís that amounted to reverence. There were a few who suspected that He was none other than the One Whose appearance the Báb had foretold.

Two years after the death of the Báb a new tragedy engulfed the community of His followers. Three Bábí youths, blaming the shah for all of the tribulations that had been visited upon the Báb and His followers, waylaid the king at his summer resort near Tehran and attempted to assassinate him. The young men were by no means professional killers. Indeed, they were not at all competent, as the clumsy manner of their attempt revealed. Inadequate weapons—short daggers and pistols loaded with tiny birdshot—caused only superficial injuries to the sovereign. The three were easily subdued by the shah's guard and were soon killed.

It was quickly established that the number of other conspirators was limited. The instigator of the plot made a full confession before his death, convincing the authorities that Bahá'u'lláh, well known as the most prominent leader of the Bábís, was completely innocent. Nevertheless, as word of the attempted murder spread through the city, the entire community of Bábís was sought out for destruction. The shah's mother was among those who cried out the loudest for their blood, and she specifically singled out Bahá'u'lláh, refusing to believe that He had not been complicit.

The new prime minister himself warned Bahá'u'lláh that He was being sought. At that time He was staying in the vicinity of Tehran as the guest of the minister, who was also a distant relative. His friends offered to hide Him from the authorities, but Bahá'u'lláh refused. Instead of fleeing, He set out towards the headquarters of the imperial army, near Tehran.

Hearing of Bahá'u'lláh's approach toward the city, the shah ordered His arrest. Seized and chained, Bahá'u'lláh was led to prison. Years later, in a letter addressed to one of the leading divines of Persia, He recalled the episode:

> By the righteousness of God! We were in no wise connected with that evil deed, and Our innocence was indisputably established by the tribunals. Nevertheless, they apprehended Us, and from Níyávarán, which was then the residence of His Majesty, conducted Us, on foot and in chains, with bared head and bare feet, to the dungeon of Tihrán. A brutal man, accom-

panying Us on horseback, snatched off Our hat, whilst We were being hurried along by a troop of executioners and officials.[4]

Crowds gathered along the way to jeer and insult Him. Some even pelted Him with stones. Among His persecutors on this occasion was an old woman who attempted to strike Him with a stone. She was frail, however, and could not keep pace. She begged the guards to give her the chance to fling her stone at Bahá'u'lláh's face. Seeing this, Bahá'u'lláh said to the guards, "'Suffer not this woman to be disappointed. Deny her not what she regards as a meritorious act in the sight of God.'"[5]

Bahá'u'lláh was thrown into the Black Pit, an infamous dungeon in Tehran. A number of other Bábís had also been arrested and were chained together with Him in the dungeon. Bahá'u'lláh later described this experience:

> We were consigned for four months to a place foul beyond comparison. As to the dungeon in which this Wronged One and others similarly wronged were confined, a dark and narrow pit were preferable. Upon Our arrival We were first conducted along a pitch-black corridor, from whence We descended three steep flights of stairs to the place of confinement assigned to Us. The dungeon was wrapped in thick darkness, and Our fellow prisoners numbered nearly a hundred and fifty souls: thieves, assassins and highwaymen. Though crowded, it had no other outlet than the passage by which We entered. No pen can depict that place, nor any tongue describe its loathsome smell. Most of these men had neither clothes nor bedding to lie on. God alone knoweth what befell Us in that most foul-smelling and gloomy place![6]

Bahá'u'lláh was forced to wear constantly one or the other of two heavy chains. So great was their weight that they left Him scarred for the rest of His life.

One of the witnesses to the horrible toll these sufferings took on Bahá'u'lláh was His own son. A boy of only eight years at the time, he was allowed to see his Father briefly at the prison. The sight of his Father struggling under the weight of the chains was heartrending and would remain a vivid memory for the remainder of his life.

Bahá'u'lláh's immediate family was not exempt from the tide of revenge that swept Tehran and its environs. Overnight His wife and children found themselves destitute, virtually every earthly possession having been taken away by the mob. At one point their deprivation was so severe that Bahá'u'lláh's wife, Navváb, could find no other food than dry flour, which she poured into the palms of her children for them to eat.

Other Bábís shared similar sufferings, and hundreds, absolutely innocent of any wrongdoing, were put to death in circumstances of extreme cruelty. Many of the executions were recorded in the government gazette in celebratory terms. The bloodbath inevitably attracted the attention of foreign visitors, virtually all of whom commented with horror on the injustices being perpetrated against the Bábís. These observers left many written accounts. One of them was penned by an Austrian officer, Captain von Goumoens, at the time in the employment of the shah. He resigned in disgust over the atrocities being committed against the Bábís. The captain wrote these words to a friend, which were later published in several European newspapers:

"... But follow me my friend, you who lay claim to a heart and European ethics, follow me to the unhappy ones who, with gouged-out eyes, must eat, on the scene of the deed, without any sauce, their own amputated ears; or whose teeth are torn out with inhuman violence by the hand of the executioner; or whose bare skulls are simply crushed by blows from a hammer; or where the *bázár* is illuminated with unhappy victims, because on right and left the people dig deep holes in their breasts and shoulders and insert burning wicks in the wounds. I saw some dragged in chains through the *bázár*, preceded by a military band, in whom these wicks had burned so deep that now the fat flickered convulsively in the wound like a newly-extinguished lamp.

"Not seldom it happens that the unwearying ingenuity of the Orientals leads to fresh tortures. They will skin the soles of the Bábís' feet, soak the wounds in boiling oil, shoe the foot like the hoof of a horse, and compel the victim to run. No cry escaped from the victim's breast; the torment is endured in dark silence by the numbed sensation of the fanatic; now he must run; the body cannot endure what the soul has endured; he falls. Give him the *coup de grâce!* Put him out of his pain! No! The executioner swings the whip, and—I myself have had to witness it—the unhappy victim of hundred-fold tortures runs! This is the beginning of the end. As for the end itself, they hang the scorched and perforated bodies by their hands and feet to a tree head-downwards, and now every Persian may try his marksmanship to his heart's content from a fixed but not too proximate distance on the noble quarry placed at his disposal. I saw corpses torn by nearly 150 bullets. The more fortunate suffered strangulation, stoning or suffocation: they were bound before the muzzle of a mortar, cut down with swords, or killed with dagger thrusts, or blows from hammers and sticks. Not only the executioner and the common people took part in the massacre: sometimes Justice would present some of the unhappy Bábís to various dignitaries and the Persian [recipient] would be well content, deeming it an honour to imbrue his own hands in the blood of the pinioned and defenceless victim. Infantry, cavalry, artillery, the *ghuláms* or guards of the King, and the guilds of butchers, bakers, etc., all took their fair share in these bloody deeds. . . .

"At present I never leave my house, in order not to meet with fresh scenes of horror. . . .

"Since my whole soul revolts against such infamy, against such abominations as recent times, according to the judgement of all, present, I will no longer maintain my connection with the scene of such crimes. . . . "[7]

Many of the Bábís who were imprisoned with Bahá'u'lláh were executed. Bahá'u'lláh's enemies, led by the shah's own mother, sought to add His name to the death list. None knew from day to day what His fate would be. Yet in spite of this the prisoners, inspired by Bahá'u'lláh's example, maintained their courage and fortitude. Bahá'u'lláh later described what went on in that dark, dismal place:

"We were all huddled together in one cell, our feet in stocks, and around our necks fastened the most galling of chains. The air we breathed was laden with the foulest impurities, while the floor on which we sat was covered with filth and infested with vermin. No ray of light was allowed to penetrate that pestilential dungeon or to warm its icy-coldness. We were placed in two rows, each facing the other. We had taught them to repeat certain verses which, every night, they chanted with extreme fervour. 'God is sufficient unto me; He verily is the All-sufficing!' one row would intone, while the other would reply: 'In Him let the trusting trust.' The chorus of these gladsome voices would continue to peal out until the early hours of the morning. Their reverberation would fill the dungeon, and, piercing its massive walls, would reach the ears of Násiri'd-Dín Sháh, whose palace was not far distant from the place where we were imprisoned. 'What means this sound?' he was reported to have exclaimed. 'It is the anthem the Bábís are intoning in their prison,' they replied. The Sháh made no further remarks, nor did he attempt to restrain the enthusiasm his prisoners, despite the horrors of their confinement, continued to display."[8]

That dungeon, with its pestilence and daily horrors, became the scene of one of the most significant spiritual events in human history. For it was here that the ministry of Bahá'u'lláh was born. Bahá'u'lláh was none other than the Promised One foretold by the Báb and prophesied in all of the holy scriptures of the world's great religions. He later recounted a series of powerful and profound spiritual experiences that occurred during His confinement:

"During the days I lay in the prison of Tihrán, though the galling weight of the chains and the stench-filled air allowed Me but little sleep, still in those infrequent moments of slumber I felt as if something flowed from the crown of My head over My breast, even as a mighty torrent that precipitateth itself upon the earth from the summit of a lofty mountain. Every limb of My body would, as a result, be set afire. At such moments My tongue recited what no man could bear to hear."

"One night in a dream, these exalted words were heard on every side: 'Verily, We shall render Thee victorious by Thyself and by Thy pen. Grieve Thou not for that which hath befallen Thee, neither be Thou afraid, for Thou art in safety. Ere long will God raise up the treasures of the earth— men who will aid Thee through Thyself and through Thy Name, wherewith God hath revived the hearts of such as have recognized Him.'"

"While engulfed in tribulations I heard a most wondrous, a most sweet voice, calling above My head. Turning My face, I beheld a Maiden—the embodiment of the remembrance of the name of My Lord—suspended in the air before Me. So rejoiced was she in her very soul that her countenance shone with the ornament of the good-pleasure of God, and her cheeks glowed with the brightness of the All-Merciful. Betwixt earth and heaven she was raising a call which captivated the hearts and minds of men. She was imparting to both My inward and outer being tidings which rejoiced My soul, and the souls of God's honored servants. Pointing with her finger unto My head, she addressed all who are in heaven and all who are on earth, saying: 'By God! This is the Best-Beloved of the worlds, and yet ye comprehend not. This is the Beauty of God amongst you, and the power of His sovereignty within you, could ye but understand. This is the Mystery of God and His Treasure, the Cause of God and His glory unto all who are in the kingdoms of Revelation and of creation, if ye be of them that perceive.'"[9]

Bahá'u'lláh kept these experiences to Himself for the time being and would not reveal His true station for some time to come. Meanwhile, His enemies continued to plot His demise. But Bahá'u'lláh was not an ordinary prisoner. Such a prominent personage could not be executed without evidence, even in that corrupt regime, and there was none. Moreover, He had a number of friends in high positions, some of whom rallied to His defense. Among them was His brother-in-law, who served as secretary of the Russian legation in Tehran. He succeeded in getting the Russian minister, Prince Dolgorouki, to intercede on behalf of Bahá'u'lláh. This act, combined with intercessions from other quarters, saved Him from execution. Instead, Bahá'u'lláh was commanded to gather His family and, within a month, leave Iran forever.

Bahá'u'lláh was forced to hasten out of the country in the dead of winter, accompanied by His nearest kin and a few officials acting as escorts. Forced to abandon nearly all of their few remaining possessions, the little group made its way to the province of Iraq, in the neighboring Ottoman Empire.

Fully aware of His divine mission, Bahá'u'lláh knew that further trials were in store. However difficult the past few years had been, the years to come would bring far greater suffering. Far from being discouraged, however, Bahá'u'lláh faced the future with complete confidence and assurance. He remarked to His companions that all of His enemies' schemes had come to nothing.

Bahá'u'lláh and His family arrived in Baghdad in April 1853. He would never see His homeland again.

CHAPTER 5

EXILE

In the days immediately following the crucifixion of Jesus Christ, it may very well have seemed to most people that He had been merely an impostor, perhaps one of many others who had made similar claims and Who, in the end, had received just punishment. To all appearances, the powers that be had won the day: the "Messiah" was dead, those closest to Him were demoralized and scattered to the winds, and those who had been sympathetic to His message silenced and disillusioned.

Such an assessment, however, would have failed to take into account Christ's true power, which was born of the Holy Spirit, and which could not be reckoned according to normal standards. This spiritual power, acting at first upon His little band of disciples, succeeded in transforming the earliest Christians into spiritual giants whose exploits would successfully establish the new faith in every corner of the ancient world. And as time passed, that same force would transform a small and persecuted community, at first only one among a multitude of contemporary cults and sects, into a great world religion. In the end, Christ was indeed triumphant.

Today millions believe that Christ possessed an authority and power that came from God. His achievements and those of His followers—in spite of their utter lack of material resources, political authority, or worldly prestige—are taken by believers today as evidence of His divine stature.

It is important to remember that this historical perspective gives us a great advantage over the people of the ancient world. Very few people in the early days, even as late as two centuries after Christ, would have predicted the future that was in store for His faith.

The following question has probably occurred to most Christians and is the theme of sermons without number:

Would *I* have believed if I had been alive during the time of Christ?

It is a sobering thing to contemplate. How many of us would have recognized in a carpenter from Nazareth our Lord and Savior, either during His lifetime or at any time during the two centuries thereafter? Would we have been moved by the story of His life and teachings, or would we have disdained Him? Would we have accepted the explanation in the Gospels of how He fulfilled the promises of the ancient prophets, or would we have clung to our own notions of how such promises were to be fulfilled? Would our hearts have been touched by His love, by His suffering, and by His sacrifice; or would we, like most everyone else, have remained indifferent?

Often these questions lead to another: If He were to return to earth today under similar circumstances, would we be prepared to recognize Him, or would we fail such a test?

The achievements of the Báb, His personality, His teachings, and His trials offer a remarkable parallel to the life of Jesus of Nazareth. The Báb was the self-proclaimed Messenger of God. His teachings were spiritually profound and challenging. During His own lifetime He succeeded in winning over to His Cause thousands upon thousands of devoted followers, many of whom, like the early Christians, were to prove with their very blood the sincerity of their faith.

Youthful, courageous, and meek, the Báb possessed a loving nature that exerted a magnetic and transforming influence over those with whom He came in contact. He carried out a brief and tumultuous ministry with unflinching resolution and, to many observers, an almost reckless disregard for His own personal safety. Although not wealthy and not of the learned or ruling classes, He, by virtue of the divine power of His personality and His pen, established a new faith that challenged the traditions and dogma of the established order.

The Báb was forced to wander throughout the course of His ministry. He experienced the adulation of the masses, only to see them turn against Him in the end. He was the object of the wrath of the established powers, the clergy in particular. In His final months, He was interrogated by the highest officials, religious and secular, who later pronounced upon Him the sentence of death. Finally, He suffered a cruel public execution, refusing to the very end to renounce His claims or compromise His doctrine.

The French writer Comte de Gobineau, a contemporary who traveled to Persia in the mid-nineteenth century, was deeply moved by what he learned of His life, His teachings, and His severe treatment at the hands of the authorities. He wrote:

"He [the Prime Minister] was picturing him [the Báb] as a vulgar charlatan, a weak dreamer who did not have courage enough to conceive, still less to direct the daring enterprises of his . . . apostles, or even to take part in them. Such a man, taken to Ṭihrán and brought face to face with the most subtle dialecticians of Islám, could not but surrender shamefully. His influence would vanish the more rapidly than if, while destroying his body, one allowed to linger in the minds of the people the phantom of a superiority which death would have consecrated. It was therefore decided to arrest him and bring him to Ṭihrán and, on the way, to exhibit him publicly in chains and humiliated; to make him debate everywhere with the Mullás, silencing him whenever he would become too audacious; briefly, to engage him in a series of unequal encounters in which he would inevitably meet defeat, as he would have been previously demoralized and heartbroken. It was a lion that they were eager to unnerve, hold in chains and strip of claws and teeth, then turn him over to the dogs to show how easily they could overpower him. Once defeated, his ultimate fate was of little importance.

"This plan was not devoid of sense, but it rested upon premises which were far from proven. It was not enough to imagine that the Báb was without courage and firmness, it was necessary that he be really so. But his conduct in the fort of Chihríq [where He was incarcerated] gave no such evidence. He prayed and worked unceasingly. His meekness was unfailing. Those who came near him felt in spite of themselves the fascinating influence of his personality, of his manner and of his speech. His guards were not free from that weakness. He (the Báb) felt that his death was near and he would frequently refer to it as to a thought that was not only familiar but even pleasant. Suppose, for a moment, that thus exhibited throughout Persia he would still remain undaunted? Suppose he would display neither arrogance nor fear but would rise far above his misfortune? Suppose that he succeeded in throwing into confusion the learned, subtle, and eloquent doctors arraigned against him? Suppose he would remain more than ever the Báb for his old followers and become so for the indifferent and even for his enemies? It was risking much in order to gain much, without doubt, but also perhaps to lose much and, after having weighed the matter with care, they dared not take the chance."[1]

Summing up the life of the Báb, A. L. M. Nicolas, another Frenchman who traveled to Persia in the years immediately after the death of the Báb, wrote:

. . . "Christians believe that if Jesus Christ had wished to come down from the cross he could have done so easily; he died of his own free will because it was written that he should and in order that the prophecies might be fulfilled. The same is true of the Báb, so the Bábís say, who, in this way, gave a clear sanction to his teachings. He likewise died voluntarily because his death was to be the salvation of humanity. . . . His life is one of the most magnificent examples of courage which it has been the privilege of mankind to behold, and it is also an admirable proof of the love which our hero felt for his fellow countrymen. He sacrificed himself for humanity, for it he gave his body and his soul, for it he endured privations, insults, torture and martyrdom. He sealed, with his very lifeblood, the covenant of universal brotherhood. Like Jesus he paid with his life for the proclamation of a reign of concord, equity and brotherly love. More than anyone he knew what dreadful dangers he was heaping upon himself. He had been able to see personally the degree of exasperation that a fanaticism, shrewdly aroused, could reach; but all these considerations could not weaken his resolve. Fear had no hold upon his soul and, perfectly calm, never looking back, in full possession of all his powers, he walked into the furnace."[2]

In all of these respects the life of the Báb showed striking parallels to that of Jesus. And there is another similarity. In the aftermath of His dramatic career, it appeared for a time as if the Báb had spent His life in vain.

The shah and his ministers, the clergy and their followers rejoiced. The Báb—an impostor in their eyes—was dead. Thousands of the new believers had been killed, including virtually all of the leading disciples. The rest of them, under relentless persecution, had been driven underground or banished. The established powers seemed in every respect to have won a resounding and complete victory over the Báb. The future, they imagined, was in their hands.

Yet the Báb had foretold His own martyrdom and had made it clear that He was the Herald of a still greater revelation from God. Indeed, the entire purpose of His ministry, according to His own testimony, had been to prepare the way for "Him Whom God would make manifest." The Báb had made it clear that this revelation was imminent and that it would bring in its wake the establishment of God's Kingdom on earth, as foretold in all of the holy scriptures of the world's major religions.

As we have seen, the light of that new revelation broke during the darkest hour of persecution, at the very moment when it seemed that all had been lost. And by the inscrutable decree of Providence, the Bearer of that light, the only survivor among the effective leaders of the Bábí Faith, had been forced to leave His native land forever. Little did His self-satisfied enemies realize that this humiliating banishment would make it possible for Bahá'u'lláh to reinvigorate the Bábí community and to prepare them for His own revelation.

Bahá'u'lláh's Arrival in Baghdad

Baghdad in the mid-nineteenth century was a city long past its heyday. Once the capital of the far-flung Abbasid dynasty (A.D. 750–1258), it boasted at its height a population of more than one million souls and was a mighty center of government, industry, art, and science. So great was its fame that the very name, particularly in the West, has come to symbolize the zenith of Islamic civilization. After a period of slow decline the city suffered sudden, severe reversal at the hands of Mongol invaders in the thirteenth and fifteenth centuries. By the time of Bahá'u'lláh's arrival, it had become a provincial capital of the Ottoman Empire, with a total population of some sixty thousand. There was little evidence at that point to suggest its former glories.

Bahá'u'lláh and His family arrived there in April 1853 after three months of travel in the dead of winter over the desolate and icy mountains of western Persia. Although the journey, coming on the heels of a horrible imprisonment, must surely have been exhausting, Bahá'u'lláh wasted no time in doing what He could to revive the spirits of the Báb's remaining followers.

The community of Bábís, grief-stricken and confused, had lost not only their beloved leader, the Báb, but also thousands of their fellow-believers, including nearly all of the most prominent disciples. Many of the faithful turned naturally to Bahá'u'lláh for inspiration and guidance, since He was virtually the only leading Bábí to have survived the brutal persecutions. Bahá'u'lláh, realizing that the community stood in grave peril of disintegration, assumed the task of reviving its demoralized remnants with characteristic ability and determination. This He did without revealing His own station.

Over time the signs of Bahá'u'lláh's spiritual eminence, leadership, and high integrity would become evident to all, provoking joy and wonder in the hearts of countless admirers and restoring hope to the beleaguered Bábís. His home would become a center of the city, where all who came, high and low alike, enjoyed His wisdom and basked in the warmth of His loving hospitality. Eventually multitudes testified to the impact of His presence in their midst.

But initially there was resistance from some quarters. That so many of the Bábís rallied around Bahá'u'lláh provoked intense envy in a few, who began campaigning for leadership. Some combined forces to undermine Bahá'u'lláh's efforts to unify the believers. Still others, well-meaning but confused and disoriented in the aftermath of the persecutions, went so far as to claim that they were the Promised One foretold by the Báb. These claims and schemes led to disruptive behavior and potentially serious dissension within the ranks of the believers.

Bahá'u'lláh's reaction was not to assert His own leadership aggressively. Rather, to everyone's complete surprise, He departed the city. Without notifying anyone,

He left in April 1854 in the company of a single servant, making His way to the mountains of Kurdistan some distance to the north. He took up residence in a cave in mountains near the town of Sulaymaniyyah, where He spent His time in prayer and meditation. Even His relatives did not know where He had gone.

This two-year period, reminiscent of the withdrawal of Moses to Sinai, of Jesus into the wilderness, and of Muḥammad's periodic retreats to the hills outside of Mecca, was spent contemplating the mission with which God had entrusted Him. That remote corner of Kurdistan offered no physical comforts of any kind. Yet, even in that desolate region, He soon attracted attention. A few people in the area took notice of His extraordinary wisdom and knowledge as well as His kindness and His captivating personality. Gradually He attracted a large circle of admirers, including some men of learning. Concealing His real identity, He was thought by some to be a Muslim mystic, or dervish. Before long His reputation for spiritual insight began to spread beyond the confines of Kurdistan. Eventually His friends and family, who had no idea where He had gone, heard tales of a remarkable saint in the district of Sulaymaniyyah. From these reports they concluded that this personage must be none other than Bahá'u'lláh and sent emissaries to plead for His return. Bahá'u'lláh considered this development a sign from God that He should resume His mission in Baghdad. "Surrendering Our will to His," He wrote, "We submitted to His injunction."[3]

He returned in March 1856 to find the Bábís even more dispirited and divided than when He had left. But there was one difference—by then the vast majority could see that those who had pretended to leadership were, in fact, utterly incapable of restoring the spirit of the new religion. Now most of the Bábís turned with a new appreciation to Bahá'u'lláh for guidance. This included almost all of the individuals who had themselves previously claimed to be the Promised One Whom the Báb had foretold.

Although Bahá'u'lláh still would not publicly announce His mission for some time, He continued to compose various writings immediately upon His return to Baghdad. These were revealed in Arabic and Persian, sometimes in combination, and always in an original and matchless style. Over the course of time they proved a means of spiritual rejuvenation for the Bábí community, as well as a source of inspiration for others.

One of the most important of these works is known as the Hidden Words. This is a compilation of verses composed in Persian and Arabic. Bahá'u'lláh states in this same work that they represent the "inner essence" of the religion of God as "revealed unto the Prophets of old."[4] The themes related in the Hidden Words also make up the ethical heart of the Bahá'í teachings, which Bahá'u'lláh would reiterate and elaborate upon for the remainder of His ministry.

The verses address humanity collectively and individually, conveying God's infinite love for humankind, the high potential with which He has invested us, and His desire that we all fulfill our true purpose, which is none other than to know and to love Him. The tone is by turns exultant, admonishing, and poignant; for while the verses tell of God's love, they also lament humanity's rejection of Him.

Telling of God's love for us, Bahá'u'lláh addresses humanity:

O SON OF MAN!
Veiled in My immemorial being and in the ancient eternity of My essence, I knew My love for thee; therefore I created thee, have engraved on thee Mine image and revealed to thee My beauty.[5]

And elsewhere:

O SON OF MAN!
I loved thy creation, hence I created thee. Wherefore, do thou love Me, that I may name thy name and fill thy soul with the spirit of life.[6]

In other verses we are reminded of our true reality, which is spiritual rather than physical. We are counseled by God to turn towards Him and to attain the station for which we were created. We are warned that we will find neither peace nor happiness unless we do so, but if we do, we are assured of eternal life.

The verses of the Hidden Words make it clear that nearness to God is dependent on faith, purity of heart, and good deeds. Time and again they exhort us to live an upright and moral life:

O SON OF SPIRIT!
My first counsel is this: Possess a pure, kindly and radiant heart, that thine may be a sovereignty ancient, imperishable and everlasting.[7]

One of the virtues we are called upon to acquire is justice, which enables an individual to investigate reality impartially and free of blind imitation:

O SON OF SPIRIT!
The best beloved of all things in My sight is Justice; turn not away therefrom if thou desirest Me, and neglect it not that I may confide in thee. By its aid thou shalt see with thine own eyes and not through the eyes of others, and shalt know of thine own knowledge and not through

the knowledge of thy neighbor. Ponder this in thy heart; how it behooveth thee to be. Verily justice is My gift to thee and the sign of My loving-kindness. Set it then before thine eyes.[8]

Other verses call upon us to show compassion and love for others. Some of them stress that we are all created equal. Others exhort humanity, and rulers in particular, to show special compassion for the poor and the oppressed. This theme resurfaces time and again in Bahá'u'lláh's writings. Failure in this regard, He warns, will invite God's wrath:

O CHILDREN OF DUST!
Tell the rich of the midnight sighing of the poor, lest heedlessness lead them into the path of destruction, and deprive them of the Tree of Wealth. To give and to be generous are attributes of Mine; well is it with him that adorneth himself with My virtues.[9]

O OPPRESSORS ON EARTH!
Withdraw your hands from tyranny, for I have pledged Myself not to forgive any man's injustice. This is My covenant which I have irrevocably decreed in the preserved tablet and sealed with My seal of glory.[10]

Certain passages make clear that, although God wishes what is best for us, we are given freedom to choose. Because of this we often become overly attached to worldly things in the mistaken belief that the pursuit of material pleasures will bring happiness. True happiness comes when we learn to love God and follow His commandments, thereby acquiring divine attributes. If we are obedient, we draw near unto God and thereby acquire eternal life; if not, we face eternal remoteness from Him, which is spiritual death.

Other verses lament that human beings have all too often forgotten God. Instead of rising to our high destiny, we have chosen to follow our baser inclinations. Such verses express God's concern for us, reminding us lovingly not to forgo eternal bliss in selfish pursuits:

O MOVING FORM OF DUST!
I desire communion with thee, but thou wouldst put no trust in Me. The sword of thy rebellion hath felled the tree of thy hope. At all times am I near to thee, but thou art ever far from Me. Imperishable glory have I chosen for thee, yet boundless shame thou hast chosen for thyself. While there is yet time, return, and lose not thy chance.[11]

Yet there is also reassurance:

O SON OF LOVE!
Thou art but one step away from the glorious heights above and from the celestial tree of love. Take thou one pace and with the next advance into the immortal realm and enter the pavilion of eternity. Give ear then to that which hath been revealed by the Pen of Glory.[12]

In other passages humanity is called upon to champion the Cause of God and to uphold His Word. These themes and many others find expression in the sublime poetic beauty of the Hidden Words.

Revival of the Bábí Community

A stream of writings poured from the pen of Bahá'u'lláh almost continually in the years that He lived in Baghdad. These writings served to invigorate the little community of Bábís. Yet as powerful as their effect was, Bahá'u'lláh's personality and His presence had an even more profound impact, for an increasing number of individuals discerned the signs of a heavenly power in Him.

Among the individuals upon whom Bahá'u'lláh's personality and presence had a profound effect was Nabíl, who would later emerge as the most eminent of the early historians of the Bahá'í Faith. In a passage from his narrative of the early days of the Bahá'í Faith, he gives an eyewitness account describing the joy and wonder that Bahá'u'lláh instilled in the hearts of the believers. His presence, and even His written words, transported them to such an extent that they became virtually oblivious to all else. Nabíl, depicting the tumult that had seized the hearts of Bahá'u'lláh's companions in the days prior to the declaration of His mission, writes,

"Many a night would [Bahá'u'lláh's amanuensis] gather them together in his room, close the door, light numerous camphorated candles, and chant aloud to them the newly revealed odes and Tablets in his possession. Wholly oblivious of this contingent world, completely immersed in the realms of the spirit, forgetful of the necessity for food, sleep or drink, they would suddenly discover that night had become day, and that the sun was approaching its zenith."[13]

These friends and companions, like Bahá'u'lláh Himself, had very little in the way of material means. Yet they basked in the presence of their Beloved:

"Many a night, no less than ten persons subsisted on no more than a penny-worth of dates. No one knew to whom actually belonged the shoes, the cloaks, or the robes that were to be found in their houses. Whoever went to the bazaar could claim that the shoes upon his feet were his own, and each one who entered the presence of Bahá'u'lláh could affirm that the cloak and robe he then wore belonged to him. Their own names they had forgotten, their hearts were emptied of aught else except adoration for their Be-loved. . . . O, for the joy of those days, and the gladness and wonder of those hours!"[14]

"So intoxicated were those who had quaffed from the cup of Bahá'u'lláh's presence," wrote Nabíl,

"that in their eyes the palaces of kings appeared more ephemeral than a spider's web. . . . The celebrations and festivities that were theirs were such as the kings of the earth had never dreamt of." "I, myself with two others, lived in a room which was devoid of furniture. Bahá'u'lláh entered it one day, and, looking about Him, remarked: 'Its emptiness pleases Me. In My estimation it is preferable to many a spacious palace, inasmuch as the be-loved of God are occupied in it with the remembrance of the Incomparable Friend, with hearts that are wholly emptied of the dross of this world.'"[15]

It should be added that Bahá'u'lláh shared fully in the privations suffered by His companions. "There was a time in 'Iráq," He affirms, "when the Ancient Beauty [He Himself] . . . had no change of linen. The one shirt He possessed would be washed, dried and worn again."[16]

Among the many others who were profoundly influenced by Bahá'u'lláh was a learned man by the name of Ismá'íl. Although very educated and accomplished in his own right, he was so impressed with Bahá'u'lláh that he could be seen every morning sweeping the doorway of Bahá'u'lláh's house. This was his way of indicating the humility he felt in relation to Bahá'u'lláh and showing his appreciation of the loftiness of Bahá'u'lláh's station. And this was before Bahá'u'lláh had proclaimed Himself a Messenger of God.

Yet another devoted admirer was one Mullá Muḥammad. He was an individual of outstanding learning and accomplishment. In the early days he noticed that Bahá'u'lláh, notwithstanding His noble lineage and high social rank, showed great humility, often serving the Bábís tea and refreshments with His own hands. Considering his own attainments, Mullá Muḥammad assumed that his knowledge was superior to that of all others, including Bahá'u'lláh. Because of this he took the place of honor in gatherings, speaking with authority on any and all issues.

One day, at a gathering in Bahá'u'lláh's house, someone asked a question. Mullá Muḥammad attempted an answer, during which the guests listened in silence. Bahá'u'lláh, Who was serving tea, was the only person to make a comment from time to time. Gradually Bahá'u'lláh's words came to dominate the discussion, while Mullá Muḥammad grew silent. He later recalled:

"His explanations were so profound and the ocean of His utterance surged with such a power that my whole being was overtaken with awe and fear. Spellbound by His words, I was plunged into a state of dazed bewilderment. After a few minutes of listening to His words—words of unparalleled wonder and majesty—I became dumbfounded. I could no longer hear his voice. Only by the movement of His lips did I know that He was still speaking. I felt deeply ashamed and troubled that I was occupying the seat of honour in that meeting. I waited impatiently until I saw that His lips were no longer moving when I knew that He had finished talking. Like a helpless bird which is freed from the claws of a mighty falcon I rose to my feet and went out. There three times I hit my head hard against the wall and rebuked myself for my spiritual blindness."[17]

Not all of the people who associated with Bahá'u'lláh were Bábís, yet almost everyone who met and came to know Him became an admirer. Eventually He became renowned in Baghdad and its environs for His learning and spiritual qualities. Some individuals were so moved by their experiences in His presence that separation from Him became extremely difficult to bear. One Persian nobleman, for instance, was so impressed that he designed for his own home an exact replica of Bahá'u'lláh's reception area in the hope that this would allow him to recapture the joy he always felt when he visited there. Yet another nobleman was heard to state: "I cannot explain it, I do not know how it is, but whenever I feel gloomy and depressed, I have only to go to the house of Bahá'u'lláh to have my spirits uplifted."[18] Yet another person who became devoted to Bahá'u'lláh was the owner of a coffee shop frequented by Him during these years. He was invited regularly to join Bahá'u'lláh for tea and became so attached to Him that he came to consider any day in which he failed to visit Him as wasted. After Bahá'u'lláh's departure from Baghdad the man was so distraught that he was never again seen drinking tea, nor did he ever visit his own coffeehouse again.

CHAPTER 6

GOD AND HISTORY

Another important work revealed by Bahá'u'lláh during His years in Baghdad is the Book of Certitude. The book was written in response to several questions posed to Bahá'u'lláh by a maternal uncle of the Báb who had not yet accepted that the Báb was a Messenger of God. The main reason for this was that he could not understand how the Báb's claims could be true when He had apparently failed to fulfill the prophecies of Islam. In the Book of Certitude Bahá'u'lláh not only vigorously upholds the Báb's claims; He also depicts all religious history as the unfoldment of one process of which God is the Author, and the ultimate goal of which is the spiritual awakening of humanity. In setting forth His thesis, Bahá'u'lláh refers to the Old and New Testaments and to the Koran, explaining the nature of the prophecies they contain and how they were indeed fulfilled. He also clarifies the primary purpose of religion and explains what humanity's response to it ought to be.

Bahá'u'lláh asserts that God's nature is far beyond human understanding. He states:

> To every discerning and illumined heart it is evident that God, the un-knowable Essence, the divine Being, is immensely exalted beyond every human attribute, such as corporeal existence, ascent and descent, egress and regress. Far be it from His glory that human tongue should adequately recount His praise, or that human heart comprehend His fathomless mystery. He is and hath ever been veiled in the ancient eternity of His Essence, and will remain in His Reality everlastingly hidden from the sight of men. . . . No tie of direct intercourse can possibly bind Him to His creatures. He standeth exalted beyond and above all separation and union, all proximity and remoteness. . . .

. . . All the Prophets of God and their chosen Ones, all the divines, the sages, and the wise of every generation, unanimously recognize their inability to attain unto the comprehension of that Quintessence of all truth, and confess their incapacity to grasp Him, Who is the inmost Reality of all things.[1]

Because human beings cannot know God directly, He has sent His Messengers and Prophets to educate humanity and lead them towards Him. Bahá'u'lláh also refers to these souls as Manifestations of God because they embody His attributes like perfect mirrors reflecting the sun.*

Among the Manifestations of God Who had appeared were Moses, Jesus, Muḥammad, and, most recently, the Báb. The Prophets are part of a single process designed by God to educate humanity. The laws and teachings they reveal are meant for our upliftment and salvation.

Mankind Has Always Rejected the Manifestations of God

The Báb's uncle was skeptical of his nephew's claim because it did not appear that He had fulfilled many well-known Islamic prophecies. Bahá'u'lláh pointed out that every Manifestation of God without exception has faced rejection and persecution, often from the very people who have been awaiting His appearance. One of the reasons for this persecution is the failure of the people to understand the true meaning of the prophecies.

Bahá'u'lláh recounts the stories of several divine Messengers, demonstrating how each was persecuted when He appeared. Jesus was persecuted by the Jews, Muḥammad by His countrymen, and the Báb by the people of Islam—the very people who had been awaiting His advent.

Why is it that the Prophets meet with rejection? For one thing, Bahá'u'lláh says, the Prophets and Messengers appear outwardly to be ordinary human beings. They have neither worldly riches nor political power. In addition, they always challenge well-established notions and beliefs, to which most of the people cling unthinkingly.

Bahá'u'lláh states that such conditions are the "clouds" referred to in the New Testament:

---

* In this volume we will use the terms *Prophet, Messenger of God,* and *Manifestation of God* interchangeably. These are all designations used by Bahá'u'lláh in reference to these Holy Beings.

And now regarding His [Christ's] words, that the Son of man shall "come in the clouds of heaven." By the term "clouds" is meant those things that are contrary to the ways and desires of men. . . . These "clouds" signify, in one sense, the annulment of laws, the abrogation of former Dispensations, the repeal of rituals and customs current amongst men, the exalting of the illiterate faithful above the learned opposers of the Faith. In another sense, they mean the appearance of that immortal Beauty in the image of mortal man, with such human limitations as eating and drinking, poverty and riches, glory and abasement, sleeping and waking, and such other things as cast doubt in the minds of men, and cause them to turn away. All such veils are symbolically referred to as "clouds.". . .

It is evident that the changes brought about in every Dispensation constitute the dark clouds that intervene between the eye of man's understanding and the divine Luminary which shineth forth from the dayspring of the divine Essence. Consider how men for generations have been blindly imitating their fathers, and have been trained according to such ways and manners as have been laid down by the dictates of their Faith. Were these men, therefore, to discover suddenly that a Man, Who hath been living in their midst, Who, with respect to every human limitation, hath been their equal, had risen to abolish every established principle imposed by their Faith—principles by which for centuries they have been disciplined, and every opposer and denier of which they have come to regard as infidel, profligate and wicked—they would of a certainty be veiled and hindered from acknowledging His truth. . . . Such men, when acquainted with these circumstances, become so veiled that without the least question, they pronounce the Manifestation of God an infidel, and sentence Him to death. You must have heard of such things taking place all down the ages, and are now observing them in these days.[2]

The People Blindly Follow the Clergy

Bahá'u'lláh singles out religious leaders for special blame. Theirs is the great responsibility of leading the faithful, yet they have always been in the vanguard of the enemies of every Prophet:

Leaders of religion, in every age, have hindered their people from attaining the shores of eternal salvation, inasmuch as they held the reins of authority in their mighty grasp. Some for the lust of leadership, others through want of knowledge and understanding, have been the cause of the deprivation of the people. By their sanction and authority, every Prophet of God hath drunk from the chalice of sacrifice, and winged His flight unto the heights of glory. What unspeakable cruelties they that have occupied the seats of authority and learning have inflicted upon the true Monarchs of the world, those Gems of divine virtue! Content with a transitory dominion, they have deprived themselves of an everlasting sovereignty. Thus, their eyes beheld not the light of the countenance of the Well-Beloved, nor did their ears hearken unto the sweet melodies of the Bird of Desire. For this reason, in all sacred books mention hath been made of the divines of every age.[3]

The people assume their share of fault, because they do not think for themselves. Instead, they act based on the expectations set by their leaders:

Unto every discerning observer it is evident and manifest that had these people in the days of each of the Manifestations of the Sun of Truth sanctified their eyes, their ears, and their hearts from whatever they had seen, heard, and felt, they surely would not have been deprived of beholding the beauty of God, nor strayed far from the habitations of glory. But having weighed the testimony of God by the standard of their own knowledge, gleaned from the teachings of the leaders of their faith, and found it at variance with their limited understanding, they arose to perpetrate such unseemly acts.[4]

Bahá'u'lláh explains that God tests humanity by revealing His Word in terms that are not always literal. He offers abundant examples of this, citing passage after passage of the Bible and the Koran and demonstrating their true meaning. For example, He refers to a passage from the New Testament wherein Jesus Christ tells the signs of His second coming:

"Immediately after the oppression of those days shall the sun be darkened, and the moon shall not give her light, and the stars shall fall from heaven, and the powers of the earth shall be shaken: and then shall appear the sign of the Son of man in heaven: and then shall all the tribes of the earth mourn, and they shall see the Son of man coming in the clouds of heaven with power and great glory. And he shall send his angels with a great sound of a trumpet."[5]

Bahá'u'lláh explains that the terms "sun" and "moon," when mentioned in the writings of the Prophets of God, do not refer solely to the sun and moon of the visible universe. These terms symbolize manifold spiritual truths.

In one particular case, the word "sun" stands for the divines who are the leaders of religion: "That the term 'sun' hath been applied to the leaders of religion is due to their lofty position, their fame, and renown. Such are the universally recognized divines of every age, who speak with authority, and whose fame is securely established." Yet once the true Sun is revealed in the form of a new Prophet, these suns go dark in the relative brightness of the new light from God. The same is true for the "moon" and "stars."

Bahá'u'lláh also interpreted these terms as symbols of the laws and teachings of God. When God sends a new Messenger, the "sun," "moon," and "stars" of the past are replaced with new teachings.

Similarly, Bahá'u'lláh states that the term "return" does not signify the literal return of an individual Messenger to earth, but the return of the same divine qualities, the same manifestation of the Holy Spirit. In that sense each new Messenger is the "return" of those Who preceded Him. When the scriptures speak of the end of the world, of the descent of Christ from heaven in the last days, of the Day of Judgment, and of the resurrection of the dead, these are also symbolic terms. The physical world will not really be destroyed, nor will the physical moon and sun go dark. The return of Christ descending from heaven is not a literal event—it means the reappearance in the world of the Christ Spirit, which comes from heaven. The Resurrection will not entail bodies of the dead coming back to life; it signifies the spiritual reawakening of those who believe and follow God's Messenger.

But why does God speak in such symbolic terms and not plainly? Profound spiritual truth cannot be stated in literal terms, superficially. Bahá'u'lláh explains that this is done to test humanity so that the sincere souls can be distinguished from those who cling blindly to tradition.

An examination of religious history validates Bahá'u'lláh's assertions. For example, the main reason the Jews persecuted Christ was that He did not appear to have fulfilled the ancient prophecies concerning the Messiah. They expected a personage who would occupy the throne of David and thus rid them of their Gentile overlords, the Romans. Yet Christ's sovereignty was not of that kind. His was a heavenly dominion, and the Kingdom of God of which He spoke was a spiritual reality.

The True Standard for Judgment

How are we to understand the scriptures? Bahá'u'lláh exhorts the seeker to investigate the Word of God unhindered by the faulty standards that prevail at the beginning of every new religion. Bahá'u'lláh makes clear that true spiritual understanding is not dependent upon human knowledge. Nor can reliance upon past traditions serve as a true guide, even if those traditions are based upon scripture. Rather, true understanding calls for rectitude of conduct, purity of heart, love of God, and a sincere desire to discover the truth:

> . . . they that tread the path of faith, they that thirst for the wine of certitude, must cleanse themselves of all that is earthly—their ears from idle talk, their minds from vain imaginings, their hearts from worldly affections, their eyes from that which perisheth. They should put their trust in God, and, holding fast unto Him, follow in His way. Then will they be made worthy of the effulgent glories of the sun of divine knowledge and understanding, and become the recipients of a grace that is infinite and unseen, inasmuch as man can never hope to attain unto the knowledge of the All-Glorious, can never quaff from the stream of divine knowledge and wisdom, can never enter the abode of immortality, nor partake of the cup of divine nearness and favor, unless and until he ceases to regard the words and deeds of mortal men as a standard for the true understanding and recognition of God and His Prophets.[6]

In the Book of Certitude Bahá'u'lláh upholds the validity of Judaism, Christianity, and Islam. He describes these faiths as integral parts of one grand unfolding process for the eventual spiritualization of the human race. He also vigorously defends the claims of the Báb, characterizing Him as the latest in the succession of divine Messengers and the Forerunner of the One foretold in all of the sacred scriptures of past ages. Moreover, He praises the heroism of the countless followers of the Báb who suffered death rather than disavow their faith. He considers the Báb's career itself as one of the greatest proofs of His divine mission.

The Book of Certitude was revealed by Bahá'u'lláh near the end of His sojourn in Baghdad. Written in a masterful style, challenging and original in its themes, it is now regarded as the most important of His voluminous writings, second only to His Most Holy Book (about which we will hear more later). Also impressive is that, although encompassing some two hundred pages, the book was revealed in the space of no more than two days and nights.

In it Bahá'u'lláh alludes to His own station, and it is clear that this book was meant to prepare the followers of the Báb for the imminent announcement that He was the Promised One.

CHAPTER 7

RENEWAL OF OPPOSITION

Bahá'u'lláh's influence, although universally acknowledged, was not welcomed by all. For some it was the cause of envy and consternation, and these individuals took steps to undermine His reputation and to provoke fresh hostilities against the community of Bábís. Among His most notable opponents in Baghdad were the Persian consul and one of the leading Islamic clerics of the area. As much as they tried, however, they never succeeded in enlisting the support either of the governor, who deeply admired Bahá'u'lláh, nor of the masses of the citizens of Baghdad. Frustrated, His opponents turned to other measures.

At one point the consul hired a man to assassinate Bahá'u'lláh. Enticed by the promise of a rich reward, this man sought out Bahá'u'lláh one day in the public bath, yet, as he himself admitted later, was so overwhelmed by His presence that he spontaneously fled the scene. He made another attempt and on that occasion, too, was so overcome with awe that he was unable to carry out his design.

This was but one of many instances in which the plottings of His enemies placed Bahá'u'lláh and the Bábís in great peril. Sometimes the plots were successful, and one or more Bábís would fall victims of violence. As time passed, the danger increased; yet through it all Bahá'u'lláh retained His composure, going about His daily business as usual and, to the dismay of His many friends, without a guard.

Another episode typifies this period because it illustrates Bahá'u'lláh's fearlessness and the impact of His personality upon those who intended to do Him bodily harm. According to the historian Nabíl, it became known at one point that Bahá'u'lláh's adversaries had convinced a group of more than a hundred Kurds to assault His house. Bahá'u'lláh refused the offer of many of the Bábís to defend Him, insisting that there was no need for it. When the Kurds appeared, disguised as a band of passing mourners, He invited them into His home and served them tea and sherbet. Bahá'u'lláh's kindness and majesty so impressed them that they left as friends, shouting as they departed, "May God curse your enemies."

The clergy also made moves to have Bahá'u'lláh killed. When these efforts were not successful they turned to other measures intended to discredit Him. On one occasion He was challenged to perform a miracle. Here is an account of the incident as 'Abdu'l-Bahá, Bahá'u'lláh's eldest son, relates it:

> It often happened that in Baghdád certain Muhammadan 'ulamá [divines], Jewish rabbis and Christians met together with some European scholars, in a blessed reunion [i.e., a meeting with Bahá'u'lláh]: each one had some question to propose, and although they were possessed of varying degrees of culture, they each heard a sufficient and convincing reply, and retired satisfied. Even the Persian 'ulamá who were at Karbilá and Najaf chose a wise man whom they sent on a mission to Him; his name was Mullá Hasan 'Amú. He came into the Holy Presence, and proposed a number of questions on behalf of the 'ulamá, to which Bahá'u'lláh replied. Then Hasan 'Amú said, "The 'ulamá recognize without hesitation and confess the knowledge and virtue of Bahá'u'lláh, and they are unanimously convinced that in all learning he has no peer or equal; and it is also evident that he has never studied or acquired this learning; but still the 'ulamá say, 'We are not contented with this; we do not acknowledge the reality of his mission by virtue of his wisdom and righteousness. Therefore, we ask him to show us a miracle in order to satisfy and tranquilize our hearts.'"
>
> Bahá'u'lláh replied, "Although you have no right to ask this, for God should test His creatures, and they should not test God, still I allow and accept this request. But the Cause of God is not a theatrical display that is presented every hour, of which some new diversion may be asked for every day. If it were thus, the Cause of God would become mere child's play.
>
> "The 'ulamás must, therefore, assemble, and with one accord, choose one miracle, and write that, after the performance of this miracle they will no longer entertain doubts about Me, and that all will acknowledge and confess the truth of My Cause. Let them seal this paper, and bring it to Me. This must be the accepted criterion: if the miracle is performed, no doubt will remain for them; and if not, We shall be convicted of imposture." The learned man, Hasan 'Amú, rose and replied, "There is no more to be said"; he then kissed the knee of the Blessed One although he was not a believer, and went. He gathered the 'ulamá and gave them the sacred message. They consulted together and said, "This man is an enchanter; perhaps he will perform an enchantment, and then we shall have nothing more to say." Acting on this belief, they did not dare to push the matter further.

This man, Ḥasan 'Amú, mentioned this fact at many meetings. After leaving Karbilá he went to Kirmánsháh and Ṭihrán and spread a detailed account of it everywhere, laying emphasis on the fear and withdrawal of the 'ulamá.

Briefly, all His adversaries in the Orient acknowledged His greatness, grandeur, knowledge and virtue; and though they were His enemies, they always spoke of Him as "the renowned Bahá'u'lláh."[1]

The episode with the 'ulamá illustrates both the courage of Bahá'u'lláh and the insincerity of His enemies. It is interesting to note that the clergy asked Him to perform a miracle, even though He had as yet only alluded to His own spiritual station and had not put forth a formal claim to leadership. That He was the object of such a demand testifies to the profound influence of His personality and His writings.

Unable to destroy Bahá'u'lláh, the Persian consul stepped up his efforts to have Him removed from the city and away from the Iranian frontier. A period of incessant activity ensued, during which he and his superiors spread infamous tales about Bahá'u'lláh and the Bábís to the Ottoman authorities. At last a message arrived from the grand vizier* with instructions for the governor. The governor requested a meeting with Bahá'u'lláh.

News of the upcoming meeting caused a flurry of rumors and hearsay. Some speculated that Bahá'u'lláh would refuse to meet with the governor; others thought that He and all of the Bábís would be handed over to the Persian authorities; still others thought that they would all be drowned in the Tigris River.

Bahá'u'lláh agreed to meet with a deputy who conveyed the news from the grand vizier—an invitation for Bahá'u'lláh to proceed to the capital city of Constantinople (today known as Istanbul, Turkey). The language of the summons was courteous.

As it turned out, the governor of Baghdad had known of the invitation for several months. He had developed a deep admiration for Bahá'u'lláh and could not bring himself to deliver the news at first. The grand vizier sent five successive commands. Only after the fifth did the governor accede to the order.

At first it appeared that Bahá'u'lláh's adversaries had at last succeeded in inflicting a humiliating defeat. They imagined an ignominious banishment from Baghdad, but this turned out to be far from what actually happened. The news of Bahá'u'lláh's impending departure caused immense distress among all classes of people, whose public gestures of support for Bahá'u'lláh made clear that they could not bear the thought of His absence.

---

* The chief minister of the Ottoman government, residing in Constantinople

The governor gave Bahá'u'lláh a sum of money to be used on the journey, an amount sufficient for Himself, His relatives, and a number of attendants. Bahá'u'lláh gave the entire sum to charity. The governor also offered a reception for Bahá'u'lláh's brother and eldest son, whom Bahá'u'lláh sent to meet with the governor. The lavishness of that occasion demonstrated the esteem that Bahá'u'lláh enjoyed among the highest circles.

In the days before His final departure from Baghdad, Bahá'u'lláh stayed in a large garden on the east bank of the Tigris River. There He received guests from every walk of life who came from the city to pay their respects and to beg Him to stay. He offered what consolation He could but firmly insisted that the time had come for Him to leave. The governor himself came to beg Bahá'u'lláh's forgiveness, asking what service he might perform for Him. Noting the tumult that had seized the inhabitants of the city, the governor remarked to Bahá'u'lláh, "'Formerly they insisted upon your departure. Now, however, they are even more insistent that you should remain.'"[2]

CHAPTER 8

THE DECLARATION
OF BAHÁ'U'LLÁH

Bahá'u'lláh stayed in the garden for twelve days before finally departing Baghdad. The Bábís were grief-stricken, for only a handful would be allowed to accompany Him and His family to Constantinople. Those who were to remain behind came to say their farewells. Through it all, in spite of the uncertain fate that awaited Him, Bahá'u'lláh remained tranquil. Once again we turn to Nabíl, who described those days:

> "Every day, ere the hour of dawn, the gardeners would pick the roses which lined the four avenues of the garden, and would pile them in the center of the floor of His blessed tent. So great would be the heap that when His companions gathered to drink their morning tea in His presence, they would be unable to see each other across it. All these roses Bahá'u'lláh would, with His own hands, entrust to those whom He dismissed from His presence every morning to be delivered, on His behalf, to His Arab and Persian friends in the city."[1]

The time had come for Bahá'u'lláh to reveal His true station. To a small group of believers He made the announcement that He was the One heralded by the Báb and foretold in the holy books of old. He was the Lord of Hosts, "He Whom God Shall make manifest," the Prince of Peace; and this was the Day of Days awaited by humanity since time immemorial.

Strange to think that the world was as oblivious to this momentous event as it was when Christ began His ministry nearly two millennia before. The Great Announcement had occurred, but in circumstances entirely unexpected by a waiting humanity.

The time for Bahá'u'lláh's final departure from the city provoked even greater demonstrations of love from the masses of the citizenry:

"The great tumult," wrote an eyewitness, "associated in our minds with the Day of Gathering, the Day of Judgment, we beheld on that occasion. Believers and unbelievers alike sobbed and lamented. The chiefs and notables who had congregated were struck with wonder. Emotions were stirred to such depths as no tongue can describe, nor could any observer escape their contagion."

Mounted on His steed, a red roan stallion of the finest breed, the best His lovers could purchase for Him, and leaving behind Him a bowing multitude of fervent admirers, He rode forth on the first stage of a journey that was to carry Him to the city of Constantinople. "Numerous were the heads," Nabíl himself a witness of that memorable scene, recounts, "which, on every side, bowed to the dust at the feet of His horse, and kissed its hoofs, and countless were those who pressed forward to embrace His stirrups." "How great the number of those embodiments of fidelity," testifies a fellow-traveler, "who, casting themselves before that charger, preferred death to separation from their Beloved! Methinks, that blessed steed trod upon the bodies of those pure-hearted souls." *"He* (God) *it was,"* Bahá'u'lláh Himself declares, *"Who enabled Me to depart out of the city* (Baghdád), *clothed with such majesty as none, except the denier and the malicious, can fail to acknowledge."* [2]

Further Exile

Bahá'u'lláh and His small group of companions traveled for a little over three months through various provinces of the Ottoman Empire, arriving in the capital city of Constantinople in August 1863. They had been invited by the sultan himself, but none knew what would happen next. Bahá'u'lláh took up residence in the city and made no attempt to contact the sultan, nor did He make entreaty of any kind.

Throughout history the courts of kings and rulers have been centers of intrigue. The seat of the Ottoman government, known as the Sublime Porte, was no exception. Schemers, malcontents, and petitioners of every description swarmed the capital, jostling and competing to further their own interests. Exiles, political refugees, businessmen, persons of prominence, and various unfortunates crowded the court, all begging favors, considerations, or patronage. Bribery, corruption, and chicanery were the rule of the day. It was expected by many that Bahá'u'lláh would use the opportunity afforded by proximity to the rulers of the empire to solicit aid for Himself. His friends encouraged Him to do so, and His enemies, particularly the Persian ambassador, feared that He might win the support, even the allegiance, of influential members of the Turkish government. But Bahá'u'lláh refused to do anything that might associate the name of His faith with such sordid dealings. He made no petition nor any other effort to make formal contact with the government. Even when ministers called upon Him, He did not take advantage of the potential openings they provided.

Nevertheless, the Persian ambassador was far too anxious to allow the situation to remain as it was. He and his allies pressed the Ottoman authorities to remove Bahá'u'lláh from the capital to a place where He would not be able to exert any influence. They used Bahá'u'lláh's silence as evidence that He was against the government. At first the government resisted. The chief minister was impressed by Bahá'u'lláh's "exemplary conduct" and considered His teachings "worthy of high esteem."[3] In the end, however, he was prevailed upon. After only a few months in Constantinople, Bahá'u'lláh and His companions were once again forced to relocate. This time it was to Adrianople, a provincial city in Ottoman-held Europe, known today as Edirne, Turkey. The move took place in weather so cold that on the road they occasionally encountered the corpses of travelers who had frozen to death. Upon arrival in Adrianople they were given poor housing. Without adequate clothing, shelter, and other necessities, the exiles suffered tremendously. Neither Bahá'u'lláh nor any of His retinue had been charged with a crime, yet they had been summarily and hastily removed. At that point it became clear that they were, in effect, prisoners of the state.

Bahá'u'lláh sent a message of stern rebuke to the Persian ambassador, upbraiding him for this unjust treatment and boldly asserting the ultimate triumph of God's Cause.

Crisis from Within

Once again Bahá'u'lláh found Himself banished, this time to Ottoman-held Europe. His arrival marked the first time in recorded history that the Founder of a world religion had set foot on the European continent. Moses, Christ, and Muḥammad had all spent the entirety of Their lives in the Middle East, although in due course each of the religions They founded has had a profound impact upon the West. Bahá'u'lláh predicted that the same pattern would repeat itself in this age, but on a vastly larger scale. Christ had stated, "For as the lightning comes from the east and shines as far as the west, so will be the coming of the Son of man." Bahá'u'lláh, apparently echoing these words, stated, "In the East the light of His Revelation hath broken; in the West have appeared the signs of His dominion. Ponder this in your hearts, O people. . . ."[4]

From Adrianople Bahá'u'lláh communicated news of His declaration of His mission to the Bábís in Persia. This announcement was greeted with joy. In a short time virtually all of them rallied to Him, for they had already come to regard Him as the leader of the faith. Indeed, quite a few had suspected that He was the Promised One, and a handful had openly professed their faith before His own declaration. It was during this period of Bahá'u'lláh's stay in Adrianople that His followers became known as *Bahá'ís*—followers of Bahá.

It had been barely twenty years since the birth of the Bábí Faith. The community of believers had survived a series of devastating calamities, including the martyrdom of the Báb, the deaths of thousands of His followers, the banishment of Bahá'u'lláh from His native land, and now His further banishment to the remote city of Adrianople. In spite of it all, the persecuted faithful had steadily regained their spirit and their sense of purpose.

At this moment the new faith faced its gravest crisis—the threat of division from within. To understand it we must retrace our steps back to Bahá'u'lláh's days in Persia.

Before His martyrdom the Báb appointed Bahá'u'lláh's half-brother Mírzá Yahyá, known as Azal, as the nominal head of the Bábí community pending the appearance of the Promised One. At the time of the Báb's death, Azal was in his late teens. He had grown up under the loving care of Bahá'u'lláh from the age of eight, when their father had died. But he shared few of Bahá'u'lláh's personal qualities. He was neither intellectually gifted nor possessed of great virtue. Rather, he was self-centered, envious, and capable of deceit. In particular, he was extremely cowardly. In the years after the death of the Báb and before Bahá'u'lláh's banishment from Persia, he spent his time in hiding, fearful of sharing the fate of so many of his fellow believers. Yet his position as head of the community was necessary, for it deflected attention from Bahá'u'lláh. This allowed Bahá'u'lláh relative freedom to see to the community's affairs.

Azal did not accompany Bahá'u'lláh into exile from Persia but did follow Him a little later. In Baghdad he had quickly perceived Bahá'u'lláh's ascending leadership and set about to undermine it. Together with a few confederates, Azal began a campaign of calumny against Bahá'u'lláh intended to harm His prestige among the Bábís and the general citizenry. It was due in large part to Azal's intrigues that Bahá'u'lláh had departed for the mountains of Kurdistan. Bahá'u'lláh never launched a counterattack. Indeed, He never even questioned Azal's position as nominal head of the faith. On the contrary, He kept silent in the face of these plots and even told others who wished to take action against Azal to be forbearing. He continued to treat Azal with kindness and generosity, ensuring that he received monetary support from His own meager resources. Azal did not take advantage of Bahá'u'lláh's absence by circulating openly, although this would have been his golden opportunity. He was far too concerned for his own safety. He remained in seclusion, sometimes in disguise, refusing to divulge his whereabouts to any but a few for fear that he would come to harm. He even went so far as to threaten with excommunication any Bábí who so much as mentioned his location. This was in striking contrast to Bahá'u'lláh's fearless public support of the Báb.

At one point the news came that a believer in Persia had been martyred. Fearing a general renewal of the persecutions, Azal left for Basra, disguised as a Jewish shoe merchant. When it soon became apparent that there was no need for alarm, he returned to Baghdad. Such was the pattern of cowardice that ruled his life.

Azal and his associates would instigate the more impressionable believers to all kinds of heinous activity. At one point Azal wrote a treatise proclaiming himself to be the prophetic successor of the Báb. One of the Bábís in Persia wrote an argument refuting this claim. Azal lashed out against this person in a new book, calling upon the believers to take his life and that of one of his admirers. Azal dispatched his own servant to Persia to do the bloody deed, which was later accomplished, albeit in Baghdad.

These infamous events brought great sorrow to Bahá'u'lláh. Azal would stop at nothing to advance his own position. Not only did he resort to murder, he did not seem to care that he was causing incalculable damage to the reputation of the new faith. He even stooped to introducing his own additions into the writings of the Báb, portraying himself as equal to God.

When the time came for Bahá'u'lláh's departure from Baghdad, Azal again did not accompany Him out of the city for fear of detection. Instead he traveled in disguise for some time, catching up with the retinue after it was well on its way. In Constantinople he and his associates continued their sordid practices, complaining to the authorities that Bahá'u'lláh was cheating them out of their share of the government's allowance. This was not the case at all, but they said so in order to damage His reputation.

Now, in Adrianople, it was becoming more and more clear that Bahá'u'lláh's sun was ascending. The masses of the Bábís now called themselves Bahá'ís, and Bahá'u'lláh, despite the intrigues of His enemies, was becoming famed even among nonbelievers for His knowledge, character, and spiritual gifts. Azal resorted to what means he could to cause Him harm.

Azal eventually concluded that there was only one thing to do. Contrary to his past habits, he began inviting Bahá'u'lláh to dine at his home. One day, as his own wife would later testify, he introduced poison into Bahá'u'lláh's tea. The effect was devastating, causing an illness that lasted for a whole month. Although the illness did not prove fatal, Bahá'u'lláh was left with a shaking hand for the rest of His life.

The time had come for Bahá'u'lláh to formally acquaint Azal with His station and demand a response. This He did by way of a written message. Azal requested and received a one-day respite to ponder his reply, after which he issued his own counter-declaration that he was the recipient of an independent revelation from God.

Only a very few sided with Azal, but this breach caused great harm to the faith. He and his handful of followers continued a campaign of abuse directed against Bahá'u'lláh, accusing Him of anti-government activity, abuse of Azal's rights, and other crimes. For a time these accusations gained currency in some circles, much to the detriment of Bahá'u'lláh's reputation. Emboldened by Bahá'u'lláh's customary patience and forbearance, and egged on by his comrades, Azal grew so bold as to challenge Bahá'u'lláh in 1867 to a public debate in order to establish which of them was the legitimate claimant to authority. Azal foolishly assumed that Bahá'u'lláh would never consent to such a public display. Now, however, the unity and prestige of the Cause of God itself were threatened, and Bahá'u'lláh immediately accepted. Then Azal's true nature once again asserted itself. Knowing that he could never best Bahá'u'lláh in open debate, he did not dare rise to the challenge that he himself had issued.

These events caused Bahá'u'lláh intense anguish, especially since His own half-brother was at the center of it all. As later events would show, Azal's attempted breach came to nothing. He would continue in his perfidious ways, never to repent, and would die years later, alone and friendless. This episode served in the end to strengthen the Cause and to prove that this revelation would be impervious to all attempts at creating schism. But the events as they unfolded made for a crisis of the gravest order.

CHAPTER 9

PROCLAMATION TO THE KINGS AND RULERS

While Bahá'u'lláh was making clear to the Bábís that He was God's new Messenger, He was also making this announcement to the world, and while in Adrianople sent many of His letters to the great rulers of His day, announcing the advent of the Day of God, calling upon them to end tyranny and oppression and to establish justice and peace in the world. This series of announcements would continue after He left the city on the next stage of His exile.

The nineteenth century was a period of unbridled ambition on the part of the great nations and empires. During this era they jockeyed for positions of eminence as world powers. Alliances were made and broken, wars fought, and huge territories absorbed, all in the name of national destiny. All but a few were ruled by despots in whose hands absolute power was concentrated. These rulers, in the main, considered their power to have been conferred upon them by God. It was, they believed, their divine right to rule, and their goal was to gain wealth and power in God's name. In this mission they found support among the academics, intellectuals, press, and other leaders of their day. That this meant indescribable hardship for the masses of humanity, and even their own subjects, they considered a necessary evil.

These sovereigns did not welcome bold challenges from their subjects. Particularly in the East, where they had the power of life and death over all, rulers seldom entertained direct accusations against them. Those individuals who dared to speak out typically met a grim fate.

Then Bahá'u'lláh, a prisoner, Himself a victim of two of these same despots, courageously issued His own judgment to them. Addressing the rulers and peoples of the earth collectively, and certain rulers individually, He rebuked the selfishness, tyranny, and unrighteousness that are the cause of humanity's agelong sufferings. He called upon these rulers to unite and, in the name of justice, establish "the Lesser Peace," wherein the nations of the earth will be reconciled among themselves.

He wrote to the shah of Persia, a vicious and fickle tyrant who had been responsible for the martyrdom of the Báb, for Bahá'u'lláh's exile, and for the deaths of thousands of Bábís. In this letter He speaks of His own motives and calls upon the shah to behave with justice:

> O King! I was but a man like others, asleep upon My couch, when lo, the breezes of the All-Glorious were wafted over Me, and taught Me the knowledge of all that hath been. This thing is not from Me, but from One Who is Almighty and All-Knowing. And He bade Me lift up My voice between earth and heaven, and for this there befell Me what hath caused the tears of every man of understanding to flow. The learning current amongst men I studied not; their schools I entered not. Ask of the city wherein I dwelt, that thou mayest be well assured that I am not of them who speak falsely. . . .
>
> Look upon this Youth, O King, with the eyes of justice; judge thou, then, with truth concerning what hath befallen Him. Of a verity, God hath made thee His shadow amongst men, and the sign of His power unto all that dwell on earth. Judge thou between Us and them that have wronged Us without proof and without an enlightening Book. They that surround thee love thee for their own sakes, whereas this Youth loveth thee for thine own sake, and hath had no desire except to draw thee nigh unto the seat of grace, and to turn thee toward the right hand of justice. Thy Lord beareth witness unto that which I declare. . . .[1]

In this same message Bahá'u'lláh prays that God will allow His imprisonment to result in freedom for humanity:

> I have seen, O Sháh, in the path of God what eye hath not seen nor ear heard. . . . How numerous the tribulations which have rained, and will soon rain, upon Me! I advance with My face set towards Him Who is the Almighty, the All-Bounteous, whilst behind Me glideth the serpent. Mine eyes have rained down tears until My bed is drenched.
>
> I sorrow not for Myself, however. By God! Mine head yearneth for the spear out of love for its Lord. . . .
>
> By God! Though weariness lay Me low, and hunger consume Me, and

the bare rock be My bed, and My fellows the beasts of the field, I will not complain, but will endure patiently as those endued with constancy and firmness have endured patiently, through the power of God, the Eternal King and Creator of the nations, and will render thanks unto God under all conditions. We pray that, out of His bounty—exalted be He—He may release, through this imprisonment, the necks of men from chains and fetters, and cause them to turn, with sincere faces, towards His face, Who is the Mighty, the Bounteous. . . .[2]

But the shah ignored the summons. The messenger who delivered it, a young follower of Bahá'u'lláh, was tortured and killed. The shah never replied.

Another recipient was the Ottoman sultan, in whose dominions Bahá'u'lláh was a prisoner. Far from begging for mercy, and far from flattering him, Bahá'u'lláh addresses the sultan in courageous and clear terms:

Beware, O King, that thou gather not around thee such ministers as follow the desires of a corrupt inclination, as have cast behind their backs that which hath been committed into their hands and manifestly betrayed their trust. Be bounteous to others as God hath been bounteous to thee, and abandon not the interests of thy people to the mercy of such ministers as these. Lay not aside the fear of God, and be thou of them that act uprightly. Gather around thee those ministers from whom thou canst perceive the fragrance of faith and of justice, and take thou counsel with them, and choose whatever is best in thy sight, and be of them that act generously. . . .

Take heed that thou resign not the reins of the affairs of thy state into the hands of others, and repose not thy confidence in ministers unworthy of thy trust, and be not of them that live in heedlessness. Shun them whose hearts are turned away from thee, and place not thy confidence in them, and entrust them not with thine affairs and the affairs of such as profess thy faith. Beware that thou allow not the wolf to become the shepherd of God's flock, and surrender not the fate of His loved ones to the mercy of the malicious. Expect not that they who violate the ordinances of God will be trustworthy or sincere in the faith they profess. Avoid them, and preserve strict guard over thyself, lest their devices and mischief hurt thee. Turn away from them, and fix thy gaze upon God, thy Lord, the All-Glorious, the Most Bountiful. He that giveth up himself wholly to God, God shall, assuredly, be with him; and he that placeth his complete trust in God, God shall, verily, protect him from whatsoever may harm him, and shield him from the wickedness of every evil plotter. . . .

Shouldst thou cause rivers of justice to spread their waters amongst thy subjects, God would surely aid thee with the hosts of the unseen and of the seen, and would strengthen thee in thine affairs. No God is there but Him. All creation and its empire are His. Unto Him return the works of the faithful. . . .

Let thine ear be attentive, O King, to the words We have addressed to thee. Let the oppressor desist from his tyranny, and cut off the perpetrators of injustice from among them that profess thy faith. By the righteousness of God! The tribulations We have sustained are such that any pen that recounteth them cannot but be overwhelmed with anguish. No one of them that truly believe and uphold the unity of God can bear the burden of their recital. So great have been Our sufferings that even the eyes of Our enemies have wept over Us, and beyond them those of every discerning person. And to all these trials have We been subjected, in spite of Our action in approaching thee, and in bidding the people to enter beneath thy shadow, that thou mightest be a stronghold unto them that believe in and uphold the unity of God.

Have I, O King, ever disobeyed thee? Have I, at any time, transgressed any of thy laws? Can any of thy ministers that represented thee in 'Iráq produce any proof that can establish My disloyalty to thee? Nay, by Him Who is the Lord of all worlds! Not for one short moment did We rebel against thee, or against any of thy ministers. Never, God willing, shall We revolt against thee, though We be exposed to trials more severe than any We suffered in the past.[3]

The sultan treated this message from Bahá'u'lláh with the same disdain as the shah had shown. He was not moved to investigate Bahá'u'lláh's case, nor was he moved to introduce any of the reforms prescribed by Him. In another message, this one to one of the sultan's ministers, Bahá'u'lláh predicted the sovereign's imminent overthrow and death. This prediction was well-known to the Bahá'ís and those who knew them. When it came true some of the latter group became believers.

Yet another message was addressed to Napoleon III, emperor of France. His arrogant response is reported to have been, "'If this man is God, I am two gods.'"[4] Bahá'u'lláh sent a second message, this time predicting the emperor's downfall:

For what thou hast done, thy kingdom shall be thrown into confusion, and thine empire shall pass from thine hands, as a punishment for that which thou hast wrought. Then wilt thou know how thou hast plainly erred. Commotions shall seize all the people in that land, unless thou arisest to help this Cause, and followest Him Who is the Spirit of God [Jesus Christ] in this, the Straight Path. Hath thy pomp made thee proud? By My Life! It shall not endure; nay, it shall soon pass away, unless thou holdest fast by this firm Cord. We see abasement hastening after thee, whilst thou art of the heedless. It behoveth thee when thou hearest His Voice calling from the seat of glory to cast away all that thou possessest, and cry out: "Here am I, O Lord of all that is in heaven and all that is on earth!"[5]

This letter was sent in 1869. Only one year later, in a swift series of events that shocked the whole world, Napoleon suffered humiliating defeat at the hands of the Prussians. He lost his power and would die in exile a few years later. Interestingly, the French agent who translated the tablet and sent it to Napoleon, aware of the promise of doom it contained, became a believer in Bahá'u'lláh as soon as it was fulfilled.

A similar warning was sent to the German kaiser, Wilhelm I, who had triumphed over the French. Calling to mind Napoleon III's fate, Bahá'u'lláh challenged Kaiser Wilhelm to meditate upon the fleeting sovereignty of this world and to behave with due humility towards God:

. . . King of Berlin! . . . Take heed lest pride debar thee from recognizing the Dayspring of Divine Revelation, lest earthly desires shut thee out, as by a veil, from the Lord of the Throne above and of the earth below. Thus counseleth thee the Pen of the Most High. He, verily, is the Most Gracious, the All-Bountiful. Do thou remember the one [Napoleon III] whose power transcended thy power, and whose station excelled thy station. Where is he? Whither are gone the things he possessed? Take warning, and be not of them that are fast asleep. He it was who cast the Tablet of God behind him, when We made known unto him what the hosts of tyranny had caused Us to suffer. Wherefore, disgrace assailed him from all sides, and he went down to dust in great loss. Think deeply, O King, concerning him, and concerning them who, like unto thee, have conquered cities and ruled over men. The All-Merciful brought them down from their palaces to their graves. Be warned, be of them who reflect.[6]

Bahá'u'lláh predicted that the current prosperity of the German nation would be followed by dire ordeals:

O banks of the Rhine! We have seen you covered with gore, inasmuch as the swords of retribution were drawn against you; and ye shall have another turn. And We hear the lamentations of Berlin, though she be today in conspicuous glory.[7]

As Bahá'u'lláh's prediction implies, the kaiser remained deaf to His call.

The czar of Russia, Alexander II, a mighty potentate and absolute ruler of vast dominions, also received the divine summons. In His message to that king Bahá'u'lláh remembered the kindness of the Russian minister, which had led to his release from prison in Tehran. He assured the king that God had destined for him a great reward on that account, provided that he would now heed His call. However, he did not.

Bahá'u'lláh also addressed Pope Pius IX in majestic language, calling upon him to recognize in this day the fulfillment of the promises of Jesus Christ:

> . . . Call thou to remembrance Him Who was the Spirit [Jesus], Who, when He came, the most learned of His age pronounced judgement against Him in His own country, whilst he who was only a fisherman believed in Him. Take heed, then, ye men of understanding heart! Thou, in truth, art one of the suns of the heaven of His names. Guard thyself, lest darkness spread its veils over thee, and fold thee away from His light. . . .
>
> Consider those who opposed the Son [Jesus], when He came unto them with sovereignty and power. How many the Pharisees who were waiting to behold Him, and were lamenting over their separation from Him! And yet, when the fragrance of His coming was wafted over them, and His beauty was unveiled, they turned aside from Him and disputed with Him. . . . None save a very few, who were destitute of any power amongst men, turned towards His face. And yet today every man endowed with power and invested with sovereignty prideth himself on His Name! In like manner, consider how numerous, in these days, are the monks who, in My Name, have secluded themselves in their churches, and who, when the appointed time was fulfilled, and We unveiled Our beauty, knew Us not, though they call upon Me at eventide and at dawn. . . .
>
> . . . The Word which the Son concealed is made manifest. It hath been sent down in the form of the human temple in this day. Blessed be the Lord Who is the Father! He, verily, is come unto the nations in His most great majesty. Turn your faces towards Him, O concourse of the righteous!
>
> . . . This is the day whereon the Rock [Peter] crieth out and shouteth, and celebrateth the praise of its Lord, the All-Possessing, the Most High, saying: "Lo! The Father is come, and that which ye were promised in the Kingdom is fulfilled!"[8]

The supreme pontiff did not respond.

Bahá'u'lláh's message to Queen Victoria is of a somewhat different character from the rest. In it He praises the queen for abolishing the slave trade and for her country's representative form of government. In this message He offers counsel as to how humanity can finally realize peace:

> O ye the elected representatives of the people in every land! Take ye counsel together, and let your concern be only for that which profiteth mankind and bettereth the condition thereof, if ye be of them that scan heedfully. Regard the world as the human body which, though at its creation whole and perfect, hath been afflicted, through various causes, with grave disorders and maladies. Not for one day did it gain ease, nay its sickness waxed more severe, as it fell under the treatment of ignorant physicians, who gave full rein to their personal desires and have erred grievously. And if, at one time, through the care of an able physician, a member of that body was healed, the rest remained afflicted as before. Thus informeth you the All-Knowing, the All-Wise.
>
> We behold it, in this day, at the mercy of rulers so drunk with pride that they cannot discern clearly their own best advantage, much less recognize a Revelation so bewildering and challenging as this. And whenever any one of them hath striven to improve its condition, his motive hath been his own gain, whether confessedly so or not; and the unworthiness of this motive hath limited his power to heal or cure.
>
> That which the Lord hath ordained as the sovereign remedy and mightiest instrument for the healing of all the world is the union of all its peoples in one universal Cause, one common Faith. This can in no wise be achieved except through the power of a skilled, an all-powerful and inspired Physician. This, verily, is the truth, and all else naught but error.[9]

Queen Victoria reportedly commented, "'If this is of God, it will endure; if not, it can do no harm.'"[10]

Bahá'u'lláh also addressed a message to the rulers of the American republics collectively, exhorting them to defend the cause of justice. Like the message to Queen Victoria, it is also different from the messages to the other rulers:

> Hearken ye, O Rulers of America and the Presidents of the Republics therein, unto that which the Dove is warbling on the Branch of Eternity. . . . Adorn ye the temple of dominion with the ornament of justice and of the fear of God, and its head with the crown of the remembrance of your Lord, the Creator of the heavens. Thus counseleth you He Who is the Dayspring of Names, as bidden by Him Who is the All-Knowing, the All-Wise. The Promised One hath appeared in this glorified Station, whereat all beings, both seen and unseen, have rejoiced. Take ye advantage of the Day of God.

Verily, to meet Him is better for you than all that whereon the sun shineth, could ye but know it. O concourse of rulers! . . . Bind ye the broken with the hands of justice, and crush the oppressor who flourisheth with the rod of the commandments of your Lord, the Ordainer, the All-Wise.[11]

The proclamation of Bahá'u'lláh to the kings and rulers of the world marked a significant stage in His unfolding ministry. Its themes would be taken up time and again throughout His remaining years as He elaborated upon the principles that would lay the foundation of an everlasting peace. That His plea fell on deaf ears at the time would not, He assured His followers, prevent God's ultimate aim from being accomplished.

CHAPTER 10

FURTHER BANISHMENT

Bahá'u'lláh's years in Adrianople followed a trajectory similar to that of the years spent in Baghdad. Despite the ill will of some Persian and Ottoman officials, and notwithstanding the treachery of His own half-brother and his handful of colleagues, Bahá'u'lláh's reputation among the populace steadily grew. Before long His spiritual power and ascendancy were recognized by high and low, Muslim and Christian. The governor of the province himself would visit Him regularly to pay his respects.

The public esteem Bahá'u'lláh came to enjoy, however, was as nothing in comparison to the love His followers had for Him. By now the word of His mission had reached the believers in Persia, and virtually all of them gave Him their unqualified allegiance. Many of the believers, now known as Bahá'ís, set out on the arduous and perilous journey from Persia in the hope of attaining His presence. Those who arrived in Adrianople were welcomed by Bahá'u'lláh and, in that corner of the Ottoman Empire, enjoyed the honor and blessing of being with Him and hearing His teachings directly. After a suitable interval most were instructed to return home and to spread the glad tidings.

All of this provoked the envy of Azal, who had effectively cut himself off from the Bahá'í community and now found himself rejected by the vast majority. Stirred to fresh intrigues, he and a few others plotted to discredit Bahá'u'lláh in the eyes of the authorities. Among their accusations was that Bahá'u'lláh was conniving with Bulgarian leaders and other European powers to capture the capital and overthrow the sultan. These "reports," although baseless, caused the authorities great fear. As a result, a new exile was ordered—this time to a place where, the authorities were certain, Bahá'u'lláh and His Cause would be doomed to oblivion.

Bahá'u'lláh and His companions had lived in Adrianople for about five years.

Then one morning, without warning, His house was surrounded by soldiers. He and His followers were informed that they must prepare to depart the city.

Bahá'u'lláh later wrote, "'The loved ones of God and His kindred were left on the first night without food . . . The people surrounded the house, and Muslims and Christians wept over Us . . . We perceived that the weeping of the people of the Son (Christians) exceeded the weeping of others—a sign for such as ponder.'"[1]

One of the companions who would share the exile described the consternation that overcame the citizens of the town. "A great tumult seized the people. All were perplexed and full of regret . . . Some expressed their sympathy, others consoled us, and wept over us . . . Most of our possessions were auctioned at half their value."[2]

A few of the foreign consuls offered assistance to Bahá'u'lláh, but He did not take advantage of their overtures. The governor of the province, who knew and admired Bahá'u'lláh, was aghast at his own government's decision. He could not bring himself to carry it out and instead deputized another official to inform Bahá'u'lláh. Before long He and several dozen of His followers were on the way to yet another place of exile in the company of Turkish escorts. Azal, caught in the web that he himself had spun, would also suffer exile, but not to the same destination as Bahá'u'lláh. He and a few others were sent to the island of Cyprus, where Azal would spend the rest of his days.

The scene of Bahá'u'lláh's departure was very much like what had occurred in Baghdad years before as masses of people turned out to bid Him farewell for the last time. The date was August 12, 1868.

Arrival in 'Akká

The city of 'Akká, also known as Acre or Accho, has existed for thousands of years. In ancient times it was known as Ptolemais. Later, under the Crusaders, it was called St. Jean d'Acre. Located on the eastern shore of the Mediterranean in what is now Israel, it was for centuries a crossroads of commerce. Relatively easy to supply and defend, it was the pride of its various rulers and the envy of their enemies. Under Ottoman rule it fell into severe decline, although its massive stone walls had enabled its defenders to thwart an attack by Napoleon in 1799.

Bahá'u'lláh entered the city in August 1868 with about seventy relatives and companions. By that time the city had deteriorated beyond even a shadow of its former glory. With narrow streets, dilapidated buildings, no sanitation, brackish water, and an utter absence of greenery, the city was a haven for vermin and disease. Its very name had become a byword for repugnance and filth; according to one proverb, a bird flying over the city would drop dead from the stench.

Its inhabitants were, for the most part, a benighted lot—poor, uneducated and fanatical. The citadel of the city, formerly a barracks, was now used as a prison. To that miserable place were sent the worst offenders of the realm. So horrendous were the conditions within the city that Bahá'u'lláh's enemies did not expect Him to survive for long.

There were two gates to the city, one by land and the other by sea. Bahá'u'lláh and His fellow exiles arrived by sea after a brief stop in the nearby port of Haifa. As they made their way into the city they were met by a throng of onlookers who had come to see and mock the "God of the Persians." A company of soldiers escorted the prisoners through the narrow streets and into the barracks. The weather was so hot and the air so rank that Bahá'u'lláh's daughter fainted as she entered the prison.

Polluted water, inadequate food, and the filthy environment soon took their toll. All but two of the prisoners became gravely ill, and three of them died. The guards refused to remove the bodies for burial without being paid, so Bahá'u'lláh offered the carpet upon which He slept to be sold to pay the expenses. Yet even after receiving payment, the guards still did not give the bodies a proper burial.

Three days after the prisoners' arrival, the sultan's decree was read to the public in the mosque. Bahá'u'lláh, His family, and companions were sentenced to life imprisonment and were forbidden to associate either with each other or with the citizens of 'Akká.

The initial phase of this imprisonment, more severe than any Bahá'u'lláh had yet experienced, marked a low point in the fortunes of His new Faith and the culmination of His sufferings. It seemed as if Bahá'u'lláh's enemies had triumphed at last, for now He was an exile in a penal colony, shorn of all possessions, completely divested of honor, without any connection to the outside world, and seemingly far from any possible influence either among His own followers or in the circles of government. At this point the vast majority of His followers did not yet know His fate. For a time there was even a rumor to the effect that He had been drowned in the sea. To an outside observer it might well have appeared that His Cause was doomed to extinction. His enemies thought so and rejoiced.

Yet this is not how Bahá'u'lláh Himself interpreted these events. He met this fate with the courage and serenity that He had shown on past occasions, predicting that the present abasement and humiliation were but a prelude to the triumph of His Cause.

"'According to what they say,'" He wrote, in reference to 'Akká, "'it is the most desolate of the cities of the world, the most unsightly of them in appearance, the most detestable in climate, and the foulest in water. It is as though it were the metropolis of the owl.'" Recounting the conditions of His confinement, He wrote, "'None knoweth what befell Us, except God, the Almighty, the All-Knowing . . . From the foundation of the world until the present day a cruelty such as this hath neither been seen nor heard of.'"3

The cruel circumstances of His arrival and captivity in 'Akká had a profound spiritual significance, portending great future developments. "'Upon our arrival,'" He would later write, "'We were welcomed with banners of light, whereupon the Voice of the Spirit cried out saying: "Soon will all that dwell on earth be enlisted under these banners."'"4

And again: "'Know thou that upon Our arrival at this Spot, We chose to designate it as the "Most Great Prison." Though previously subjected in another land (Ṭihrán) to chains and fetters, We yet refused to call it by that name. Say: Ponder thereon, O ye endued with understanding!'"5

Bahá'u'lláh had been subjected to banishment upon banishment until at last He arrived in the Holy Land, the place so closely associated with scriptural prophecies concerning the establishment of God's Kingdom. It was a land of expectation for Christians, Jews, and Muslims. Indeed, one group of German Christians settled across the bay in Haifa, arriving only months after Bahá'u'lláh, to found a colony in anticipation of Christ's imminent return. To this day one can visit the homes they built. Some of the lintels are inscribed with verses expressing their hopes for His advent. One, for example, reads, *"Der Herr ist Nahe,"* meaning "The Lord is Nigh."

Among those who had foreseen the future of this land was the prophet Isaiah, who had written that "The wilderness and the solitary place shall be glad for them, and the desert shall rejoice, and blossom as the rose. It shall blossom abundantly, and rejoice even with joy and singing: the glory of Lebanon shall be given unto it, the excellency of Carmel and Sharon, they shall see the Glory of the Lord, and the excellency of our God."6

Amos had said, "The Lord will roar from Zion, and utter His voice from Jerusalem; and the habitations of the shepherds shall mourn, and the top of Carmel shall wither."7

Micah had predicted the stages by which Bahá'u'lláh would arrive in this chosen land: "from Assyria, and from the fortified cities, and from the fortress even to the river, and from sea to sea, and from mountain to mountain."8

And King David had sung the praises of the One Who would appear in one of his psalms: "Lift up your heads, O ye gates, even lift them up, ye everlasting doors; and the King of Glory shall come in. Who is this King of Glory? The Lord of Hosts, he is the King of Glory."9

Referring to 'Akká, the Prophet Muḥammad had said, "'Blessed the man that hath visited 'Akká, and blessed he that hath visited the visitor of 'Akká.'" "'He that raiseth therein the call to prayer, his voice will be lifted up unto Paradise.'"[10]
Bahá'u'lláh's son 'Abdu'l-Bahá would state years later,

> When Bahá'u'lláh came to this prison in the Holy Land, the wise men realized that the glad tidings which God gave through the tongue of the Prophets two or three thousand years before were again manifested, and that God was faithful to His promise; for to some of the Prophets He had revealed and given the good news that "the Lord of Hosts should be manifested in the Holy Land." All these promises were fulfilled; and it is difficult to understand how Bahá'u'lláh could have been obliged to leave Persia, and to pitch His tent in this Holy Land, but for the persecution of His enemies, His banishment and exile."[11]

The Reason for Bahá'u'lláh's Imprisonment

Bahá'u'lláh, like all of the Messengers and holy ones before Him, had become the object of hatred and ridicule to all but a relatively small number of followers. But what had His crime been, other than to call people to God?
He writes,

> More grievous became Our plight from day to day, nay, from hour to hour, until they took Us forth from Our prison and made Us, with glaring injustice, enter the Most Great Prison. And if anyone ask them: "For what crime were they imprisoned?", they would answer and say: "They, verily, sought to supplant the Faith with a new religion!" . . . If this be My crime, then Muḥammad, the Apostle of God, committed it before Me, and before Him He Who was the Spirit of God [Jesus Christ], and yet earlier He Who conversed with God [Moses]. And if My sin be this, that I have exalted the Word of God and revealed His Cause, then indeed am I the greatest of sinners! Such a sin I will not barter for the kingdoms of earth and heaven.[12]

His purpose was not to decry or undermine the religions of the past, but rather to fulfill their promise of the day when God would unite all humanity under the shelter of one faith. Only then will the human race enjoy true happiness and prosperity:

The Ancient Beauty* hath consented to be bound with chains that mankind may be released from its bondage, and hath accepted to be made a prisoner within this most mighty Stronghold that the whole world may attain unto true liberty. He hath drained to its dregs the cup of sorrow, that all the peoples of the earth may attain unto abiding joy, and be filled with gladness. This is of the mercy of your Lord, the Compassionate, the Most Merciful. We have accepted to be abased, O believers in the Unity of God, that ye may be exalted, and have suffered manifold afflictions, that ye might prosper and flourish. He Who hath come to build anew the whole world, behold, how they that have joined partners with God have forced Him to dwell within the most desolate of cities![13]

Bahá'u'lláh would spend some twenty-four years—the remaining third of His life and more than half of His total ministry—in 'Akká and the surrounding area. In that time the fortunes of His faith would be restored, His humiliation would be reversed, and His Cause would be set firmly on the road towards ultimate triumph.

---

* One of Bahá'u'lláh's designations.

CHAPTER 11

YEARS OF CONFINEMENT

At first the citizens of 'Akká treated Bahá'u'lláh and His followers with scorn. Their minds had been poisoned by the authorities, who characterized the Bahá'ís as enemies of God and of Islam. This general hostility, in addition to the strict confinement, made life extremely difficult for the exiles. Two of Azal's followers had been sent with them into prison. These individuals immediately set about doing what they could to spread rumors about Bahá'u'lláh and to add in other ways to the prisoners' miseries.

It was not long before the Bahá'ís in Persia learned the whereabouts of Bahá'u'lláh. Some of them set out almost immediately on the journey to 'Akká. In those days travel in the Middle East was an arduous and hazardous affair. For those who traveled on foot, as some did, the journey took months in each direction. And they had no idea whether they would actually be permitted to see Bahá'u'lláh when they arrived.

It turned out to be very difficult for the pilgrims to enter the city. The authorities kept careful watch at the gates. Even when the city was successfully entered, it was virtually impossible to gain admittance into the citadel itself. To make matters worse, the two followers of Azal took lodgings directly over the land gate and made it their business to notify the officials whenever anyone they suspected of being a Bahá'í sought to enter.

So most of the believers who came to 'Akká in those early days were unable, after such a long and perilous trip, to enter Bahá'u'lláh's presence. Standing across the vast moat outside the citadel, they waited in the hope of obtaining a glimpse of Bahá'u'lláh behind the bars of His cell, where He would wave to them. There is a story of one such individual who had to content himself with the hope of seeing Him from afar. But he was elderly and nearly blind, and he was unable to see

Bahá'u'lláh's hand as He waved His handkerchief through the bars of the window. This pitiful incident brought tears to the eyes of Bahá'u'lláh and His family.

During Bahá'u'lláh's incarceration in 'Akká there was another terrible loss—the death of His young son Mírzá Mihdí. Deeply loved by Bahá'u'lláh and the believers for his purity of heart and high character, he had shared his father's trials and exiles from the time he was a small child. In 'Akká he developed the habit of pacing the roof of the citadel in the evenings to pray and meditate. One night, deep in reflection, he failed to notice an open skylight and fell through it to the floor below, striking a wooden crate that pierced his chest. He was twenty-two years old.

The sound of the crash brought Bahá'u'lláh and several others to him. A physician was summoned, but he was unable to help. One eyewitness recalled that Bahá'u'lláh asked His son what his wish was. The reply was, "'I wish the people of Bahá [the Bahá'ís] to be able to attain Your presence.'" "'And so it shall be,'" Bahá'u'lláh replied. "'God will grant your wish.'"[1] Mírzá Mihdí died on June 23, 1870. Bahá'u'lláh and the believers were heartbroken.

True to the promise, conditions changed within a few months. Troop movements in the region made it necessary for the Ottoman authorities to use the barracks. The prisoners were removed from the citadel and were given lodging in various parts of the city. This improved their condition a great deal.

But the followers of Azal were still afoot and restless. The two who had been consigned to prison with the Bahá'ís were eventually joined by a third, and together they made every effort to ally themselves with individuals who could help them in their schemes to discredit Bahá'u'lláh. They even went to the length of adding to Bahá'u'lláh's writings passages that were inflammatory and seditious. They succeeded in creating an atmosphere of suspicion and danger in which the Bahá'ís were forced to exist.

Before long the patience of the Bahá'ís was near the breaking point. Bahá'u'lláh told His followers to be patient and not to retaliate under any circumstances. When one believer arrived from Beirut and announced his intent to deal with the mischief-makers, Bahá'u'lláh ordered him to return home immediately, which he did. Others, however, unable to restrain themselves, decided to take action. A handful of believers, seven in all, set upon the three adversaries and killed them.

As news of the murders got out, the whole city was thrown into tumult. The people of 'Akká, already deeply suspicious of the Bahá'ís, thanks in no small measure to the efforts of the murdered men, were now fired with uncontrollable animosity towards them. The situation was so bad that even the Bahá'í children could not venture into the street without being chased and pelted with stones.

Bahá'u'lláh, Who had strictly forbidden any acts of revenge against Azal's followers, and Who had always shown the utmost forbearance towards them, was plunged into deep anguish because of what His own followers had done. Their act betrayed the most fundamental principles of His faith and damaged its reputation more than anything any outside enemy could have done.

Stricken with sorrow, He lamented, "My captivity can bring on Me no shame. Nay, by My life, it conferreth on Me glory. That which can make Me ashamed is the conduct of such of My followers as profess to love Me, yet in fact follow the Evil One."[2]

Later He would reiterate this point, saying:

"My imprisonment doeth Me no harm, neither the tribulations I suffer, nor the things that have befallen Me at the hands of My oppressors. That which harmeth Me is the conduct of those who, though they bear My name, yet commit that which maketh My heart and My pen to lament."[3]

He also wrote, returning to this theme,

I sorrow not for the burden of My imprisonment. Neither do I grieve over My abasement, or the tribulation I suffer at the hands of Mine enemies. By My life! They are My glory, a glory wherewith God hath adorned His own Self. Would that ye know it! . . .

My sorrows are for those who have involved themselves in their corrupt passions, and claim to be associated with the Faith of God, the Gracious, the All-Praised.

It behoveth the people of Bahá to die to the world and all that is therein, to be so detached from all earthly things that the inmates of Paradise may inhale from their garment the sweet smelling savor of sanctity, that all the peoples of the earth may recognize in their faces the brightness of the All-Merciful, and that through them may be spread abroad the signs and tokens of God, the Almighty, the All-Wise. They that have tarnished the fair name of the Cause of God, by following the things of the flesh—these are in palpable error![4]

An investigation followed in which it was soon discovered that the seven erring believers had acted alone. Bahá'u'lláh was cleared of any responsibility in the matter, and the guilty parties were sent back to prison.

In spite of this incident, the populace gradually learned that the Personage in their midst was no ordinary prisoner. They came to appreciate His remarkable wisdom and kindness as well as His majestic presence. The change in attitude also had much to do with the character and behavior of Bahá'u'lláh's eldest son, 'Abbas, who would come to be known as 'Abdu'l-Bahá, meaning "the Servant of Bahá."

Now a young man in his late twenties, 'Abdu'l-Bahá increasingly dealt with the public on His father's behalf, so that Bahá'u'lláh would be free to tend to the affairs of the Faith. Over time 'Abdu'l-Bahá's patience, kindliness, and humanitarianism warmed the hearts of many an erstwhile foe.

Among those who experienced a transformation of attitude was Shaykh Maḥmúd, the chief Islamic official of 'Akká. Enraged at the presence in his city of these enemies of God and Islam, he decided that he must take action as a leader of the people.

Determined to find and kill Bahá'u'lláh himself, Shaykh Maḥmúd hid a weapon under his cloak, then made his way to the citadel and demanded entry. The guards could not refuse such a prominent person, so he was admitted. He asked to see Bahá'u'lláh, Whose cell lay at the top of a flight of stairs. An attendant went upstairs to seek permission for the shaykh to enter Bahá'u'lláh's presence. He returned moments later with a message from Bahá'u'lláh to the effect that the shaykh should first divest himself of that which he was carrying. This reply astonished the shaykh, but it did not change his heart. He later made another attempt, this time intending to kill Bahá'u'lláh with his own hands. The response from Bahá'u'lláh this time was that he should first purify his heart.

The shaykh was stunned. Who is this man, he asked himself, who knows the secrets of hearts? He could not bring himself to enter Bahá'u'lláh's presence that day.

Later the shaykh had a dream that made him understand Bahá'u'lláh was the fulfillment of the prophecy of the coming of the Lord to 'Akká. Upon his third attempt to visit Bahá'u'lláh he was a changed man and was taken to Bahá'u'lláh's chamber. There and then he threw himself at Bahá'u'lláh's feet and declared his belief in Him. The shaykh remained a staunch believer from that day forward.[5]

Many high officials came to know and admire both Bahá'u'lláh and 'Abdu'l-Baha. The governor became so enamored that he begged Bahá'u'lláh for the honor of performing some service for Him. Bahá'u'lláh advised him to repair the city's ancient aqueduct, which had fallen into disrepair. Its restoration provided fresh water to 'Akká's inhabitants, who came to believe that since Bahá'u'lláh's arrival the very air of the city had improved. That governor's successor likewise became a friend, going so far as to imply that he would not object if Bahá'u'lláh were to decide to leave the city for the surrounding countryside.

The Most Holy Book

Early in the year 1873, when Bahá'u'lláh had been in 'Akká for nearly five years, He revealed the Most Holy Book, which contains the laws and ordinances that would serve as the basis for the development of the Bahá'í Faith and as the framework for a future world civilization. He described this work, unique in the sacred scriptures of the world in both style and range, as "'the source of true felicity'" and the "'Unerring Balance.'" He ranked it as His foremost work, "'. . . a heaven which We have adorned with the stars of Our commandments,'" and His "'weightiest testimony unto all people, and the proof of the All-Merciful unto all who are in heaven and all who are on earth.'"[6]

The Most Holy Book was revealed in Arabic and is held by those familiar with that language to be incomparable in its power, compactness, and enchanting beauty of expression. Even in its English translation these qualities come across to some extent, for the language is both compelling and exalted. The originality of presentation, wherein themes and exhortations of very different kinds, linked by common threads, are interspersed in quick succession, is remarkable and fascinating. The majesty of tone and rapid, changing flow give the overall effect of a rushing torrent or of a rapidly changing series of panoramas, each providing a new spiritual vista. To read it is an unforgettable experience.

The Most Holy Book, or Kitáb-i-Aqdas, covers a range of essential issues. It sheds light on the purpose of divine law and on the necessity for humanity to be attentive to the Word of God. It upholds the validity of all of the divinely revealed religions, affirming their essential teachings regarding the oneness of God, personal morality, and love for others. It abrogates laws no longer in accord with the needs of this age. It proclaims new laws that are appropriate to humanity's present stage of development and that are designed to foster the unification of the peoples of the world. Such laws deal with the individual's relationship to God, with matters that benefit the individual directly, and with interpersonal and other social relationships, asserting high and uncompromising moral values.

The Most Holy Book includes exhortations, particularly to rulers and ecclesiastics, on the imperatives of justice, order, and peace and delineates essential principles for achieving them. It foreshadows the unification of the world's peoples, the establishment of universal peace, and the emergence of a new world order, establishing the basic framework for a just system of governance. Furthermore, and perhaps most significantly, it establishes a new covenant between God and humanity, providing the Bahá'í Faith with continued leadership after Bahá'u'lláh's passing and, through new and unprecedented interpretive and legislative institutions, the means for continued, orderly development with the full assurance that the integrity and unity of His Cause will be safeguarded.

The Most Holy Book is not lengthy, but its themes are profound, encompassing many aspects of the Bahá'í Faith. For this reason we shall refer to it time and again in this volume. Explanations of specific teachings will be found in later chapters.

Departure from 'Akká

The city of 'Akká had been the scene of some of the most dramatic events in the ministry of Bahá'u'lláh. Over the course of some nine years the humiliating circumstances of His arrival and His days within the citadel gave way to relative freedom. The hatred on the part of the public changed to genuine esteem. The Bahá'ís were not subjected to the same abuses as when they first arrived, and most were pursuing gainful trade and employment. These developments marked yet another instance of a recurring pattern whereby crisis was transformed into victory.

Nonetheless it could not be said that life in the city was pleasant. For one thing, Bahá'u'lláh had been a lifelong lover of nature. As a young man He had loved horseback riding and the countryside. 'Akká, utterly barren, afforded not so much as a glimpse of greenery. When nine years had gone by He made a remark about this. 'Abdu'l-Bahá, deeply touched by this comment, took steps to secure a location in the countryside for Him to reside. When Bahá'u'lláh left 'Akká to take up residence there, He met no opposition from the authorities, even though the sultan's decree was still nominally in force.

Bahá'u'lláh would reside at this place in the countryside for two years. Then an opportunity came to rent, and later purchase, another more spacious home not far away. The mansion was located in the vicinity of a garden known as Bahjí, meaning "Delight," and the Bahá'ís came to call it by that name. The original owner had fled the area after an outbreak of plague. Bahjí would be Bahá'u'lláh's residence from 1879 until His passing some thirteen years later.

The mansion of Bahjí was near the city of 'Akká, but it was surrounded by natural beauty. Among its pleasant features was a stand of tall pines, some of which are still there today. From His room on the second floor of the mansion He could see the Mediterranean Sea and, in the distance, Mount Carmel.

Although Bahá'u'lláh was nominally still a prisoner, this change in circumstances was no less than miraculous. He and His companions had arrived in 'Akká only a few years before, condemned to perpetual imprisonment within the citadel. They had been met with jeers and insults and made to suffer the harshest privations imaginable. At that time few observers would have predicted a complete reversal of the situation. Yet in the earliest days after their arrival Bahá'u'lláh had written, "'Fear not. These doors shall be opened. My tent shall be pitched on Mount Carmel, and the utmost joy shall be realized.'"[7] And so it was. At Bahjí Bahá'u'lláh occasionally received prominent persons of all kinds who came with humble spirit to partake of His wisdom and His kind hospitality. He now enjoyed a prestige that excited consternation in His foes and awe in His friends. It was almost as if the tribulations of only a few years before had been blotted from memory. Thus did the long established pattern assert itself yet again, transforming abasement into conspicuous glory and defeat into undeniable victory.

Dr. John Esslemont, in his book *Bahá'u'lláh and the New Era*, offers a memorable depiction of life at Bahjí during this period:

> Having in His earlier years of hardship shown how to glorify God in a state of poverty and ignominy, Bahá'u'lláh in His later years at Bahjí showed how to glorify God in a state of honor and affluence. The offerings of hundreds of thousands of devoted followers placed at His disposal large funds which He was called upon to administer. Although His life at Bahjí has been described as truly regal, in the highest sense of the word, yet it must not be imagined that it was characterized by material splendor or extravagance. The Blessed Perfection* and His family lived in very simple and modest fashion, and expenditure on selfish luxury was a thing unknown in that household. Near His home the believers prepared a beautiful garden called Riḍván, in which He often spent many consecutive days or even weeks, sleeping at night in a little cottage in the garden. Occasionally He went further afield. He made several visits to 'Akká and Haifa, and on more than one occasion pitched His tent on Mount Carmel, as He had predicted when imprisoned in the barracks at 'Akká.[8]

For the believers, Bahjí truly lived up to its name, "Delight." Increasing numbers made their way there from points all over the Middle East, but especially Persia, staying in the precincts of the mansion and enjoying the incalculable blessing of nearness to Him. With enraptured hearts they listened to His words, witnessed the outpouring of sacred verses, and partook of His infinite love. By their written accounts it is clear that, for them, this was heaven.

Believers who later attempted to describe what it was like to be with Bahá'u'lláh found it very difficult to do so. Even those who did not give Him their allegiance were deeply affected; they were inevitably awed and humbled when in His presence. It was common for individuals to come intending to ask certain questions, only to find themselves so overwhelmed as to forget them completely. This even happened to His foes. Often such persons would later attribute Bahá'u'lláh's mysterious influence over them to sorcery!

One of the well-known early believers was named Ḥaydar-'Alí. He enjoyed the blessing of meeting Bahá'u'lláh on a number of occasions and observed His interactions with His guests:

---

* An appellation referring to Bahá'u'lláh.

"Although he [Bahá'u'lláh] showed much compassion and loving-kindness, and approached anyone who came to His presence with tender care and humbleness, and often used to make humorous remarks to put them at ease, yet in spite of these, no one, whether faithful or disbelieving, learned or unlettered, wise or foolish, was able to utter ten words in His presence in the usual everyday manner. Indeed, many would find themselves to be tremulous with an impediment in their speech.

"Some people asked permission to attain His presence for the sole purpose of conducting arguments and engaging in controversies. As a favour on His part, and in order to fulfil the testimony and to declare conclusively the proofs, He gave these permission to enter the court of His majesty and glory. As they entered the room, heard His voice welcoming them in, and gazed at His countenance beaming with the light of grandeur, they could not help but prostrate themselves at His door. They would then enter and sit down. When He showed them where to sit, they would find themselves unable to utter a word or put forward their questions. When they left they would bow to Him involuntarily. Some would be transformed through the influence of meeting Him and would leave with the utmost sincerity and devotion, some would depart as admirers, while others would leave His presence, ignorant and heedless, attributing their experience to pure sorcery.

". . . To be brief, the bounties which were vouchsafed to a person as a result of attaining His presence were indescribable and unknowable. The proof of the sun is the sun itself."[9]

Some people might attribute descriptions of Bahá'u'lláh given by the believers to their impressionable state. After all, they might argue, if one expects to meet God's Messenger then one is predisposed to be impressed. Ḥaydar-'Alí, noting this, made this comment:

"When a believer describes what he has experienced in the presence of Bahá'u'lláh, his impressions may be interpreted as being formed through his attitude of self-effacement and a feeling of utter nothingness in relation to Him. But to what can it be attributed when one enters into His presence as an antagonist and leaves as a believer, or comes in as an enemy but goes out as a friend, or comes to raise controversial arguments, but departs without saying anything and, due to wilful blindness, attributing this to magic?"[10]

Ḥaydar-'Alí recorded many memorable descriptions of his encounters with Bahá'u'lláh. Here is one such description of what it was like to be in His presence:

"His blessed person appeared in the form of a human being, but His very movements, His manners, His way of sitting or standing, eating or drinking, even His sleep or wakefulness, were each a miracle to me. Because His perfections, His exalted character, His beauty, His glory, His most excellent titles and most august attributes revealed to me that He was peerless and without parallel. He was matchless with no one to join partners with Him, unique with no peer or equal, the One and Single without a deputy . . . I saw a Person Who, from the human point of view, was like the rest of humanity. However, if one were to add the love, mercy and compassion of all the peoples of the world together, they would appear as a drop when compared with the ocean of His tender mercy and loving-kindness. I even seek God's forgiveness for making such a comparison. Similarly, if one brought together all the knowledge of science, crafts, philosophy, politics, natural history and divinity possessed by mankind, it would seem, in comparison with His knowledge and understanding, as an atom compared to the sun. If one weighed the might and power of kings, rulers, Prophets and Messengers against His omnipotence and sovereignty, His grandeur and glory, His majesty and dominion, they would be as insignificant as a touch of moisture compared with the waters of the sea . . . As I observed every one of His attributes, I discovered my inability to emulate Him, and realized that all the peoples of the world will never be able to attain to His perfections."[11]

PART 2

SOME BASIC TEACHINGS OF BAHÁ'U'LLÁH

CHAPTER 12

THE OCEAN OF HIS WORDS

Bahá'u'lláh's years at Bahjí were noteworthy for the constant stream of writings that poured from His pen. His writings are sacred scripture, direct revelation from God. He has compared them to a vast ocean, and they are indeed voluminous, comprising over the course of His forty-year ministry a total of some one hundred volumes.

In His writings Bahá'u'lláh deals with virtually every aspect of spiritual reality and the human condition. He wrote in various styles, always in superb language. Often He wrote replies to letters sent to Him by believers. His mastery of both Persian and Arabic was absolute. His works were hailed in His own day by friend and stranger as masterpieces of literary expression. Even His enemies conceded this. This ability would have been an extraordinary achievement in its own right, especially with regard to literary Arabic, which normally required a lifetime of intensive study and practice to acquire. But it is all the more remarkable when one realizes that Bahá'u'lláh was not a scholar. He received little formal education while growing up.

As the son of a nobleman, Bahá'u'lláh received a traditional aristocratic education. This meant a rudimentary exposure to the Koran and to the works of some Persian poets and a concentration on penmanship. Functional literacy was all that was normally required for a person of His position. In addition, young nobles typically learned such skills as riding, fencing, and hunting, for these were in keeping with their station in life. This was quite different from the training received by religious scholars, who often devoted their entire lives to the acquisition of Arabic and to refining their stylistic skill. Such persons also spent years studying philosophy and theology, and in the end only a few were ever regarded as having attained thorough knowledge of these subjects.

Bahá'u'lláh was considered a prodigy because of His apparently effortless mastery of literary forms of Arabic and His profound insight into religious and social issues. People were amazed to learn that He had never received formal religious training. Bahá'u'lláh Himself asserted that His knowledge was bestowed upon Him by God and that His writings were the greatest proof of His claim to Prophethood after His own person. In His letter to the shah of Persia, to which we have already referred, He stated that His learning was not of this world and challenged the shah to verify for himself that He had received no formal education.

Many observers were astonished at the ease with which Bahá'u'lláh referenced the works of other writers, often referring to them in depth even though He had never actually read them. He stated that this ability was divinely conferred: "Thou knowest full well," He wrote to one believer,

> that We perused not the books which men possess and We acquired not the learning current amongst them, and yet whenever We desire to quote the sayings of the learned and of the wise, presently there will appear before the face of thy Lord in the form of a tablet all that which hath appeared in the world and is revealed in the Holy Books and Scriptures. Thus do We set down in writing that which the eye perceiveth. Verily His knowledge encompasseth the earth and the heavens.[1]

The way in which Bahá'u'lláh composed His writings was also remarkable. He usually dictated to His secretary in a continuous flow, often speaking so rapidly that the secretary could barely keep up with Him. Eyewitnesses testified to the awesome spiritual power that filled the room whenever He revealed the Word of God. At such times His words came out like a rushing torrent. This He did sometimes for hours on end, even under the most adverse conditions such as illness, grief, or exhaustion.

"Day and night," an eyewitness wrote, "the Divine verses were raining down in such number that it was impossible to record them. Mírzá Áqá Ján [Bahá'u'lláh's secretary] wrote them as they were dictated, while the Most Great Branch* was continually occupied in transcribing them. There was not a moment to spare."[2]

> "A number of secretaries," Nabíl has testified, "were busy day and night and yet they were unable to cope with the task. Among them was Mírzá Báqir-i-Shírází. . . . He alone transcribed no less than two thousand verses every day. He labored during six or seven months. Every month the equivalent of several volumes would be transcribed by him and sent to Persia. About twenty volumes, in his fine penmanship, he left behind as a remembrance for Mírzá

---

* 'Abdu'l-Bahá, Bahá'u'lláh's eldest son.

Áqá Ján." Bahá'u'lláh, Himself, referring to the verses revealed by Him, has written: *"Such are the outpourings . . . from the clouds of Divine Bounty that within the space of an hour the equivalent of a thousand verses hath been revealed."* . . . *"I swear by God!"* He, in another connection has affirmed, *"In those days the equivalent of all that hath been sent down aforetime unto the Prophets hath been revealed." "That which hath already been revealed in this land* (Adrianople)," He, furthermore, referring to the copiousness of His writings, has declared, *"secretaries are incapable of transcribing. It has, therefore, remained for the most part untranscribed."*[3]

Another believer left the following description of the process of revelation:

"I recall that as Mírzá Áqá Ján was recording the words of Bahá'u'lláh at the time of revelation, the shrill sound of his pen could be heard from a distance of about twenty paces. . . .*

"Mírzá Áqá Ján had a large ink-pot the size of a small bowl. He also had available about ten to twelve pens and large sheets of paper in stacks. In those days all letters which arrived for Bahá'u'lláh were received by Mírzá Áqá Ján. He would bring these into the presence of Bahá'u'lláh and, having obtained permission, would read them. Afterwards the Blessed Beauty† would direct him to take up his pen and record the Tablet which was revealed in reply . . .

"Such was the speed with which he used to write the revealed Word that the ink of the first word was scarcely yet dry when the whole page was finished. It seemed as if someone had dipped a lock of hair in the ink and applied it over the whole page. None of the words was written clearly and they were illegible to all except Mírzá Áqá Ján. There were occasions when even he could not decipher the words and had to seek the help of Bahá'u'lláh. When revelation had ceased, then . . . Mírzá Áqá Ján would rewrite the Tablet in his best hand and dispatch it to its destination . . ."[4]

When Bahá'u'lláh was finished His secretaries would make a clean copy. Occasionally He made corrections due to errors made by the assistants. Then the document would sometimes receive a seal indicating His approval. Thus, for the first time in the history of religion, the personally authenticated writings of a Messenger of God are available for anyone to read and study.

---

* The pen was made of reed, hence the sound it made as it scratched over the paper.
† An appellation referring to Bahá'u'lláh.

CHAPTER 13

SPIRITUAL TRUTHS

In His writings Bahá'u'lláh affirms many ancient truths, sheds light on age-old questions, and opens new vistas of understanding. Through them, He has infused a fresh spirit into the religion of God and provided guidance for the individual and for humanity as a whole.

Let us review some of Bahá'u'lláh's basic teachings about spiritual reality. It should be emphasized at the outset that this is only a summary. The purpose here is to touch upon the fundamentals as a means of encouraging further personal investigation.

We have already mentioned that Bahá'u'lláh taught that there is only one God. He stated that "God in His Essence and in His own Self hath ever been unseen, inaccessible, and unknowable."[1] God is neither male nor female, although the limitations and conventions of our language and many others have led us to refer to Him in the masculine. He is personal, meaning that He is conscious and rational and has a will and a purpose. Although He is not a person, He is also not some mindless force, as some people believe.

God is eternal, omniscient, almighty, and omnipresent. He is not the same as His creation, but distinct and transcendent. He is infinitely exalted above human conception:

> To every discerning and illuminated heart it is evident that God, the unknowable Essence, the Divine Being, is immensely exalted beyond every human attribute, such as corporeal existence, ascent and descent, egress and regress. Far be it from His glory that human tongue should adequately recount His praise, or that human heart comprehend His fathomless mystery. He is, and hath ever been, veiled in the ancient eternity of His Essence, and

will remain in His Reality everlastingly hidden from the sight of men. "No vision taketh in Him, but He taketh in all vision; He is the Subtile, the All-Perceiving.". . .[2]

God is the Creator of all things. His creation is infinite, has always existed, and will always continue to exist:

As to thy question concerning the origin of creation. Know assuredly that God's creation hath existed from eternity, and will continue to exist forever. Its beginning hath had no beginning, and its end knoweth no end.[3]

Know thou of a truth that the worlds of God are countless in their number, and infinite in their range. None can reckon or comprehend them except God, the All-Knowing, the All-Wise.[4]

God has imbued all of creation with the signs of His attributes. Yet of all created things, humanity has been endowed with unique capacities:

Whatever is in the heavens and whatever is on the earth is a direct evidence of the revelation within it of the attributes and names of God, inasmuch as within every atom are enshrined the signs that bear eloquent testimony to the revelation of that Most Great Light. Methinks, but for the potency of that revelation, no being could ever exist. How resplendent the luminaries of knowledge that shine in an atom, and how vast the oceans of wisdom that surge within a drop! To a supreme degree is this true of man, who, among all created things, hath been invested with the robe of such gifts, and hath been singled out for the glory of such distinction. For in him are potentially revealed all the attributes and names of God to a degree that no other created being hath excelled or surpassed.[5]

Having created the world and all that liveth and moveth therein, He, through the direct operation of His unconstrained and sovereign Will, chose to confer upon man the unique distinction and capacity to know Him and to love Him—a capacity that must needs be regarded as the generating impulse and the primary purpose underlying the whole of creation. . . . Upon the inmost reality of each and every created thing He hath shed the light of one of His names, and made it a recipient of the glory of one of His attributes. Upon the reality of man, however, He hath focused the radiance of all of His names and attributes, and made it a mirror of His own Self. Alone

of all created things man hath been singled out for so great a favor, so enduring a bounty.[6]

That the attributes of God are fully mirrored in humanity echoes the biblical
teaching that we are created in God's image. In the Hidden Words, Bahá'u'lláh
expresses this concept, speaking as the voice of God: "Veiled in My immemorial
being and in the ancient eternity of My essence, I knew My love for thee; therefore I created thee, have engraved on thee Mine image and revealed to thee My
beauty."[7]

Human beings have been created to know and to love God. Each person is
endowed with an immortal soul. The purpose of this physical existence is to acquire divine attributes that will prepare us for the eternal life to come. But we
cannot know God directly because He is far above our understanding. For this
reason God manifests Himself to us through His Prophets:

> The door of the knowledge of the Ancient of Days being thus closed in
> the face of all beings, the Source of infinite grace, according to His saying,
> "His grace hath transcended all things; My grace hath encompassed them
> all," hath caused those luminous Gems of Holiness to appear out of the
> realm of the spirit, in the noble form of the human temple, and be made
> manifest unto all men, that they may impart unto the world the mysteries of
> the unchangeable Being, and tell of the subtleties of His imperishable Es-
> sence.
>
> These sanctified Mirrors, these Day Springs of ancient glory, are, one and
> all, the Exponents on earth of Him Who is the central Orb of the universe,
> its Essence and ultimate Purpose. From Him proceed their knowledge and
> power; from Him is derived their sovereignty. The beauty of their counte-
> nance is but a reflection of His image, and their revelation a sign of His
> deathless glory. They are the Treasuries of Divine knowledge, and the Re-
> positories of celestial wisdom. Through them is transmitted a grace that is
> infinite, and by them is revealed the Light that can never fade. . . . These
> Tabernacles of Holiness, these Primal Mirrors which reflect the light of
> unfading glory, are but expressions of Him Who is the Invisible of the
> Invisibles. By the revelation of these Gems of Divine virtue all the names
> and attributes of God, such as knowledge and power, sovereignty and do-
> minion, mercy and wisdom, glory, bounty, and grace, are made manifest.[8]

The Manifestations of God are not equal to Him. They are not God incarnate,
for God is far too exalted ever to incarnate His Essence. Rather, They are like

perfect mirrors reflecting God's attributes. They are the Revealers of His Word. In that sense, to know Them is to know God. Their purpose is to educate and uplift the souls, to guide our social and spiritual evolution, and to show us the way to eternal life. In each age They appear, revealing laws and teachings appropriate for that time:

> Men at all times and under all conditions stand in need of one to exhort them, guide them and to instruct and teach them. Therefore He hath sent forth His Messengers, His Prophets and chosen ones that they might acquaint the people with the divine purpose underlying the revelation of Books and the raising up of Messengers, and that everyone may become aware of the trust of God which is latent in the reality of every soul.[9]

Progressive Revelation

In His writings Bahá'u'lláh offers an entirely new way of understanding how God has intervened in human history through a succession of Prophets. He calls this concept "progressive Revelation,"[10] which is the process whereby God has sent Messengers to reveal His Word in every age. All of the Messengers are part of a process whose ultimate goal is the unification and salvation of humanity. They all teach the same fundamental spiritual truths, but They also reveal new laws and teachings that are appropriate to the time in which They appear. For this reason there are differences in what the Messengers have revealed. But these differences have nothing to do with the relative qualities of the Messengers, for They all possess the same knowledge, power, and capacities.

Bahá'u'lláh has specifically mentioned certain Manifestations of God Who have appeared to humanity. Among Them were Abraham, Moses, Christ, and Muḥammad. More recently, the Báb and Bahá'u'lláh appeared. Bahá'ís also accept Zoroaster, Buddha, and Krishna as Manifestations of God. And Bahá'u'lláh assures us that God has sent countless Messengers throughout the ages, even before recorded history: "Know thou that the absence of any reference to them is no proof that they did not actually exist. That no records concerning them are now available should be attributed to their extreme remoteness, as well as to the vast changes which the earth hath undergone since their time."[11]

Some believe that not all of these Messengers could have been sent by God, because They taught contradictory things. Bahá'u'lláh ascribes such apparent differences chiefly to misunderstandings on the part of Their followers. Another reason for the differences is that the religious truths the Messengers taught are relative, for each subsequent Messenger sheds new light on spiritual reality and revises particular laws according to the needs of the time.

Bahá'u'lláh states,

> There can be no doubt whatever that the peoples of the world, of whatever race or religion, derive their inspiration from one heavenly Source, and are the subjects of one God. The difference between the ordinances under which they abide should be attributed to the varying requirements and exigencies of the age in which they were revealed. All of them, except a few which are the outcome of human perversity, were ordained of God, and are a reflection of His Will and Purpose.[12]

The Bahá'í writings liken the appearance of the Messengers of God to the annual cycle of the seasons. The appearance of the Prophet is, like the springtime, a season of renewal and rebirth. The spiritual power released by His appearance to humanity is like the sun's effect in the natural world, creating a fresh impetus for growth. Gradually the sun moves to its zenith, and the world of nature matures in full summer splendor. Then there is the gradual decline of fall, which is followed by the latency of winter, but spring eventually returns, and the cycle begins anew. Similarly, each of the Messengers of God infuses the human world with fresh spiritual capacities. After a while His teachings begin to show their full effects in the world, usually long after His own lifetime. Then the initial freshness and energy gradually begin to fade, and the time comes for another Messenger. If we examine the lives of Moses, Christ, and Muḥammad, we can see this principle at work. Each brought a renewed spiritual force into the world, and in each case Their teachings became the basis for fundamental advancements in human religious and social life. It is important to state here that the need for spiritual renewal does not imply that the Messengers Themselves are no longer relevant, nor does it imply that Their teachings are no longer true. The successive appearances of the Messengers of God are simply part of an ongoing process for humanity's education.

Bahá'u'lláh explains God's motive in sending down these Messengers, or Prophets:

> The purpose of the one true God in manifesting Himself is to summon all mankind to truthfulness and sincerity, to piety and trustworthiness, to resignation and submissiveness to the Will of God, to forbearance and kindliness, to uprightness and wisdom. His object is to array every man with the mantle of a saintly character, and to adorn him with the ornament of holy and goodly deeds.[13]

In a passage of one of His writings Bahá'u'lláh refers to God as the "All-Knowing Physician."[14] He also uses the metaphor of the divine physician in reference to the Prophets, Whose task is to spiritually heal an afflicted humanity. The Prophets have unique knowledge and expertise, and Their spiritual remedy must be followed if the well-being of the whole human race is to be achieved.

According to the Bahá'í teachings, the Prophets invariably appear at a time and place when the true spirit of religion is at its lowest ebb. One of the signs of Their divine power is Their ability to transform a people who have lost the true meaning of faith and are clinging to outworn or misbegotten beliefs and practices. For example, Moses appeared to a people in bondage whose religious practice was little more than polytheism and whose moral and social life was decadent. That same people built a great nation upon the foundation of God's law as revealed through Moses. In a later age Christ appeared to that same people, who by then were once again suffering under the yoke of the oppressor. What is more, Christ criticized the religious leaders of the time for their superficial understanding of the Torah. His message eventually reached far beyond the confines of the Jewish world and became the underpinning for still further changes in humanity's social and spiritual evolution.

In the Western world there is often a tendency to think of Muḥammad as a fanatical warmonger. Most people in Europe and the United States do not think of Him as Christ-like at all. We must realize that He has been the victim of centuries of misunderstanding. In fact, the Prophet is rightly considered by His followers to be the very embodiment of wisdom, justice, and righteousness. His character was blameless and His personality profoundly spiritual and attractive. Muḥammad announced His prophetic mission to the peoples of Arabia at a time when that peninsula was the domain of savage and warlike tribes. Steeped in ignorance and superstition, they had languished at the periphery of history for many centuries. Then, in the course of a single generation, Muḥammad succeeded in uniting these feuding clans through the power of the Word of God as revealed in the Koran. As a result, the warlike tribes became like another people with a new social and spiritual ethic. The new religion spread through the Middle East to parts of Africa, Europe, and Asia. The Koran itself speaks to more than just issues of theology. It addresses issues of personal conduct as well as social issues, emphasizing justice and care for the poor and the oppressed. At its height the civilization that resulted was the envy of the world. Islamic advances in philosophy, science, literature, and government, making their way to Europe by way of returning Crusaders and through Moorish Spain, were a foundation of the Western Renaissance. Just as most Westerners refrain from judging Christ by the actions of His more fanatical followers, we should not allow the actions of modern-day Islamic fanatics to cloud our judgment of Muḥammad and the Koran.

We have already noted the decadent conditions existing in Persia when the Báb and Bahá'u'lláh appeared. According to Bahá'í writings, that country was chosen among others not because of its innate worthiness or because of any inherent superiority, but, ironically, because of its degeneracy and perversity so that the spiritually regenerative power of Their revelations would be plainly demonstrated.

What Distinguishes the Prophets

In the Book of Certitude Bahá'u'lláh points out that, to outward seeming, the Prophets are ordinary men. They eat, sleep, feel pain, and in general share with us all of the joys and sorrows of the human condition. These human characteristics, however, do not change the fact that their inner reality is altogether different from that of other human beings. Indeed, as Bahá'u'lláh states, their humanness is itself a test for humanity, for only those with spiritual perception can understand and appreciate Their words and acts.

It is also clear that the various Prophets live within specific cultural contexts. They share a language with the people among whom They live, and They share in the cultural and religious milieu into which they are born. Their teachings are tailored to some extent to the beliefs and perceptions of Their audience, but that is not to say that Their own understanding is limited by this, nor that They remain within the confines of prevalent viewpoints. Rather, they always challenge contemporary attitudes, and for that reason They inevitably meet with rejection by the masses.

What is it that separates the Prophets from other teachers and philosophers? Bahá'u'lláh states several differences that distinguish Them from ordinary men.

As we have seen, the Prophets are Manifestations of the attributes and qualities of God. Bahá'u'lláh makes clear that They do not achieve this station as the result of Their own desire or effort. They are chosen by God, and the very nature of Their souls is different from ours. They occupy a rank infinitely exalted above that of ordinary human beings. Infallible in word and deed, possessing divine knowledge, They act as channels of the Holy Spirit to humanity. Theirs is a station that no ordinary person can ever hope to attain. For these reasons Their words and acts are considered to be the pure expression of God's Will.

The Manifestations of God typically show evidence of high character and extraordinary knowledge, even from childhood. In the Gospel of Luke, Jesus' parents, after a long search, find Him engaged in conversation with elders in the Temple, who are astonished at the boy's understanding of scripture. Muḥammad was known as al-Amín, meaning "the Trusted One," and when disputes arose He, even as a young and relatively poor man, was sought by the people because of His sense of justice. We have already seen some of the extraordinary qualities displayed by both the Báb and Bahá'u'lláh while still very young. Bahá'u'lláh indicated that He was aware of His own station from early childhood, although His ministry would not begin until later in life.

The Word of God

Another distinction is that the Messengers of God reveal His Word to humanity. The nature of the Word of God is altogether different from human utterance. Bahá'u'lláh explains that the Word has unique creative power and alone is capable of effecting spiritual transformation in the human heart. The Word of God holds within it the keys to infinite spiritual knowledge. Indeed, the Word of God is the source of all other knowledge, and its effects are felt in every human undertaking. Bahá'u'lláh has written,

> The Word of God is the king of words and its pervasive influence is incalculable. It hath ever dominated and will continue to dominate the realm of being. The Great Being saith: The Word is the master key for the whole world, inasmuch as through its potency the doors of the hearts of men, which in reality are the doors of heaven, are unlocked. . . . It is an ocean inexhaustible in riches, comprehending all things. Every thing which can be perceived is but an emanation therefrom.[15]

The Word of God is not to be equated with mere words. It is the expression of God's creative power that guides and shapes human development. In the following passage Bahá'u'lláh expounds the creative power of the Word of God:

> Every word that proceedeth out of the mouth of God is endowed with such potency as can instill new life into every human frame, if ye be of them that comprehend this truth. All the wondrous works ye behold in this world have been manifested through the operation of His supreme and most exalted Will, His wondrous and inflexible Purpose. Through the mere revelation of the word "Fashioner," issuing forth from His lips and proclaiming His attribute to mankind, such power is released as can generate, through successive ages, all the manifold arts which the hands of man can produce. This, verily, is a certain truth. No sooner is this resplendent word uttered, than its animating energies, stirring within all created things, give birth to the means and instruments whereby such arts can be produced and perfected.[16]

Calling attention to the marvelous acceleration of the growth of human knowledge in His own day, Bahá'u'lláh explains that it is the direct result of His revelation. He also predicts even greater things to come:

> All the wondrous achievements ye now witness are the direct consequences of the Revelation of this Name. In the days to come, ye will, verily, behold things of which ye have never heard before. Thus hath it been decreed in the Tablets of God, and none can comprehend it except them whose sight is sharp. . . . Well is it with them that apprehend this truth.[17]

Evidence of the transformative power of the Word of God can be seen in its effects on those who sincerely believe in it. This influence is far different from any ordinary ideology or philosophy. For example, in the Gospels and in the book of Acts, the effect of Christ's teaching upon His earliest followers is apparent. Hardly any of those who believed in Him were persons of prominence or wealth. Some had led morally questionable lives before coming into contact with Him. Yet these same people were utterly transformed by their faith and experienced profound spiritual changes. Many of them devoted the rest of their lives to preaching the good news, and many paid with their lives for this. Eventually, like a great tree that had begun as a little seed, Christ's Word permeated the Mediterranean world. A morally and spiritually distinctive community of believers arose, and theirs eventually became the chief religion of the West. Few living in Jesus' time would have foreseen such a destiny for the religion, but its spread is now understood by many to be an evidence of His divine mission.

In nineteenth-century Persia thousands of individuals sacrificed their lives rather than recant their belief in the Báb and Bahá'u'lláh. In this day and time we tend to equate martyrdom with blind, unthinking fanaticism, or perhaps with some warped and pitiful dependence by weak-minded souls on a despotic leader who promises heaven in exchange for their lives and material resources. This is understandable, as there have been plenty of examples of such pathetic behavior in recent history. However, the Bábís and Bahá'ís do not belong in that category, as an unbiased examination of their history will show. These people did not harbor a death wish, and they usually avoided trouble whenever possible. Bahá'u'lláh strictly instructed His followers not to foment sedition or to take up arms against anyone, even in defense of their own lives. This made them easy victims, but their steadfastness was proof of the power of their faith. Their only motives were to stand up for the truth and to help build a new world order based on divine teachings. They knew that change sometimes requires the highest sacrifice, and they were willing to lay down their lives in order to achieve it. In this light it is clear that their choice was not born of some kind of mental perversion, but rather from the noblest of motives. We can think of parallel examples of this kind of sacrifice, such as the early Christians and those who, in our own time, gave their lives for the American and other civil rights movements.

In the Book of Certitude Bahá'u'lláh calls attention to the behavior of those who, in every age, have remained faithful to the Cause of God despite the persecutions they have been made to suffer and the antagonism of those who have rejected the Prophets. He makes it clear that the behavior of such people, on the one hand, and their persecutors on the other, lays bare the true spiritual station of both parties.

The Word of God as revealed by the Prophets, or Manifestations of God, has a unique power over the human heart. The Prophets have other qualities that separate them from other philosophers and teachers. They have the capacity to foresee future events. In the Gospels, for example, there are numerous instances of Christ's prophetic foresight. One of the best known is His prophecy concerning the destruction of Jerusalem. He also foresaw His own betrayal, death, and resurrection. The Báb predicted His own martyrdom as well as the very year when Bahá'u'lláh's ministry would begin. We have already seen that Bahá'u'lláh had this same prophetic power. He foretold the downfall of Napoleon III as a result of his arrogant response to Bahá'u'lláh's message. Likewise He foretold the overthrow of Sultan 'Abdu'l-'Azíz. He foresaw the sufferings that would be visited upon Germany. He predicted His own eventual liberation from confinement within the citadel of 'Akká. And He predicted many other things, a number of which will be covered in later chapters.

Bahá'u'lláh made other profound statements about the power of the Word of God. For example, He made clear that the Prophets do not merely predict future events. In some cases such events come about because it is Their will that it be so. Such prophecies convey a sense of the profound power of the Word of God. They are not mere predictions in the normal sense. They show clear cause and effect. As we have seen, for example, various rulers lost their power as a consequence of their behavior. Such examples demonstrate the dynamic force of the Word of God in influencing the course of human events. Revelation of God's Word is a power unique to the Manifestations of God.

The Significance of Bahá'u'lláh's Revelation

As He was preparing to leave Baghdad Bahá'u'lláh announced that He was the One Whose advent had been foretold by the Báb. He also was the One foretold in the holy books of all previous religious Dispensations.

Judaism, Christianity, and Islam all anticipate a time when good will finally triumph over evil. That era of fulfillment is known by several terms such as the "Last Day," the "Day of Judgment," the "Day of Resurrection,"[18] and so on. In some cases this is associated with the establishment of God's Kingdom; in others with the end of the world and the ascension of the righteous into heaven and eternal bliss. Some believers anticipate the appearance of a messianic figure: the Messiah, the Lord of Hosts, or the Return of Christ. Others expect that God Himself will appear to put an end to evil. Branches of other religions, including Buddhism, Hinduism, and Zoroastrianism, have similar traditions in which a great figure appears to establish this victory. The same can be said of various indigenous religions in many parts of the world.

Bahá'u'lláh taught that His coming signaled the fulfillment of all of these ancient promises. His purpose in coming is none other than to usher in God's Kingdom on earth, wherein humanity will live in peace, justice, and unity under God's Law.

Bahá'u'lláh has written,

> The time foreordained unto the peoples and kindreds of the earth is now come. The promises of God, as recorded in the holy Scriptures, have all been fulfilled. Out of Zion hath gone forth the Law of God, and Jerusalem, and the hills and land thereof, are filled with the glory of His Revelation. Happy is the man that pondereth in his heart that which hath been revealed in the Books of God, the Help in Peril, the Self-Subsisting. Meditate upon this, O ye beloved of God, and let your ears be attentive unto His Word, so that ye may, by His grace and mercy, drink your fill from the crystal waters of constancy, and become as steadfast and immovable as the mountain in His Cause.
>
> . . . This is the Day which the Pen of the Most High hath glorified in all the holy Scriptures. There is no verse in them that doth not declare the glory of His holy Name, and no Book that doth not testify unto the loftiness of this most exalted theme. Were We to make mention of all that hath been revealed in these heavenly Books and holy Scriptures concerning this Revelation, this Tablet would assume impossible dimensions.[19]

Other passages from Bahá'u'lláh's writings extol the greatness of His revelation:

> Great indeed is this Day! The allusions made to it in all the sacred Scriptures as the Day of God attest its greatness. The soul of every Prophet of God, of every Divine Messenger, hath thirsted for this wondrous Day. All the divers kindreds of the earth have, likewise, yearned to attain it.[20]

The excellence of this Day is immensely exalted above the comprehension of men, however extensive their knowledge, however profound their understanding.[21]

"Peerless is this Day, for it is as the eye to past ages and centuries, and as a light unto the darkness of the times."[22]

Referring to His own station Bahá'u'lláh writes,

Verily I say, this is the Day in which mankind can behold the Face, and hear the Voice, of the Promised One. The Call of God hath been raised, and the light of His countenance hath been lifted up upon men. It behoveth every man to blot out the trace of every idle word from the tablet of his heart, and to gaze, with an open and unbiased mind, on the signs of His Revelation, the proofs of His Mission, and the tokens of His glory.[23]

It is worth repeating here that Bahá'u'lláh did not consider Himself in any way superior to the Messengers of God Who came before Him. The only difference between Their revelations and His is the relative outpouring of God's Word and the special time of fulfillment that He has inaugurated.

Bahá'u'lláh explains that all of the Messengers reveal the same Holy Spirit. In this way Their stations are one and the same, even though They go by different names and have distinct individual identities.

This may seem to contradict what we have read in other scriptures. In the Bible we find passages that seem to equate Jesus with God and others that imply that He is subordinate to God. In the Koran it is made perfectly clear that Muḥammad is not God. Bahá'u'lláh explains that all of the Prophets have a human nature as well as a divine nature. Sometimes They speak with the voice of God, but this does not mean that They are the same as God. Bahá'u'lláh touches upon this in the following passage, which is part of a prayer: "'When I contemplate, O my God, the relationship that bindeth me to Thee, I am moved to proclaim to all created things 'verily I am God!'; and when I consider my own self, lo, I find it coarser than clay!'"[24]

Bahá'u'lláh states time and again that He is God's chosen Messenger and the Manifestation of His attributes, but He is not God Himself. In a later chapter we will examine how other scriptures support this concept.

God's Call to Humanity

Bahá'u'lláh warned us not to judge the Word of God according to human standards and beliefs. On the contrary, the Word of God is itself the standard by which all else is to be judged. For that reason we must take care not to summarily reject a Prophet because His teachings do not conform with our own prior expectations or wishes. The tendency on the part of human beings to do just that is the main reason for the sufferings of all of God's Messengers. The consequences reverberate down through centuries and ages, for humanity itself then becomes deprived of the influence of Their teachings.

Bahá'u'lláh taught that we must investigate the truth for ourselves with sincerity and purity of motive. This is what God expects—not blind adherence to the opinions of others, or tradition, or personal prejudices, or anything else that might stand in the way of our recognition of the Manifestation of God. We have already discussed the qualities of a true seeker as described by Bahá'u'lláh in the Book of Certitude. These include uprightness of conduct and genuine love for God.

All of this having been said, Bahá'u'lláh clearly did not fulfill the prophecies of past scriptures in the way that was generally expected. How could He be the Return of the Spirit of Christ, the Messiah, the Lord of Hosts, when the things that were to come to pass in the last days have apparently not yet occurred? How can we reconcile His claim with the usual interpretation of scriptures?

We have already glimpsed how Bahá'u'lláh dealt with issues of prophecy and the proofs of Prophethood in the Book of Certitude and other writings. Bahá'u'lláh Himself upholds the validity of the Bible and of the Koran as the revealed Word of God. There is ample evidence that His interpretation is precisely what was intended, even though it differs from prevailing understandings. We shall return to this theme later. However, to better understand the relationship of Bahá'u'lláh to the scriptures of other Manifestations of God, it is important first to deal with other aspects of His life and teachings.

CHAPTER 14

THE REALITY OF THE SOUL

Bahá'u'lláh affirms that God created humanity out of love. Our purpose is to know and to love God in return. The aim of this life is to acquire faith, love of God, and other spiritual qualities in preparation for the eternal life to come. For in reality we are spiritual beings, and this material existence is only a prelude to our future life.

Bahá'u'lláh stated that it is impossible for us to completely understand the nature of the life beyond. We cannot possibly imagine something different from anything we have ever experienced. Bahá'u'lláh makes this point in striking fashion. "The world beyond," He writes, "is as different from this world as this world is different from that of the child while still in the womb of its mother."[1]

This analogy is worth pondering. The purpose of life in the womb is to prepare the unborn child for life in the outer world. During this time the child is developing senses and capacities that are necessary for its continued existence and prosperity. All the while the child is oblivious to this fact. Even if there were some way it might imagine a "life to come," how could the child ever truly comprehend the vastness and wonders of the world beyond its mother's womb?

The same is true of the world beyond this. If we face death with fear and trepidation, it is only because we, like the unborn child, are ignorant of what awaits us. In the Hidden Words, Bahá'u'lláh says, "I have made death a messenger of joy to thee. Wherefore dost thou grieve?"[2]

Bahá'u'lláh taught that every human being possesses a rational soul, which is the true seat of our personality and consciousness. The soul survives physical death and exists forevermore in the world of the spirit.

This concept is very difficult to grasp, especially since the soul cannot be perceived with our senses in the same way that we can observe and understand physical phenomena. It is extremely hard for some people to imagine how it could be possible to continue to exist after death. These difficulties cause many to doubt the existence of the soul and of the life hereafter. Some people addressed Bahá'u'lláh with questions about these matters. Here is how Bahá'u'lláh answered the issue on one occasion:

Thou hast asked Me whether man, as apart from the Prophets of God and His chosen ones, will retain, after his physical death, the self-same individuality, personality, consciousness, and understanding that characterize his life in this world. If this should be the case, how is it, thou hast observed, that whereas such slight injuries to his mental faculties as fainting and severe illness deprive him of his understanding and consciousness, his death, which must involve the decomposition of his body and the dissolution of its elements, is powerless to destroy that understanding and extinguish that consciousness? How can any one imagine that man's consciousness and personality will be maintained, when the very instruments necessary to their existence and function will have completely disintegrated?

Know thou that the soul of man is exalted above, and is independent of all infirmities of body or mind. That a sick person showeth signs of weakness is due to the hindrances that interpose themselves between his soul and his body, for the soul itself remaineth unaffected by any bodily ailments. Consider the light of the lamp. Though an external object may interfere with its radiance, the light itself continueth to shine with undiminished power. In like manner, every malady afflicting the body of man is an impediment that preventeth the soul from manifesting its inherent might and power. When it leaveth the body, however, it will evince such ascendancy, and reveal such influence as no force on earth can equal. Every pure, every refined and sanctified soul will be endowed with tremendous power, and shall rejoice with exceeding gladness.[3]

And in other passages He describes the wonders of the life to come. For example:

And now concerning thy question regarding the soul of man and its survival after death. Know thou of a truth that the soul, after its separation from the body, will continue to progress until it attaineth the presence of God, in a state and condition which neither the revolution of ages and centuries, nor the changes and chances of this world, can alter. It will endure as long as the Kingdom of God, His sovereignty, His dominion and power will endure. It will manifest the signs of God and His attributes, and will reveal

His loving-kindness and bounty. The movement of My Pen is stilled when it attempteth to befittingly describe the loftiness and glory of so exalted a station. The honor with which the Hand of Mercy will invest the soul is such as no tongue can adequately reveal, nor any other earthly agency describe. Blessed is the soul which, at the hour of its separation from the body, is sanctified from the vain imaginings of the peoples of the world. Such a soul liveth and moveth in accordance with the Will of its Creator, and entereth the all-highest Paradise. The Maids of heaven, inmates of the loftiest mansions, will circle around it, and the Prophets of God and His chosen Ones will seek its companionship. With them that soul will freely converse, and will recount unto them that which it hath been made to endure in the path of God, the Lord of all worlds. If any man be told that which hath been ordained for such a soul in the worlds of God, the Lord of the throne on high and of earth below, his whole being will instantly blaze out in his great longing to attain that most exalted, that sanctified and resplendent station. . . .[4]

Many other passages like these describe the heavenly joys to come. But they also make clear that happiness in the spiritual world is dependent upon certain conditions. It comes when we live up to what God expects of us in this world. We must walk "in the ways of God."[5]

Heaven and Hell

What of the concepts of heaven and hell? The Bahá'í scriptures state that the next world is real, but it is not a physical place. We cannot perceive its existence through our physical senses because it is a different reality. It exists on a different plane than the physical universe, but the two are connected and affect each other in certain ways.

The human soul is part of that spiritual world. The soul comes into existence at the moment of conception. It is ultimately dependent for its progress and happiness upon its relationship with God. Heaven, then, is a spiritual state of nearness to God. Hell is remoteness from God.

Heaven and hell are metaphors for the relative spiritual condition of the soul. The Bahá'í scriptures state that the soul is never static. It progresses in this world and continues to progress in the life beyond, attaining ever greater perfections and closer communion with God. In this physical world progress is dependent on our own volition. If we choose to turn to God, we can progress. If not, we become the victim of our lesser nature and fail to attain true happiness. Bahá'u'lláh writes, "'Where is Paradise, and where is Hell?' Say: 'The one is reunion with Me; the other thine own self. . . .'"[6]

CHAPTER 15

THE PATH OF
SPIRITUAL PROGRESS

Bahá'u'lláh taught that spiritual progress is dependent upon certain conditions. The most important is our own conscious effort to attain it. In this respect the human being in this world is quite different from the unborn child, who has no choice in the matter of its physical development. Spiritual growth is open to all who sincerely strive. He wrote to one individual,

> And now, concerning thy question regarding the creation of man. Know thou that all men have been created in the nature made by God, the Guardian, the Self-Subsisting. . . . All that which ye potentially possess can, however, be manifested only as a result of your own volition. Your own acts testify to this truth.[1]

Yet as important as volition and striving are, no matter how much they try, human beings cannot attain spiritual progress or eternal life alone and unaided. The Manifestations of God appear so that They may teach us how to achieve our purpose and thereby attain eternal happiness:

The Prophets and Messengers of God have been sent down for the sole purpose of guiding mankind to the straight Path of Truth. The purpose underlying Their revelation hath been to educate all men, that they may, at the hour of death, ascend, in the utmost purity and sanctity and with absolute detachment, to the throne of the Most High. The light which these souls radiate is responsible for the progress of the world and the advancement of its peoples.[2]

To recognize the Manifestation of God means to have faith in Him and to obey His teachings. The opening page of the Most Holy Book contains the following passage:

> The first duty prescribed by God for His servants is the recognition of Him Who is the Dayspring of His Revelation and the Fountain of His laws, Who representeth the Godhead in both the Kingdom of His Cause and the world of creation. Whoso achieveth this duty hath attained unto all good; and whoso is deprived thereof hath gone astray, though he be the author of every righteous deed. It behooveth everyone who reacheth this most sublime station, this summit of transcendent glory, to observe every ordinance of Him Who is the Desire of the world. These twin duties are inseparable. Neither is acceptable without the other. Thus hath it been decreed by Him Who is the Source of Divine inspiration.[3]

The Manifestations of God reveal teachings conducive not only to individual spiritual progress but also to the advancement of human society. To turn away from such teachings is to ignore the only sure means for happiness:

> They whom God hath indued with insight will readily recognize that the precepts laid down by God constitute the highest means for the maintenance of order in the world and the security of its peoples. He that turneth away from them is accounted among the abject and foolish. We, verily, have commanded you to refuse the dictates of your evil passions and corrupt desires, and not to transgress the bounds which the Pen of the Most High hath fixed, for these are the breath of life unto all created things. The seas of Divine wisdom and Divine utterance have risen under the breath of the breeze of the All-Merciful. Hasten to drink your fill, O men of understanding! . . .
> O ye peoples of the world! Know assuredly that My commandments are the lamps of My loving providence among My servants, and the keys of My mercy for My creatures. Thus hath it been sent down from the heaven of the Will of your Lord, the Lord of Revelation. Were any man to taste the sweetness of the words which the lips of the All-Merciful have willed to utter, he would, though the treasures of the earth be in his possession, renounce them one and all, that he might vindicate the truth of even one of His command-

ments, shining above the Dayspring of His bountiful care and loving-kindness.[4]

All human societies provide in some way for the education of their children. In this way they ensure that their young ones will acquire the knowledge, skills, and moral development necessary for prosperous and happy lives. Likewise, God provides for His children—that is, humanity—through the appearance of divine Teachers, Who lay the groundwork for our spiritual education and eternal happiness.

But children differ in their inclinations. Although all may have access to education, not all have the same capacity. And there are always those who, due to immaturity or other defects of character, either do not apply themselves or completely refuse to avail themselves of the opportunity. Our relationship to the divine Teachers is the same. We have the power to choose whether we will benefit from Their teachings.

Many of the teachings are, in fact, laws that God expects us to observe. We might not always understand the full significance or meaning of such laws, but that does not excuse us. We must have faith that they are intended for our benefit, and we must strive to apply them and better understand them over the course of time.

Once again, children provide an example of this principle. Parents must set rules for their offspring, although the children themselves do not understand the reasons for the rules until much later in life. The disciplines that may appear harsh and restrictive to a child are in reality the basis of prosperity and lifelong happiness. It is only in the fullness of time that they are able to appreciate the wisdom of this parental guidance.

The same principle holds true in our relationship with the Manifestations of God. Like loving parents, They teach us what we need to do to achieve our own prosperity and happiness. Out of faith, we accept and follow Their guidance and thereby attain true happiness.

True Freedom

Freedom is one of the most important aspects of happiness. All human beings desire to be free, but there is a difference between the kind of freedom that leads to dissolution and misery, and that which comes from adherence to correct principles. Only the latter is real and lasting:

. . . True liberty consisteth in man's submission unto My commandments, little as ye know it. Were men to observe that which We have sent down unto them from the Heaven of Revelation, they would, of a certainty, attain unto perfect liberty. Happy is the man that hath apprehended the Purpose of God in whatever He hath revealed from the Heaven of His Will that pervadeth all created things. Say: The liberty that profiteth you is to be found nowhere except in complete servitude unto God, the Eternal Truth. Whoso hath tasted of its sweetness will refuse to barter it for all the dominion of earth and heaven.[5]

Although Bahá'u'lláh emphasizes the importance of obedience to God's teachings, this does not mean that we are expected to follow them blindly. In the Bahá'í teachings faith is defined as conscious knowledge expressed in action. Human beings are equipped with a rational faculty that allows them to investigate the reality of things. God expects us to do just that and not to blindly imitate the beliefs or opinions of others.

At the same time, it is important to realize that human understanding is fallible. If it were not, then everyone would always agree on everything. The Manifestations of God provide essential principles and teachings to point us in the right spiritual and moral direction, yet within this framework of guidance we are expected to develop our own understanding and attempt to apply the teachings in our lives as best we can. Sincerity and persistence are essential, and God helps those who turn towards Him.

Self-Knowledge and Mastery of Self

Spiritual growth is impossible without self-knowledge. Bahá'u'lláh writes that "man should know his own self and recognize that which leadeth unto loftiness or lowliness, glory or abasement, wealth or poverty."[6]

Because humanity was created by a loving God, and because the purpose of this physical life is to acquire spiritual qualities for the life beyond, our essential nature is, therefore, spiritual. But we also have another nature, a physical, "lower," or "animal" side. This aspect of our nature is responsible for baser desires and for the kinds of selfish impulses that destroy spirituality. Among these impulses are excessive attachment to material things, carnal desires, and the like. Other impulses that destroy spirituality include the instincts for aggression and violence.

Such forms of selfishness are the very antithesis of godliness. It is impossible to allow such qualities to flourish and to also have true love for God and for others.

The challenge of life is to overcome our lesser nature and to reflect increasingly the attributes of the spirit.

Detachment

Bahá'u'lláh often calls upon us to be detached from the things of this world. In many instances He reminds us that this physical life is only temporary and that its pleasures are as nothing in comparison with the joys of the spirit:

> The world is but a show, vain and empty, a mere nothing, bearing the semblance of reality. Set not your affections upon it. Break not the bond that uniteth you with your Creator, and be not of those that have erred and strayed from His ways. Verily I say, the world is like the vapor in a desert, which the thirsty dreameth to be water and striveth after it with all his might, until when he cometh unto it, he findeth it to be mere illusion.[7]

> Rejoice not in the things ye possess; tonight they are yours, tomorrow others will possess them. Thus warneth you He Who is the All-Knowing, the All-Informed. Say: Can ye claim that what ye own is lasting or secure? Nay! By Myself, the All-Merciful . . . The days of your life flee away as a breath of wind, and all your pomp and glory shall be folded up as were the pomp and glory of those gone before you. Reflect, O people! What hath become of your bygone days, your lost centuries? Happy the days that have been consecrated to the remembrance of God, and blessed the hours which have been spent in praise of Him Who is the All-Wise. By My life! Neither the pomp of the mighty, nor the wealth of the rich, nor even the ascendancy of the ungodly will endure. All will perish, at a word from Him.[8]

> The generations that have gone on before you—whither are they fled? And those round whom in life circled the fairest and the loveliest of the land, where now are they? Profit by their example, O people, and be not of them that are gone astray.

> Others ere long will lay hands on what ye possess, and enter into your habitations. Incline your ears to My words, and be not numbered among the foolish.

> For every one of you his paramount duty is to choose for himself that on which no other may infringe and none usurp from him. Such a thing—and

to this the Almighty is My witness—is the love of God, could ye but perceive it.

Build ye for yourselves such houses as the rain and floods can never destroy, which shall protect you from the changes and chances of this life. This is the instruction of Him Whom the world hath wronged and forsaken.[9]

By detachment is not meant, however, that we should force ourselves to endure excessive deprivations. On the contrary, Bahá'u'lláh assures us that it is perfectly acceptable to enjoy the things of this world, as long as we remember God and follow His teachings.

Nor does detachment imply that we should not be concerned with the affairs of the world. Rather, we should devote ourselves to the betterment of humanity and service to others. Bahá'u'lláh called upon the monks and other ascetics to be a part of society, stating: "The pious deeds of the monks and priests among the followers of the Spirit [Jesus]—upon Him be the peace of God—are remembered in His presence. In this Day, however, let them give up the life of seclusion and direct their steps towards the open world and busy themselves with that which will profit themselves and others."[10]

Purity and Uprightness of Conduct

A constant theme that is found throughout Bahá'u'lláh's writings is the importance of good conduct and purity of heart. We shall see many examples of exhortations to this effect in the chapters to come. The following provides an example:

Be generous in prosperity, and thankful in adversity. Be worthy of the trust of thy neighbor, and look upon him with a bright and friendly face. Be a treasure to the poor, an admonisher to the rich, an answerer of the cry of the needy, a preserver of the sanctity of thy pledge. Be fair in thy judgment, and guarded in thy speech. Be unjust to no man, and show all meekness to all men. Be as a lamp unto them that walk in darkness, a joy to the sorrowful, a sea for the thirsty, a haven for the distressed, an upholder and defender of the victim of oppression. Let integrity and uprightness distinguish all thine acts. Be a home for the stranger, a balm to the suffering, a tower of strength for the fugitive. Be eyes to the blind, and a guiding light unto the feet of the erring. Be an ornament to the countenance of truth, a crown to the brow of fidelity, a pillar of the temple of righteousness, a breath of life to the body of mankind, an ensign of the hosts of justice, a luminary above the horizon of virtue, a dew to the soil of the human heart, an ark on the ocean of knowledge, a sun in the heaven of bounty, a gem on the diadem of wisdom, a shining light in the firmament of thy generation, a fruit upon the tree of humility.[11]

Justice

We have already seen that Bahá'u'lláh upheld justice as "the best beloved of all things."[12] The principle of justice operates on many levels. In one sense it indicates the capacity to investigate truth free of the hindrance of tradition and dogma.

Ultimately, it is God Who determines what is right and wrong, and His standard must be applied. In the Most Holy Book Bahá'u'lláh warns the ecclesiastics to investigate His Cause with justice:

O leaders of religion! Weigh not the Book of God with such standards and sciences as are current amongst you, for the Book itself is the unerring Balance established amongst men. In this most perfect Balance whatsoever the peoples and kindreds of the earth possess must be weighed, while the measure of its weight should be tested according to its own standard, did ye but know it.[13]

In the Most Holy Book He also calls upon the kings and rulers of the world to embrace His Cause:

O kings of the earth! He Who is the sovereign Lord of all is come. The Kingdom is God's, the omnipotent Protector, the Self-Subsisting. Worship none but God, and, with radiant hearts, lift up your faces unto your Lord, the Lord of all names. This is a Revelation to which whatever ye possess can never be compared, could ye but know it.

We see you rejoicing in that which ye have amassed for others and shutting out yourselves from the worlds which naught except My guarded Tablet can reckon. The treasures ye have laid up have drawn you far away from your ultimate objective. This ill beseemeth you, could ye but understand it. Wash from your hearts all earthly defilements, and hasten to enter the Kingdom of your Lord, the Creator of earth and heaven, Who caused the world to tremble and all its peoples to wail, except them that have renounced all things and clung to that which the Hidden Tablet hath ordained. . . .

Ye are but vassals, O kings of the earth! He Who is the King of Kings hath appeared, arrayed in His most wondrous glory, and is summoning you unto Himself, the Help in Peril, the Self-Subsisting. Take heed lest pride deter you from recognizing the Source of Revelation, lest the things of this world shut you out as by a veil from Him Who is the Creator of heaven. Arise, and serve Him Who is the Desire of all nations, Who hath created you through a word from Him, and ordained you to be, for all time, the emblems of His sovereignty.

By the righteousness of God! It is not Our wish to lay hands on your kingdoms. Our mission is to seize and possess the hearts of men. Upon them the eyes of Bahá are fastened. To this testifieth the Kingdom of Names, could ye but comprehend it.[14]

Justice also has a social dimension. Indeed, one of the aims of the Bahá'í Faith is to establish divine justice in the world. Time and again Bahá'u'lláh addresses this theme. In some instances He grieves at the pervasive tyranny in the world: "Justice is, in this day, bewailing its plight, and Equity groaneth beneath the yoke of oppression. The thick clouds of tyranny have darkened the face of the earth, and enveloped its peoples."[15]

In other instances He lauds the principle of justice:

"The light of men is Justice. Quench it not with the contrary winds of oppression and tyranny. The purpose of justice is the appearance of unity among men." "No radiance can compare with that of justice. The organization of the world and the tranquillity of mankind depend upon it." "O people of God! That which traineth the world is Justice, for it is upheld by two pillars, reward and punishment. These two pillars are the sources of life to the world." "Justice and equity are two guardians for the protection of man. They have appeared arrayed in their mighty and sacred names to maintain the world in uprightness and protect the nations."[16]

Another important theme related to justice is that of reward and punishment. "Justice hath a mighty force at its command," writes Bahá'u'lláh. "It is none other than reward and punishment for the deeds of men. By the power of this force the tabernacle of order is established throughout the world, causing the wicked to restrain their natures for fear of punishment."[17] Bahá'u'lláh calls upon humanity to establish order in the world based upon justice and on the principle of reward and punishment.

The principle of reward and punishment also holds true in our personal lives. "The essence of wisdom," He stated, "is the fear of God, the dread of His scourge and punishment, and the apprehension of His justice and decree."[18]

It might seem contradictory that we should both love and fear God. If God is compassionate and merciful, then why fear Him? Again we turn to the example of a loving parent. The parent sincerely wants what is best for the child and does not desire to inflict punishment. Yet sometimes it is necessary for the child's own good and in fair retribution for a wrong. God can forgive any sin, yet it is foolish to assume that our actions are without consequences. Indeed, the results of our actions become immediately apparent the moment we depart this world:

> It is clear and evident that all men shall, after their physical death, estimate the worth of their deeds, and realize all that their hands have wrought. I swear by the Day Star that shineth above the horizon of Divine power! They that are the followers of the one true God shall, the moment they depart out of this life, experience such joy and gladness as would be impossible to describe, while they that live in error shall be seized with such fear and trembling, and shall be filled with such consternation, as nothing can exceed. Well is it with him that hath quaffed the choice and incorruptible wine of faith through the gracious favor and the manifold bounties of Him Who is the Lord of all Faiths. . . .[19]

When humanity as a whole develops the fear of God, true justice becomes possible. Bahá'u'lláh states, "'The fear of God hath ever been a sure defence and a safe stronghold for all the peoples of the world. It is the chief cause of the protection of mankind, and the supreme instrument for its preservation.'"[20]

In future chapters we will explore the theme of justice as it relates to Bahá'u'lláh's vision of a world civilization.

Future Manifestations of God

Yet another significant teaching of Bahá'u'lláh is that God will continue to guide humanity throughout successive ages through the appearance of more Messengers. Bahá'u'lláh described human society as an "ever-advancing civilization."[21] God will never abandon us, for He will always send us His divine Teachers. But Bahá'u'lláh also indicates that there will not be another Messenger of God for at least one thousand years after His own lifetime.

These are some of Bahá'u'lláh's essential teachings. We shall explore them and a number of other principles of spiritual growth in greater depth in later chapters.

CHAPTER 16

FINAL YEARS

During His final years Bahá'u'lláh continued to correspond with His followers, who sent Him countless messages of loyalty and devotion. Such letters usually included petitions for His blessings. Often they contained questions, and in many cases the believers would tell Bahá'u'lláh of services they had rendered to the Cause of God, asking that Bahá'u'lláh accept them.

The believers who addressed Him came from virtually every conceivable background. Among them were people of considerable status—wealthy merchants, the learned, and government officials. But others were of the humble classes, such as artisans and menial workers. Often these were illiterate and had to ask their more educated fellow-believers to write to Bahá'u'lláh on their behalf.

Bahá'u'lláh showered His love and encouragement upon all, whether high or low, exhorting them to live according to the highest moral principles and to be steadfast in service to the Cause of God. Indeed, the most tender and loving words were often addressed to the humblest of His followers. For example, He once received a letter from a believer named Muḥammad-'Alí. This individual was illiterate and expressed regret at his own lack of education. Nevertheless, he had suffered much in service to the Cause and poured out his sorrows in his letter. Bahá'u'lláh's reply reveals the depths of sympathy and love that characterized His relationship with His followers:

The living waters of My mercy, O 'Alí, are fast pouring down, and Mine heart is melting with the heat of My tenderness and love. At no time have I been able to reconcile Myself to the afflictions befalling My loved ones, or to any trouble that could becloud the joy of their hearts. . . .

The words thou hadst written have, as soon as they were read in My Presence, caused the ocean of My fidelity to surge within Me, and the breeze of My forgiveness to be wafted over thy soul, and the tree of My loving-kindness to overshadow thee, and the clouds of My bounty to rain down upon thee their gifts. . . . I sorrow for thee in thy grief, and lament with thee in thy tribulation. . . . I bear witness to the services thou hast rendered Me, and testify to the various troubles thou hast sustained for My sake. All the atoms of the earth declare My love for thee.[1]

Bahá'u'lláh expressed His love for 'Alí, indicating that his services had been accepted and revealing a prayer for this humble believer to recite. 'Alí was then encouraged to persevere in his services with complete reliance on God.

During Bahá'u'lláh's years in 'Akká the Bahá'í community steadily expanded in size. Communities of believers were established throughout Persia, in India, and in Russian Turkistan. Although most of the original converts to the Faith were from Muslim backgrounds, this period saw increasing numbers of Jews and Zoroastrians, as well as a few individuals of Christian background, embrace the new religion. These believers came from traditions of long-standing mutual animosity, but their common acceptance of Bahá'u'lláh as the Promised One of all Ages and their devotion to His teachings transformed their bitterness into love. Separation gave way to unity, and the new community grew from strength to strength. Bahá'u'lláh Himself considered this one of the greatest proofs of the power of the Word of God.

Bahá'u'lláh's public reputation also grew. Although He remained a prisoner in name, He was now famed throughout the region of Syria for His wisdom. Many believers and people of other faiths visited Bahjí, seeking the honor of meeting Him personally and benefiting from His guidance. Bahá'u'lláh's success provoked hostility and persecution from the rulers and the clergy, who feared His growing influence and the clear evidences of the honor and prestige now accorded Him by people from all walks of life. They continued to spread rumors about Him and to foment persecution of His followers, especially in Persia. News of His followers' sufferings inevitably caused Bahá'u'lláh tremendous grief. He counseled them to be patient, even as He was patient, and to trust in God. He also promised that their sacrifices would not be forgotten by God. Through them the Cause of God would be made victorious, and they would all enjoy the fruits of their own steadfastness in the world beyond.

Among the many visitors to Bahjí were several Europeans. One of them was Edward Granville Browne, an Englishman who would later become one of the most eminent orientalists of his time, whose works are still read by students of the Middle East even today. As a youth Browne had read reports about the Báb written by a European visitor in Persia. He had become so attracted by the story of the

Báb's faith that he eventually dedicated himself to learning all that he could about the new religion. In 1888 he journeyed to Persia and met with many of the Bahá'ís, including some individuals who had known the Báb personally. In 1890 he set out for Ottoman territory to meet Bahá'u'lláh.

In his journal, parts of which were later published, Browne commented on the remarkable atmosphere of spirituality that pervaded Bahjí. He noted the serenity, happiness, and utter devotion of the believers whom he met, including several who had suffered severe persecutions for their faith. But his aim was to meet Bahá'u'lláh, and this request was soon granted. Browne wrote a memorable depiction of this meeting. From his own words the power of Bahá'u'lláh's presence is clear. This is all the more impressive because Browne was neither a Bahá'í nor an Easterner; rather, he was very much a Western intellectual. We might reasonably expect that he would not ordinarily have confessed to spiritual stirrings unless they had been too great to be excluded from his account. As an academic he would have known that such sentiments would be scorned by many of his peers.

His account is valuable in part because critics would often attribute Bahá'u'lláh's spiritual presence to careful advance preparation of His guests. This is true even today—many who hear or read the accounts of those who attained His presence, desiring to offer some "rational" explanation, assume that the visitors were psychologically "programmed" in advance to expect an overwhelming spiritual experience. If that were true, then such experiences would not be due to spiritual forces at all. Browne makes clear that this did not happen in his case. In fact, he states that he was not even certain if or when the interview was to take place. Yet the account is impressive indeed. Here is his testimony:

> ". . . my conductor paused for a moment while I removed my shoes. Then, with a quick movement of the hand, he withdrew, and, as I passed, replaced the curtain; and I found myself in a large apartment, along the upper end of which ran a low divan, while on the side opposite to the door were placed two or three chairs. Though I dimly suspected whither I was going and whom I was to behold (for no distinct intimation had been given to me), a second or two elapsed ere, with a throb of wonder and awe, I became definitely conscious that the room was not untenanted. In the corner where the divan met the wall sat a wondrous and venerable figure. . . . The face of him on whom I gazed I can never forget, though I cannot describe it. Those piercing eyes seemed to read one's very soul; power and authority sat on that ample brow; while the deep lines on the forehead and face implied an age which the jet-black hair and beard flowing down in indistinguishable luxuriance almost to the waist seemed to belie. No need to

ask in whose presence I stood, as I bowed myself before one who is the object of a devotion and love which kings might envy and emperors sigh for in vain!

"A mild dignified voice bade me be seated, and then continued:— 'Praise be to God that thou hast attained! . . . Thou hast come to see a prisoner and an exile . . . We desire but the good of the world and the happiness of the nations; yet they deem us a stirrer up of strife and sedition worthy of bondage and banishment . . . That all nations should become one in faith and all men as brothers; that the bonds of affection and unity between the sons of men should be strengthened; that diversity of religion should cease, and differences of race be annulled—what harm is there in this? . . . Yet so it shall be; these fruitless strifes, these ruinous wars shall pass away, and the "Most Great Peace" shall come . . . Do not you in Europe need this also? Is not this that which Christ foretold? . . . Yet do we see your kings and rulers lavishing their treasures more freely on means for the destruction of the human race than on that which would conduce to the happiness of mankind . . . These strifes and this bloodshed and discord must cease, and all men be as one kindred and one family . . . Let not a man glory in this, that he loves his country; let him rather glory in this, that he loves his kind . . .'

"Such, so far as I can recall them, were the words which, besides many others, I heard from Behá [Bahá'u'lláh]. Let those who read them consider well with themselves whether such doctrines merit death and bonds, and whether the world is more likely to gain or lose by their diffusion."[2]

During His later years Bahá'u'lláh made four trips to Haifa, the port city located across the bay from 'Akká. In 1891 He visited the city for three months. One day, while on Mount Carmel, He pointed to a spot on the mountainside and told His son 'Abdu'l-Bahá that a mausoleum should be built on that site to contain the remains of the Báb. At this time, the Báb's remains and coffin had been hidden by the believers, carried from place to place, for over forty years. It would still be many years before Bahá'u'lláh's request could be carried out, but it was eventually accomplished. Today the Shrine of the Báb, a beautiful, majestic, golden-domed edifice, stands on the very spot that Bahá'u'lláh indicated.

It is believed that during this same trip Bahá'u'lláh visited the Cave of Elijah, where a Christian monastery stands today. On a spot near the entrance of the cave, He revealed the Tablet of Carmel, one of His most beautiful and memorable writings. The tablet lauds in jubilant tones the Day in which God's ancient promises are now fulfilled, extols the greatness of the new revelation, and, in poetic language, establishes Carmel itself as the world center of the Bahá'í Faith.

At the time He revealed the Tablet of Carmel Bahá'u'lláh had a little less than a year remaining in His life. He spent the time revealing scripture with unabated energy, assuring friend and foe of the eventual triumph of God's new faith.

Another significant work from this period was written to one of the fiercest enemies of the Bahá'í Faith in Persia. Shaykh Muḥammad-Taqí had been personally responsible for inflicting much suffering on the believers in the city of Iṣfahán. His father had done the same before him, committing such cruel atrocities that Bahá'u'lláh had addressed him as "the Wolf." Bahá'u'lláh wrote a volume, known as the Epistle to the Son of the Wolf, which stands as His own summation of His life's work. In it He reveals His own perspective on the achievements of a four-decade ministry and sets forth His vision for the future of His faith.

Bahá'u'lláh, severely rebuking the son of the Wolf, called upon him to repent and seek God's forgiveness for his injustices. Bahá'u'lláh then established the complete innocence of the persecuted Bahá'ís and repeated many of His own previous exhortations to the believers to avoid sedition and to lead upright lives. He vigorously denied accusations that He claimed to be God and, after recounting His own sufferings and those of His followers, forthrightly stated His purpose:

> Briefly, this Wronged One hath, in the face of all that hath befallen Him at their hands, and all that hath been said of Him, endured patiently, and held His peace, inasmuch as it is Our purpose, through the loving providence of God—exalted be His glory—and His surpassing mercy, to abolish, through the force of Our utterance, all disputes, war, and bloodshed, from the face of the earth. Under all conditions We have, in spite of what they have said, endured with seemly patience, and have left them to God.[3]

Bahá'u'lláh upbraided Shaykh Muḥammad-Taqí and his father in strong terms for having passed judgment against Him without having made adequate inquiry as to the true nature of His claims. Bahá'u'lláh recounted the history of the Bahá'í community, which had clearly grown and prospered under His guidance and in spite of His enemies. He foretold that the shaykh and those like him would eventually lose their power and influence. He called upon him to "rend asunder the veils of idle fancies" and assured him that the Cause of God would triumph in the end: "This Cause is too evident to be obscured, and too conspicuous to be concealed. It shineth as the sun in its meridian glory."[4]

Bahá'u'lláh continued to meet with the believers and to shower His love and blessings upon them. To a few He intimated that the span of His earthly life was drawing to a close. Then, in the early hours of May 29, 1892, in His seventy-fifth year, Bahá'u'lláh breathed His last. His forty-year ministry, unique in the annals of religious history for its dramatic events and unprecedented outpouring of revelation, was over. A telegram bearing the news to the sultan of Turkey, 'Abdu'l-

Ḥamíd, the tyrant who still nominally held Him prisoner, began with the words: "'the Sun of Bahá has set.'"[5]

Crowds of people came to Bahjí to pay their respects. These included government officials, men of learning, rich and poor, and leaders of all kinds. Jews, Christians, Muslims, and others joined in tribute to the great Personage now gone from their midst. For a full week such people came and went. From as far away as Cairo and Damascus people sent poems and tributes in honor of Bahá'u'lláh. Although most did not recognize Him as the Redeemer of the world, they were all aware to some degree of His greatness.

Their grief, however, was as nothing compared to that of the thousands of Bahá'ís in various countries who poured out expressions of sorrow. Nabíl, the great historian to whose writings we have referred many times in this volume, described the agony into which all of the believers and other admirers of Bahá'u'lláh were plunged:

> "Methinks, the spiritual commotion set up in the world of dust had caused all the worlds of God to tremble. . . . My inner and outer tongue are powerless to portray the condition we were in. . . . In the midst of the prevailing confusion a multitude of the inhabitants of 'Akká and of neighboring villages, that had thronged the fields surrounding the Mansion, could be seen weeping, beating upon their heads, and crying aloud their grief."[6]

How different this state of affairs was from the day in 1868 when Bahá'u'lláh had first arrived in the prison city of 'Akká! On that summer day He had been met by a throng of people who had come for the sole purpose of cursing and reviling Him and His followers. Subjected to strict confinement, He had not been allowed even to leave His cell.

Now, twenty-four years later in 1892, the situation was entirely different. The sultan's decree had long since become a dead letter. Bahá'u'lláh had spent His final years loved and respected by all but a handful of inveterate enemies. He had been able to come and go as He pleased. At His passing multitudes came to honor His memory. Yet on the day of His passing He was still nominally a prisoner of the Ottoman government. He had never been officially released from His sentence of perpetual confinement. Once again, Bahá'u'lláh had emerged from apparent defeat to undeniable triumph.

Bahá'u'lláh was laid to rest in a small house adjacent to the mansion of Bahjí. Since then this site has been visited by increasing numbers of people from every part of the earth. Today it is a beautiful shrine, considered by Bahá'u'lláh's millions of followers to be the holiest spot on earth.

CHAPTER 17

THE LIFE OF A PROPHET

The Founders of all of the world's great religions lived extraordinary lives. Bahá'ís believe that these Messengers not only revealed God's Word to humanity but also exemplified in Their lives and conduct, to a degree impossible for ordinary mortals, the qualities and virtues that God desires for us to attain.

These Messengers represent everything that is noble and good. Their conduct points the way for us all, offering a glimpse of what it means to be truly human. They show us how to meet tests and difficulties, how to behave in prosperity and in adversity, how to love our neighbor, how to forgive and show mercy, and also how and when to act with justice. They show us the true meaning of success, of power, and of distinction. They reveal the road to eternal life by walking it Themselves.

Bahá'u'lláh, God's latest Messenger, is in the same ranks as the great Prophets Who have gone before. He cannot be considered a mere philosopher, thinker, or mystic. The proof lies in His words and His deeds, as close examination proves.

Like all of the other Messengers, Bahá'u'lláh was chosen by God to be the bearer of a new revelation. "Not of Mine own volition," He wrote, "have I revealed Myself, but God, of His own choosing, hath manifested Me."[1]

He was destined, like Moses, Christ, and Muḥammad before Him, to bear great sufferings for the sake of His divine mission. For well over four decades He endured every kind of misfortune. In the days of the Báb, before declaring His own station, He was brutally beaten, shorn of His possessions, and imprisoned under chains that left Him scarred for life. He was exiled four times, betrayed by His own half-brother, driven into a self-imposed retreat for two years in the mountains of Kurdistan, poisoned nearly to death, consigned by the authorities to the dreadful prison of 'Akká, and subjected to incessant abuse and calumny.

"Recall thou to mind My sorrows," He has written, recounting His lifelong sufferings,

> My cares and anxieties, My woes and trials, the state of My captivity, the tears that I have shed, the bitterness of Mine anguish, and now My imprisonment in this far-off land. . . .
>
> By the righteousness of God! Every morning I arose from My bed, I discovered the hosts of countless afflictions massed behind My door; and every night when I lay down, lo! My heart was torn with agony at what it had suffered from the fiendish cruelty of its foes. With every piece of bread the Ancient Beauty breaketh is coupled the assault of a fresh affliction, and with every drop He drinketh is mixed the bitterness of the most woeful of trials. He is preceded in every step He taketh by an army of unforeseen calamities, while in His rear follow legions of agonizing sorrows.
>
> Such is My plight, wert thou to ponder it in thine heart. Let not, however, thy soul grieve over that which God hath rained down upon Us. Merge thy will in His pleasure, for We have, at no time, desired anything whatsoever except His Will, and have welcomed each one of His irrevocable decrees.[2]

Bahá'u'lláh bore these afflictions for one reason—so that all humanity might become illumined with faith and live together in peace and harmony. But He, like the Ones before Him, lived His life in relative obscurity, His revelation unacknowledged by an indifferent and distracted humanity:

> We have accepted to be tried by ills and troubles, that ye may sanctify yourselves from all earthly defilements. Why, then, refuse ye to ponder Our purpose in your hearts? By the righteousness of God! Whoso will reflect upon the tribulations We have suffered, his soul will assuredly melt away with sorrow. Thy Lord Himself beareth witness to the truth of My words. We have sustained the weight of all calamities to sanctify you from all earthly corruption, and ye are yet indifferent.[3]

During His lifetime Bahá'u'lláh had called upon His followers to spread the news of the new faith. He asked that they not grieve when the time came for His spirit to ascend to the world beyond but rest assured of His unfailing blessings and protection.

> Let not your hearts be perturbed, O people, when the glory of My Presence is withdrawn, and the ocean of My utterance is stilled. In My presence

amongst you there is a wisdom, and in My absence there is yet another, inscrutable to all but God, the Incomparable, the All-Knowing. Verily, We behold you from Our realm of glory, and will aid whosoever will arise for the triumph of Our Cause with the hosts of the Concourse on high and a company of Our favored angels.[4]

Bahá'u'lláh's greatest legacy to humanity is His revelation, a body of sacred scripture unequaled in either volume or scope in any other religion. In these writings Bahá'u'lláh affirms the great spiritual truths revealed by past Messengers. He also lays down the essential principles and laws necessary to lead humanity towards its long-awaited destiny, promised by all of the Prophets and sages of old. The Day in which we live, He announces, will witness the advent of God's Kingdom on earth. In the end it will not matter that Bahá'u'lláh Himself was subjected to suffering, nor that most of humanity was oblivious to Him in His own time. Nor will it matter that humanity, caught up in materialism, nationalism, racism, and a host of other ills, was, for the most part, utterly incapable of appreciating the remedy that was being offered by the Divine Physician and instead pursued imaginary solutions of their own devising. Addressing humanity as a whole, Bahá'u'lláh states that God's Faith will ultimately prevail:

Who is the man amongst you that can rival Me in vision or insight? Where is he to be found that dareth to claim to be My equal in utterance or wisdom? No, by My Lord, the All-Merciful! All on the earth shall pass away; and this is the face of your Lord, the Almighty, the Well-Beloved.[5]

PART 3

FOUNDATIONS OF UNITY

CHAPTER 18

THE COVENANT

One of the last and most significant scriptures that Bahá'u'lláh revealed before His passing is known as the Book of the Covenant. In it He affirms for the last time the fundamental aims of His Cause, calls attention to the body of His scripture as a source of continuing guidance to humanity, and calls upon His followers to live up to the high principles and ideals that will foster unity and love in the world.

The Book of the Covenant opens with a reminder that the things of this world are fleeting and that true value lies in things of the spirit. It is the treasures of the spirit, and not earthly riches, that Bahá'u'lláh has brought to humanity.

Bahá'u'lláh then describes His own motive in revealing God's Word and exhorts the peoples of the world to conduct themselves according to His teachings:

> The aim of this Wronged One in sustaining woes and tribulations, in revealing the Holy Verses and in demonstrating proofs hath been naught but to quench the flame of hate and enmity, that the horizon of the hearts of men may be illumined with the light of concord and attain real peace and tranquillity. From the dawning-place of the divine Tablet the daystar of this utterance shineth resplendent, and it behoveth everyone to fix his gaze upon it: We exhort you, O peoples of the world, to observe that which will elevate your station. Hold fast to the fear of God and firmly adhere to what is right.[1]

Bahá'u'lláh goes on to state that "The religion of God is for love and unity," and warns humanity, "make it not the cause of enmity or dissension."[2] He refers humanity to His own scriptures as the source of the transformative power necessary for this age, and calls upon all people to hear His counsels for their own benefit and for the benefit of the world:

That which is conducive to the regeneration of the world and the salvation of the peoples and kindreds of the earth hath been sent down from the heaven of the utterance of Him Who is the Desire of the world. Give ye a hearing ear to the counsels of the Pen of Glory. Better is this for you than all that is on the earth. Unto this beareth witness My glorious and wondrous Book.[3]

In the Book of the Covenant Bahá'u'lláh takes a step that is without parallel in any of the world's great religions. He explicitly and irrefutably designates His successor, Who, although not a Prophet of God, is to serve as the sole source of guidance to the Bahá'í community and to be responsible for the development of the Bahá'í Faith. This appointment inaugurated what is referred to as the Lesser Covenant, or Covenant of Bahá'u'lláh, a spiritual law with a practical function whereby the unity and integrity of the Bahá'í Faith are preserved and guaranteed.

The Bahá'í teachings explain that there are two kinds of covenants in religion: the Greater Covenant and the Lesser Covenant. The Greater Covenant has been in operation since time immemorial, and consists of God's promise never to abandon humanity to its own devices, but to send down His Messengers to reveal laws and teachings for our benefit. In return, humanity must turn to God's Messengers and obey Their teachings. The aim of this covenant is to provide the means for humanity's individual and collective salvation. It is this covenant, realized through the succession of Messengers and Prophets, that is the motivating force behind humanity's spiritual and social advancement, and this will continue to be so for as long as humanity exists.

The Lesser Covenant is unique to the Bahá'í revelation. It consists of the provisions made by Bahá'u'lláh to ensure that His Cause will never be subjected to the schisms and factionalism that have undermined all other religions.

If we examine the history of other religions we can easily see that schisms invariably occurred within a short time after the passing of their Founders. As long as Christ was alive, for example, there was very little possibility of a degree of disunity that might result in permanent division within the ranks of His followers. He Himself was there to make sure of that, and His disciples naturally recognized Him as their leader. Later, however, differences of opinion arose as to some of the fundamental principles of Christ's Faith. Christ left no clear instructions as to how the church should be administered or how doctrinal disputes should be resolved. Most scholars believe that early signs of the emergence of separate schools of thought are observable in the Acts of the Apostles and in the various epistles of the New Testament. Some of the early Christians understood Christ's comment to Simon to mean that he had been appointed by Jesus to head the church (whence the name Peter, "the Rock," by which he has been known ever since).* But this was disputed even in the early days. In time, various versions of Christianity, often representing extremely different points of doctrine, asserted themselves and vied for preeminence. It was not for several centuries that predominant Christian doctrines as we now know them were fully formed. These were upheld mainly by Roman Catholicism and the Greek Orthodox Church. These two creeds succeeded in claiming the allegiance of most Christians for an extended period of time, but they were by no means the only branches of Christianity to survive and thrive. The Protestant Reformation of the sixteenth century resulted in an explosion of new creeds and a reinterpretation of some of the basic church doctrines. Since then Christianity has been subject to seemingly infinite divisions.

A similar thing happened in Islam. During His lifetime Muḥammad accomplished what had seemed unimaginable—the unification of the warring tribes and clans of the Arabian Peninsula. Their transformation into a new community was based on their common belief in God's Word as revealed in the Koran. This achievement was hailed even by Muḥammad's contemporaries as a miracle in its own right. As long as He lived, there was no cause for disunity, for Muḥammad, as God's Chosen Messenger, was present to oversee the community's affairs. Immediately upon His death schisms began to emerge. Like Christ, Muḥammad left no explicit, unequivocal written instructions as to how the community of Islam should be administered after His passing. Some believed He had indicated that the successorship should fall to His youthful cousin 'Ali, who was also His son-in-law and one of the first to believe in Him. Others disputed this claim, preferring instead to elect a more experienced leader from among the ranks of the companions of the Prophet. The proponents of the latter viewpoint prevailed, electing Abu Bakr as the first "rightly guided" Caliph of Islam. 'Ali was the fourth person elected to the same post, but by then the breach was irreversible. The two main sects of Islam, Sunní and S͟hí'ih, trace their origins to these times. And many variations of both have emerged in the intervening centuries.

---

* Matt. 16:13–19: "When Jesus came into the coasts of Caesarea Philippi, he asked his disciples, saying, Whom do men say that I the Son of man am? And they said, Some say that thou art John the Baptist: some, Elias; and others, Jeremias, or one of the prophets. He saith unto them, But whom say ye that I am? And Simon Peter answered and said, Thou art the Christ, the Son of the living God. And Jesus answered and said unto him, Blessed art thou, Simon Bar-jona: for flesh and blood hath not revealed it to thee, but my Father which is in heaven. And I say also unto thee, That thou art Peter, and upon this rock I will build my church; and the gates of hell shall not prevail against it. And I will give unto thee the keys of the kingdom of heaven: and whatsoever thou shalt bind on earth shall be bound in heaven: and whatsoever thou shalt loose on earth shall be loosed in heaven."

Bahá'u'lláh makes it clear that the divisions that have assailed the divine religions have nothing to do with failure on the part of their Founders. On the contrary, the Founders deliberately withheld explicit and binding guidance concerning succession because humanity was not yet ready to bear it. After all, there are two parties to any covenant. In the case of the Greater Covenant, God sends His Messengers, but humanity has the corresponding obligation to recognize and obey Them. In the case of the Lesser Covenant, Bahá'u'lláh has made provisions for ensuring the unity of His Faith. But faithful adherence to these provisions requires a great degree of spiritual discipline and understanding. Only in this age, as humanity approaches its maturity, are we ready to bear the weighty responsibility to maintain the unity and integrity of the Cause of God.

Bahá'u'lláh maintains that His Cause will not suffer schism and disunity as has been the case in the past. Almost immediately after the declaration of His mission He began to refer to the new covenant that would ensure the inviolable unity of the Bahá'í Faith. This was necessary because humanity's destiny is to unite under the shelter of one universal religion, a goal that could not be achieved if the Faith itself were to be divided into sects and denominations.

Bahá'u'lláh's Covenant centers around the person of His eldest son, 'Abdu'l-Bahá, Whom He appointed as His successor and Interpreter of His Word. As successor and head of the Bahá'í Faith, 'Abdu'l-Bahá alone possessed the authority to give binding guidance to the Bahá'ís on all matters pertaining to the Faith, including interpretation of Bahá'u'lláh's writings and the practical implementation of His teachings among the community of believers.

This development came as no surprise to the Bahá'ís. Bahá'u'lláh had alluded to this in the Most Holy Book when He called upon His followers to turn after His own passing to "Him Whom God hath purposed, Who hath branched from this Ancient Root."[4] Nor did this appointment surprise the many officials and citizens who knew 'Abdu'l-Bahá. He was renowned for His extraordinary intellect, wisdom, humanitarianism, and spiritual qualities.

His given name was 'Abbas, and He was known to most people as 'Abbas Effendi—"Effendi" being a title of respect roughly equivalent to the English "Sir" or "Mister." Born on the very same day that the Báb had declared His mission in Shíráz, He was to share in all of His father's trials and sufferings. He was only a child when Bahá'u'lláh was imprisoned in the Black Pit of Tehran. Almost overnight, Bahá'u'lláh and His family were reduced from wealth to dire poverty and were made the targets of abuse. The children were not spared their share of tests, as 'Abdu'l-Bahá later recounted:

"At that time of dire calamities and attacks mounted by the enemies I was a child of nine [according to the lunar calendar in use at the time]. They threw so many stones into our house that the courtyard was crammed with them . . . Mother took us for safety to another quarter, and rented a house in a back alley where she kept us indoors and looked after us. But one day our means of subsistence were barely adequate, and mother told me to go to my aunt's house, and ask her to find us a few qiráns [silver coins] . . . I went and my aunt did what she could for us. She tied a five-qirán piece in a handkerchief and gave it to me. On my way home someone recognized me and shouted: 'Here is a Bábí'; whereupon the children in the street chased me. I found refuge in the entrance to a house . . . There I stayed until nightfall, and when I came out, I was once again pursued by the children who kept yelling at me and pelted me with stones . . . When I reached home I was exhausted. Mother wanted to know what had happened to me. I could not utter a word and collapsed."[5]

At about this same time 'Abdu'l-Bahá persuaded His relatives to allow Him to go to the prison to see His father. Many years later He recalled the visit, which had left a deep and lasting impression:

"They sent me with a black servant to His blessed presence in the prison. The warders indicated the cell, and the servant carried me in on his shoulders. I saw a dark, steep place. We entered a small, narrow doorway, and went down two steps, but beyond those one could see nothing. In the middle of the stairway, all of a sudden we heard His blessed voice: 'Do not bring him in here,' and so they took me back. We sat outside, waiting for the prisoners to be led out. Suddenly they brought the Blessed Perfection out of the dungeon. He was chained to several others. What a chain! It was very heavy. The prisoners could only move it along with great difficulty. Sad and heart-rending it was."[6]

'Abdu'l-Bahá accompanied Bahá'u'lláh into exile shortly thereafter. In Baghdad He grew from a child into a youth of remarkable ability, a fact widely acknowledged. He became well known amongst the religious and civil leaders of the city, and from time to time composed treatises on various subjects which were praised for their erudition and literary merit. He also developed into an outstanding supporter of His father. This was based upon personal integrity as much as on intellect and other talents. 'Abdu'l-Bahá was well aware of His father's station as a Manifestation of God even before Bahá'u'lláh made this fact known publicly. Shortly after the family's arrival in Baghdad, 'Abdu'l-Bahá recognized Bahá'u'lláh as the One Whose coming had been foretold by the Báb. At the time He was but a child of eight or nine.

As time passed, 'Abdu'l-Bahá assumed greater and greater responsibilities. In particular, Bahá'u'lláh often called upon Him to deal with governmental authorities, prominent persons, and other members of the public. 'Abdu'l-Bahá increasingly became His father's shield, taking on all kinds of issues and problems, allowing Bahá'u'lláh the necessary time to reveal sacred scriptures. In His very public role 'Abdu'l-Bahá's keen sense of justice, His love for all people, and His wisdom were on display for the world to see. 'Abdu'l-Bahá's activities, which brought Him into contact with people of all faiths and from every stratum of society, increased at each stage of Bahá'u'lláh's imprisonment and exile, reaching their culmination in the final years before His passing. One of those who met Him during Bahá'u'lláh's lifetime was Edward Granville Browne. This is the same person who met Bahá'u'lláh and left the memorable record to which we have already referred. Here is Browne's recollection of 'Abdu'l-Bahá when He was about forty-six years old, at the prime of His life:

> Seldom have I seen one whose appearance impressed me more. A tall strongly-built man holding himself straight as an arrow, with white turban and raiment, long black locks reaching almost to the shoulder, broad powerful forehead indicating a strong intellect combined with an unswerving will, eyes keen as a hawk's, and strongly-marked but pleasing features—such was my first impression of 'Abbás Efendí, 'the master' (Áká) as he *par excellence* is called by the Bábís.* Subsequent conversation with him served only to heighten the respect with which his appearance had from the first inspired me. One more eloquent of speech, more ready of argument, more apt of illustration, more intimately acquainted with the sacred books of the Jews, the Christians, and the Muhammedans, could, I should think, scarcely be found even amongst the eloquent, ready, and subtle race to which he belongs. These qualities, combined with a bearing at once majestic and genial, made me cease to wonder at the influence and esteem which he enjoyed even beyond the circle of his father's followers. About the greatness of this man and his power no one who had seen him could entertain a doubt.[7]

The relationship between Bahá'u'lláh and 'Abdu'l-Bahá was characterized by deep mutual love and admiration. But this was not the same as a normal father-son relationship. 'Abdu'l-Bahá was fully aware that Bahá'u'lláh was not merely His father, but the Manifestation of God. He considered Himself as nothing compared to His father, and observers were often amazed at the reverence He would

---

* Browne mistakenly referred to them as Bábís; by this time they called themselves Bahá'ís.

show. For example, when 'Abdu'l-Bahá traveled from 'Akká to Bahjí He often rode on a horse or a donkey. As soon as He came within sight of the mansion of Bahjí, however, He would always dismount and finish the remainder of the journey on foot as a sign of reverence for Bahá'u'lláh. This devotion was fully reciprocated, for Bahá'u'lláh, as soon as He saw 'Abdu'l-Bahá in the distance, would summon the believers to go out and escort Him to the mansion. Bahá'u'lláh frequently paid tribute to His son's extraordinary gifts and in both word and deed showed the depth of His love for Him.

As early as the Baghdad years, Bahá'u'lláh designated His son as "the Mystery of God" in recognition of His incomparable spiritual station. This title signifies that, although 'Abdu'l-Bahá is not a Manifestation of God, He manages to blend and completely harmonize the incompatible characteristics of a human nature with superhuman knowledge and perfection.[8] Bahá'u'lláh later conferred upon His son the title "Most Great Branch," "Branch" being the term He used in reference to His male descendants. In referring to 'Abdu'l-Bahá by that title or as "the Master," Bahá'u'lláh prepared the community for the role that 'Abdu'l-Bahá would play in years to come.

The Center of the Covenant

'Abdu'l-Bahá is known as the Center of the Covenant. He was not a Manifestation of God, but neither was He an ordinary human being. Just as His father was the perfect mirror of the attributes of God, 'Abdu'l-Bahá was the embodiment of true servitude to God and the perfect exemplar of spiritual qualities. Occupying a station below the Prophets but above the rest of humanity, His is a unique position in religious history. Although His writings and talks are not considered to be equal to those of Bahá'u'lláh, they are considered to be infallibly guided and are therefore regarded as sacred scripture. Among 'Abdu'l-Bahá's most important functions were to see to the development of the Bahá'í Faith and to ensure the preservation of its unity and doctrinal integrity.

Many who met and came to know 'Abdu'l-Bahá, especially those from the Western countries, were so impressed that they found it difficult to believe that He was not a Prophet. Upon meeting Him some believed that they had encountered one of the great figures from the Old Testament, and still others went so far as to state openly their belief that He was the return of Christ. But 'Abdu'l-Bahá took great pains to emphasize that He was merely the Servant of Bahá'u'lláh. After Bahá'u'lláh's passing He chose for Himself the name 'Abdu'l-Bahá, which means "Servant of Bahá."

He continually emphasized service as His primary aim. When asked about His own station, and especially when praised by people who wished to exalt Him unduly, He would reply in words such as these:

"My name is 'Abdu'l-Bahá [Servant of Bahá]. My qualification is 'Abdu'l-Bahá. My reality is 'Abdu'l-Bahá. My praise is 'Abdu'l-Bahá. Thraldom to the Blessed Perfection [Bahá'u'lláh] is my glorious and refulgent diadem, and servitude to all the human race my perpetual religion . . . No name, no title, no mention, no commendation have I, nor will ever have, except 'Abdu'l-Bahá. This is my longing. This is my greatest yearning. This is my eternal life. This is my everlasting glory."[9]

CHAPTER 19

THE MINISTRY OF 'ABDU'L-BAHÁ BEGINS

'Abdu'l-Bahá remained nominally a prisoner after His father's passing in 1892, but for several years He enjoyed a relative degree of freedom and resided in 'Akká. He also made trips to the city of Haifa. He was recognized by high and low as a leading citizen of the area and became more renowned than ever for His philanthropy and upright conduct. In spite of this, His situation took a steady and then dramatic turn for the worse as the direct result of the efforts of enemies within and outside of the Faith. A very small number of Bahá'ís who were unwilling to accept 'Abdu'l-Bahá's leadership and desired power and recognition for themselves conspired with more narrow-minded government and religious leaders in a campaign of defamation. Their hope was to undermine 'Abdu'l-Bahá's authority, perhaps even to encompass His death, and thereby create an opportunity to seize control of the Faith.

Among the leading conspirators was 'Abdu'l-Bahá's own half-brother Muḥammad-'Alí. Bahá'u'lláh had conferred upon him in the Book of the Covenant a rank second only to that of 'Abdu'l-Bahá, which implied that he would eventually lead the Faith should he survive Him. Interestingly, Bahá'u'lláh made this rank contingent upon Muḥammad-'Alí's fidelity to the Covenant. This was prompted by acts he had perpetrated even before Bahá'u'lláh's passing that revealed him to be a person possessed with an insatiable desire for power and a willingness to stoop to outrageous acts to acquire it. For example, he once composed texts glorifying his own station and attempted to pass them off as Bahá'u'lláh's writings. Bahá'u'lláh, in making Muḥammad-'Alí's rank contingent upon his conduct, apparently foresaw that he would not be equal to the challenge of obedience to the Covenant.

141

Showing a character strangely reminiscent of Bahá'u'lláh's half-brother Azal, Muḥammad-'Alí apparently was not satisfied with the hope of future leadership. He and a few others broadcast a series of calumnies with the aim of portraying 'Abdu'l-Bahá as vain, corrupt, and blasphemous. They circulated stories that 'Abdu'l-Bahá claimed to be a Messenger of God and later fabricated rumors that He claimed to be God Himself. They also alleged that He was busily preparing a revolt against the government and was using His religious activities as a screen.

Sadly, these rumors gained currency in certain circles in spite of the integrity for which 'Abdu'l-Bahá had been known for many years. Vicious reports, buttressed by documents alleging the grossest of crimes, eventually made their way to the Ottoman seat of government in Constantinople, and in 1904 a commission of inquiry was established to look into the matter. The members of the commission set out for 'Akká.

It soon became clear that 'Abdu'l-Bahá was in grave peril. Spies were posted on the streets near His home to watch His activities morning and night. Many friends and supplicants who had frequented His house were so frightened that they ceased their visits. 'Abdu'l-Bahá, fearing for the safety of the Bahá'ís, dispatched almost all of those residing in 'Akká to Egypt and other locales. He also ceased allowing visits on the part of believers from elsewhere. The time came when He was virtually alone.

The commission of inquiry summoned Him, and He answered the charges, all of them preposterous, to their satisfaction. For a time things quieted down, and life began to return to normal. But then in 1906 events affecting the Ottoman government inspired 'Abdu'l-Bahá's enemies to renew their attacks.

In these years the government was gravely threatened by crises from within and pressures from without. Already known in Western circles as the "Sick Man of Europe," the once mighty Ottoman dominions were slowly disintegrating under the weight of years of mismanagement and corruption. Added to this was the steadily building pressure from rising powers such as Russia, Germany, and Great Britain, which were now entering the high tide of their influence and were eager to exploit Ottoman weakness. The sultan, 'Abdu'l-Ḥamíd, struggling to maintain control of his empire, became acutely sensitive to any reports of rebellion. In a renewed effort, the enemies of 'Abdu'l-Bahá resurrected some of the charges and succeeded yet again in getting a response from Constantinople. The sultan established another commission of inquiry, which made its way to 'Akká immediately.

But this commission, very much under the influence of 'Abdu'l-Bahá's ill-wishers, chose to believe the charges on the flimsiest of reasoning. Rumors began to circulate that 'Abdu'l-Bahá would be exiled to the remote desert in Tripolitania, to be cut off from the world. These stories emboldened some people to molest and threaten other Persian Bahá'ís in the vicinity. Yet through the entire crisis 'Abdu'l-

Bahá displayed calmness and courage, assuring the Bahá'ís that the danger would pass.

Then, one day, the members of the commission boarded a ship that was to take them back to the capital. The ship set out across the bay in the direction of 'Akká, surely to take 'Abdu'l-Bahá prisoner, as observers thought. The Bahá'ís waited in despair, but 'Abdu'l-Bahá was seen serenely walking in the courtyard of His house. Suddenly the ship changed direction and, in the waning light of sunset, headed for the open sea and disappeared over the horizon.

It turned out that news of a grave crisis in the capital had forced the commission to beat a hasty return to Constantinople. A series of events had been initiated that would culminate in revolution, led by a group known as the Young Turks. 'Abdu'l-Ḥamíd was too distracted by intrigues closer to home to deal with the case of 'Abdu'l-Bahá. Soon the sultan was deposed, and he would spend the remainder of his life in close confinement.

Just as doom seemed to be closing in on 'Abdu'l-Bahá, the danger had been miraculously averted. Soon the new regime issued a decree that all of the political and religious prisoners of 'Abdu'l-Ḥamíd be freed forthwith. This decree included 'Abdu'l-Bahá.

The year was 1908. 'Abdu'l-Bahá was now sixty-four years old. For fifty-six years, from the time He had been a boy of eight, He had been a prisoner and an exile. Now, for the first time in all those many long years, He was finally free.

CHAPTER 20

'ABDU'L-BAHÁ IN THE WEST

In the lifetime of Bahá'u'lláh the Bahá'í Faith spread through many Asiatic countries and parts of Africa. The early years of 'Abdu'l-Bahá's ministry witnessed the spread of the Faith into Europe and America, thanks to the efforts of a number of intrepid believers. In 1894 an American, Thornton Chase, became the first believer in the United States. Soon there were communities of Bahá'ís in New York, Montreal, London, Paris, and other cities.

While still a prisoner 'Abdu'l-Bahá began to receive new believers and interested seekers visiting from Europe and America. In 'Abdu'l-Bahá's presence, basking in His love and wisdom, they experienced a sense of joy and upliftment that they found impossible to describe. Filled with awe and wonder, most returned to their homes fully determined to do what they could to share the news of the Bahá'í Faith with others.

We are fortunate to have many accounts written by these visitors. Among them was Mrs. Phoebe Hearst, who visited 'Akká in 1899. Her memories are typical of many who visited 'Abdu'l-Bahá in the Holy Land:

> It seems to me a real Truthseeker would know at a glance that He is the Master! Withal, I must say He is the Most Wonderful Being I have ever met or ever expect to meet in this world. Tho He does not seek to impress one at all, strength, power, purity, love and holiness are radiated from His majestic, yet humble, personality, and the spiritual atmosphere which surrounds Him and most powerfully affects all those who are blest by being near Him, is indescribable. His ideas and sentiments are of the loftiest and most chaste character, while His great love and devotion for humanity surpass anything I have ever before encountered.[1]

Upon attaining His freedom in 1908 'Abdu'l-Bahá began to contemplate undertaking a journey through the countries of the West. Its purpose would be to proclaim the Bahá'í Faith and its principles and also to consolidate the newly emerging groups of Bahá'ís in various cities. In 1910 He set out with a small group of companions on a sojourn without rival in religious history. For three years, interspersed with stays in Egypt, He would travel through the countries of Europe and North America, meeting with the Bahá'ís and sharing the message of the Bahá'í Faith with countless others of every conceivable background.

The arduous journey, during which He maintained a constant schedule of interviews, talks, receptions, and other meetings, often left Him ill and exhausted. Yet He pressed on and frequently displayed a level of energy and resilience that astonished those around Him. His travels took Him to France and Great Britain; then, after a rest in Egypt, He traveled across the Atlantic to Canada and the United States, where He visited cities from coast to coast. Then He returned to Europe before heading back to Egypt and then home. During the course of His travels He gave public talks in churches, synagogues, mosques, universities, societies for specific social causes, conferences and conventions of various kinds, charitable institutions, hotels, private residences, and many other venues. His comings and goings attracted the attention of the press and brought Him into contact with some of the leading figures of the time, such as Andrew Carnegie, Alexander Graham Bell, Admiral Peary, and Theodore Roosevelt.

The sheer physical demands of such an undertaking would have proved daunting, if not impossible, to a young person in the prime of life. But 'Abdu'l-Bahá was at this time in the evening of His life, His constitution taxed by many years of hardship. It is also worth remembering that He had spent virtually His entire life as a prisoner. He had never given a sermon or a public talk even to people in His own part of the world, let alone to Westerners.

In spite of these seeming disadvantages, 'Abdu'l-Bahá moved with ease through every circle of society, spreading the news of the new religion and describing its essential teachings. In most cases He was warmly welcomed, and, due to His breadth of knowledge and powerful spiritual qualities, created deep and lasting impressions upon those who met Him.

One eyewitness, Howard Colby Ives, was a Unitarian minister who had many opportunities to observe 'Abdu'l-Bahá's interactions with the public. Eventually he became a Bahá'í. Here is his description of one episode in 1912:

> Dublin [New Hampshire] is a beautiful mountain Summer resort where gathers each year a colony of wealthy intellectuals from Washington, D.C. and from various large centers. 'Abdu'l-Bahá's stay in that place for a period of three weeks offers another evidence of His unique power of adaptation to

every environment; His dominant humility in every group, which, while seeming to follow He really led, and His manifest all-embracing knowledge.

Picture, if you can, this Oriental, fresh from more than fifty years of exile and prison life, suddenly placed in an environment representing the proudest culture of the Western world. Nothing in His life, one would reasonably presume, had offered a preparation for such a contact.

Not to His youth had been given years of academic and scholastic training. Not to His young manhood had been supplied those subtle associations during His formative years. Not upon His advancing age had been bestowed the comforts and leisure that invite the mind's expanse. . . .

How, then, can it be explained that in this environment He not only mingled with these highest products of wealth and culture with no slightest embarrassment to them or to Him, but He literally outshone them in their chosen field.

No matter what subject was brought up He was perfectly at home in its discussion, yet always with an undercurrent of modesty and loving consideration for the opinions of others. I have before spoken of His unfailing courtesy. . . . He "saw the Face of His Heavenly Father in every face" and reverenced the soul behind it. How could one be discourteous if such an attitude was held towards everyone![2]

Another account was written by Sara Louisa, Lady Blomfield, after 'Abdu'l-Bahá visited her home in London in 1911:

> A silence as of love and awe overcame us, as we looked at Him; the gracious figure, clothed in a simple, white garment . . . His hair and short beard were of that snowy whiteness which had once been black; His eyes were large, blue-grey with long, black lashes and well-marked eyebrows; His face was a beautiful oval with warm, ivory-coloured skin, a straight, finely-modelled nose, and firm, kind mouth. These are merely the outside details by which an attempt is made to convey an idea of His arresting personality.
>
> His figure was of such perfect symmetry, and so full of dignity and grace, that the first impression was that of considerable height. He seemed an incarnation of loving understanding, of compassion and power, of wisdom and authority, of strength, and of a buoyant youthfulness, which somehow defied the burden of His years; and such years!
>
> One saw, as in a clear vision, that He had so wrought all good and mercy that the inner grace of Him had grown greater than all outer sign, and the radiance of this inner glory shone in every glance, and word, and movement as He came with hands outstretched.[3]

Let it not be imagined, however, that all observers were well-disposed towards the Bahá'í Faith. One clergyman, Reverend James T. Bixby, wrote a hostile article entitled "What is Behaism?" for the *North American Review* while 'Abdu'l-Bahá was touring North America. Yet this individual, although deeply disturbed at the appearance of a new, non-Christian religion, could not help but express personal admiration for 'Abdu'l-Bahá Himself:

> In the brief personal acquaintance with the head of the new faith, with which I have been honored, Abbas has impressed me as a man of great mental ability, tact, and persuasive power; friendly in disposition, affable in his manners, and amiable and progressive in his spirit. He is wisely putting the emphasis in the Behai community more and more on those great principles of international fellowship and friendly relations between diverse faiths and races that best realize the essence of the Christian spirit. Moreover, he has practically exemplified these principles in his own pacific conduct and charitable activities. The description that visitors to Akka have given of his daily personal benefactions is, indeed, beautiful and impressive.[4]

These are but a few of the countless testimonies to the powerful effect of 'Abdu'l-Bahá upon those with whom He came in contact.

CHAPTER 21

SOME OTHER BASIC TEACHINGS

In the course of His ministry 'Abdu'l-Bahá vigorously promoted and explained Bahá'u'lláh's teachings. Let us now review some more of the essential Bahá'í beliefs.

We have already seen that the Bahá'í Faith teaches the existence of one God, Who has revealed Himself to humanity over the course of history through a series of Messengers, or Manifestations, each of Whom reveals laws and teachings appropriate for the time in which They appear. These Manifestations of God provide the impetus for humanity's progress.

The age in which we live, according to Bahá'u'lláh, is to witness the culmination of humanity's social evolution—that is, the unification of the peoples of the world as citizens of one homeland and members of one faith. It is the age of humanity's spiritual maturation as well, in which a new world order founded upon God's Law will guarantee justice and prosperity for each and every human being. This is the age of the long-awaited advent of God's Kingdom on earth.

The spirit that animates all of the teachings of the Bahá'í Faith is love. Love is the cause of creation itself, the motivating principle behind the appearance of the Prophets, and the key to eternal life. The Bahá'í writings state:

> Know thou of a certainty that Love is the secret of God's holy Dispensation, the manifestation of the All-Merciful, the fountain of spiritual outpourings. Love is heaven's kindly light, the Holy Spirit's eternal breath that vivifieth the human soul. Love is the cause of God's revelation unto man, the vital bond inherent, in accordance with the divine creation, in the realities of things. Love is the one means that ensureth true felicity both in this world and the next. Love is the light that guideth in darkness, the living link that uniteth God with man, that assureth the progress of every illumined

soul. Love is the most great law that ruleth this mighty and heavenly cycle, the unique power that bindeth together the divers elements of this material world, the supreme magnetic force that directeth the movements of the spheres in the celestial realms. Love revealeth with unfailing and limitless power the mysteries latent in the universe. Love is the spirit of life unto the adorned body of mankind, the establisher of true civilization in this mortal world, and the shedder of imperishable glory upon every high-aiming race and nation.[1]

All of the teachings of the Bahá'í Faith are built upon the foundation of love. The same is true for the teachings of all of the divinely revealed religions.

The True Meaning of Life

The reality of human beings is spiritual, and the key to our happiness is to develop our spiritual capacities and draw near to God. This process is conducive not only to happiness in the life beyond, but also in this world. Our spiritual progress depends upon our own efforts to know and love God, to love and serve others, and to lead lives characterized by the highest moral standards. In the end, each of us must answer to God for our own actions. Bahá'u'lláh writes, "Bring thyself to account each day ere thou art summoned to a reckoning; for death, unheralded, shall come upon thee and thou shalt be called to give account for thy deeds."[2]

The only sure means for spiritual progress is to accept God's Manifestation for this day and to strive to abide by His teachings. As we have already mentioned in an earlier chapter, spiritual progress requires sincerity of intent, selflessness, and eager effort. Another requirement is detachment from the world in the sense that we must not allow worldy things to become a barrier between ourselves and God. Yet another prerequisite is adherence to justice, which Bahá'u'lláh defines in part as the ability to discern the truth for ourselves and not to blindly imitate others.

Many passages in the Bahá'í writings make clear that each of us must assume responsibility for our own spiritual growth. But this is not to say that salvation comes entirely through our own efforts. Our progress is always dependent upon God's love and mercy. Bahá'u'lláh upheld the principle of salvation by grace in the sense that we can never by our own deeds truly deserve eternal life. Nevertheless, God expects each of us to respond to Him. We are responsible for choosing whether to love and serve God. If we choose correctly, we can then progress spiritually and feel His love for us in our lives, as the following verse from Bahá'u'lláh suggests: "Love Me, that I may love thee. If thou lovest Me not, My love can in no wise reach thee. Know this, O servant."[3]

Prayer

Bahá'ís are called upon to pray every day. Prayer is spiritual communion with God. It is characterized by love, trust, and the realization of our dependence upon Him for all things.

Human beings often face tests and difficulties in life and find themselves in need of assistance. In such circumstances we are advised to appeal to God for help, and we are assured that such prayers, like all prayers offered with true love and sincerity, are answered. We also supplicate God for spiritual growth. But prayer is not simply asking God to do things for us. In its highest form it is a communion born of pure love without desire for anything but nearness to God. Indeed, we may, full of faith and trust in God, ask only to be content with God's will, and give thanks and praise to Him for whatever befalls us. In the Hidden Words, Bahá'u'lláh teaches that our relationship to God should be such that we desire for ourselves only what God wants, because this is what is best for us:

O SON OF SPIRIT!
Ask not of Me that which We desire not for thee, then be content with what We have ordained for thy sake, for this is that which profiteth thee, if therewith thou dost content thyself.[4]

Prayer has a profound effect. The very act of communion has an influence upon the individual. Prayer helps to make a person more and more spiritual and steadfast in God's love. Prayer also has an effect beyond the individual. The following statement by Bahá'u'lláh affirms both points:

Intone, O My servant, the verses of God that have been received by thee, as intoned by them who have drawn nigh unto Him, that the sweetness of thy melody may kindle thine own soul, and attract the hearts of all men. Whoso reciteth, in the privacy of his chamber, the verses revealed by God, the scattering angels of the Almighty shall scatter abroad the fragrance of the words uttered by his mouth, and shall cause the heart of every righteous man to throb. Though he may, at first, remain unaware of its effect, yet the virtue of the grace vouchsafed unto him must needs sooner or later exercise its influence upon his soul. Thus have the mysteries of the Revelation of God been decreed by virtue of the Will of Him Who is the Source of power and wisdom.[5]

The Báb, Bahá'u'lláh, and 'Abdu'l-Bahá all revealed prayers that are recited by Bahá'ís. These prayers number in the hundreds. Even though Bahá'ís may also pray in their own words, the revealed prayers, because they are the Word of God, have a special spiritual power. They have additional value in that they show us how we should address God and indicate the kinds of things for which we should pray. In these respects they are similar to the Lord's Prayer revealed by Jesus Christ. Some prayers of Bahá'u'lláh follow:

O my God! O my God! Unite the hearts of Thy servants, and reveal to them Thy great purpose. May they follow Thy commandments and abide in Thy law. Help them, O God, in their endeavor, and grant them strength to serve Thee. O God! Leave them not to themselves, but guide their steps by the light of Thy knowledge, and cheer their hearts by Thy love. Verily, Thou art their Helper and their Lord.

My God, my Adored One, my King, my Desire! What tongue can voice my thanks to Thee? I was heedless, Thou didst awaken me. I had turned back from Thee, Thou didst graciously aid me to turn towards Thee. I was as one dead, Thou didst quicken me with the water of life. I was withered, Thou didst revive me with the heavenly stream of Thine utterance which hath flowed forth from the Pen of the All-Merciful.

O Divine Providence! All existence is begotten by Thy bounty; deprive it not of the waters of Thy generosity, neither do Thou withhold it from the ocean of Thy mercy. I beseech Thee to aid and assist me at all times and under all conditions, and seek from the heaven of Thy grace Thine ancient favor. Thou art, in truth, the Lord of bounty, and the Sovereign of the kingdom of eternity.

Thy name is my healing, O my God, and remembrance of Thee is my remedy. Nearness to Thee is my hope, and love for Thee is my companion. Thy mercy to me is my healing and my succor in both this world and the world to come. Thou, verily, art the All-Bountiful, the All-Knowing, the All-Wise.

Fasting

Bahá'ís are also called upon to undertake a period of fasting every year. For nineteen days, from March 2 through 20, Bahá'ís between the ages of fifteen and seventy abstain from all food and drink from dawn until sunset.* The purpose of the fast, during which special prayers are recited, is to promote attention to spiritual matters and to deepen the relationship of the believer with God. The physical deprivation symbolizes one's detachment from the things of this world and reminds one of the sufferings of others.

Reading the Sacred Writings

Bahá'u'lláh exhorts humanity to read and study His writings regularly. "Immerse yourselves in the ocean of My words," He has written, "that ye may unravel its secrets, and discover all the pearls of wisdom that lie hid in its depths."[6]

Bahá'u'lláh taught that the Word of God, as an expression of the Holy Spirit, has creative and transformative powers. As such, the Word of God is not to be taken merely at face value; rather, "its meaning can never be exhausted."[7] The Word of God opens door after door of insight into divine mysteries. Every person has the duty to undertake thoughtful study of it and to strive to understand its many meanings.

Bahá'u'lláh also advises His followers to read and study the Word of God together:

> Gather ye together with the utmost joy and fellowship and recite the verses revealed by the merciful Lord. By so doing the doors to true knowledge will be opened to your inner beings, and ye will then feel your souls endowed with steadfastness and your hearts filled with radiant joy.[8]

It is not enough just to believe in God, nor is it enough to pray and read the scriptures daily. Real spiritual transformation cannot occur until a person takes action in a sincere desire to live up to God's teachings. Bahá'u'lláh reaffirms the essential virtues that have been emphasized in every divine revelation. He calls upon us all to lead pure and upright lives, to observe justice, and to do good for others.

In countless passages the Bahá'í writings describe the qualities and attributes

---

* Exemption from fasting is granted to travelers under certain conditions; to those who are ill; to women who are either pregnant, nursing, or menstruating; and to those engaged in heavy labor.

that God desires for everyone to attain. A few examples from Bahá'u'lláh's writings follow:

O SON OF SPIRIT!
My first counsel is this: Possess a pure, kindly and radiant heart, that thine may be a sovereignty ancient, imperishable and everlasting.[9]

Let truthfulness and courtesy be your adorning. Suffer not yourselves to be deprived of the robe of forbearance and justice, that the sweet savors of holiness may be wafted from your hearts upon all created things.[10]

If ye meet the abased or the down-trodden, turn not away disdainfully from them, for the King of Glory ever watcheth over them and surroundeth them with such tenderness as none can fathom except them that have suffered their wishes and desires to be merged in the Will of your Lord, the Gracious, the All-Wise. O ye rich ones of the earth! Flee not from the face of the poor that lieth in the dust, nay rather befriend him and suffer him to recount the tale of the woes with which God's inscrutable Decree hath caused him to be afflicted. By the righteousness of God! Whilst ye consort with him, the Concourse on high will be looking upon you, will be interceding for you, will be extolling your names and glorifying your action. Blessed are the learned that pride not themselves on their attainments; and well is it with the righteous that mock not the sinful, but rather conceal their misdeeds, so that their own shortcomings may remain veiled to men's eyes.[11]

It is Our wish and desire that every one of you may become a source of all goodness unto men, and an example of uprightness to mankind. Beware lest ye prefer yourselves above your neighbors. Fix your gaze upon Him Who is the Temple of God amongst men. He, in truth, hath offered up His life as a ransom for the redemption of the world. He, verily, is the All-Bountiful, the Gracious, the Most High. If any differences arise amongst you, behold Me standing before your face, and overlook the faults of one another for My name's sake and as a token of your love for My manifest and resplendent Cause. We love to see you at all times consorting in amity and concord within the paradise of My good-pleasure, and to inhale from your acts the fragrance of friendliness and unity, of loving-kindness and fellowship. Thus counselleth you the All-Knowing, the Faithful. We shall always be with you; if We inhale the perfume of your fellowship, Our heart will assuredly rejoice, for naught else can satisfy Us. To this beareth witness every man of true understanding.[12]

Such exhortations are an evidence of the essential unity of the divinely revealed religions, for the Messengers of God have always called the people to righteousness. Such passages reassert the values that have always been at the core of true religion.

CHAPTER 22

THE PRINCIPLE OF ONENESS

Each age has different requirements. For this reason we find among the teachings of the Messengers of God specific laws and principles that are suited for the eras in which They appear. These change over time as humanity's condition evolves. Some are purely personal in nature, but many of them affect human interactions. It is essential that these laws be observed in each respective religious Dispensation, for they are the expression of God's will for that time. Obedience to them ensures not only personal salvation but also the collective progress of society.

Today it is Bahá'u'lláh Who has revealed the laws and principles necessary for humanity's present stage of development. Among the most essential laws and principles are the oneness of God and the oneness of religion, the oneness of humanity, and the equality of women and men.

The Oneness of God and the Oneness of Religion

These two principles have already been discussed in earlier chapters. Bahá'u'lláh states that this is the age in which all religions will be reconciled, when all of humanity will gather under the shelter of one faith. He teaches that the religion of God has always been one. We recall that Bahá'u'lláh emphasized the essential unity of all of the Messengers of God, even though in each age They revealed what was necessary at that time.

Each successive stage in religious history has been part of God's great plan for human salvation. Therefore we should revere all of the Prophets. Moreover, all should show genuine love and goodwill towards the members of different religions. Bahá'u'lláh gives the following exhortation: "'Consort with the followers of all religions in a spirit of friendliness and fellowship.'"[1]

The Oneness of Humanity

Every religion has some version of the Golden Rule. They all teach brotherly love and consideration for others out of recognition that all people are God's children and deserve to be treated as we ourselves would wish to be treated.

One of the signs of maturity in any person is the increased capacity to consider the feelings of others and to show them genuine care. Most individuals, as they develop from childhood through adolescence and into adulthood, learn to love other people, such as relatives, friends, and others.

In many cases such love is based upon a sense of reciprocity. We love our friends because they love us. We love our family because of the love they have shown us. We occasionally make sacrifices for others with the understanding that they will do so too, should the need arise. Even when it comes to the larger society, we are often willing to give of ourselves to some extent so that, in due course, we may also benefit in some way.

The Messengers of God teach us that true love—the love that is born of the Holy Spirit—is not dependent upon a sense of reciprocity. It is selfless and unconditional. Those who are animated by such unselfish love are indiscriminate— they do not limit it to certain individuals. Such love seeks neither reward nor recognition. It inspires us to love our enemies as well as our friends, regardless of their feelings for us.

Bahá'u'lláh teaches that human beings should develop true, spiritual love for all humanity. This kind of love, He asserts, derives from our love for God and from our awareness of His love for all humanity.

In certain passages Bahá'u'lláh explains that the knowledge of self is the same as the knowledge of God, for the soul is the mirror of God's qualities. It follows, then, that if we truly love God, we must also love all of His children, who are created in His image.

The time has come, Bahá'u'lláh states, for the principle of the oneness of humanity to be understood and accepted. This is a spiritual principle that has profound implications for individual life and the ordering of society. True justice and peace can only come about when this principle is universally accepted and applied.

To understand and accept the oneness of humanity means that we must fully embrace the notion that all human beings, regardless of race, creed, class, or any other variation of background, are the children of the same Divine Father. Prejudices of any kind are unacceptable, as is any behavior that gives unfair advantage to some group or groups at the expense of others.

In the Hidden Words we find the following verse:

O CHILDREN OF MEN!
Know ye not why We created you all from the same dust? That no one should exalt himself over the other. Ponder at all times in your hearts how ye were created. Since We have created you all from one same substance it is incumbent on you to be even as one soul, to walk with the same feet, eat with the same mouth and dwell in the same land, that from your inmost being, by your deeds and actions, the signs of oneness and the essence of detachment may be made manifest. Such is My counsel to you, O concourse of light! Heed ye this counsel that ye may obtain the fruit of holiness from the tree of wondrous glory.[2]

Elsewhere Bahá'u'lláh states,

The utterance of God is a lamp, whose light is these words: Ye are the fruits of one tree, and the leaves of one branch. Deal ye one with another with the utmost love and harmony, with friendliness and fellowship. He Who is the Daystar of Truth beareth Me witness! So powerful is the light of unity that it can illuminate the whole earth. The One true God, He Who knoweth all things, Himself testifieth to the truth of these words.

Exert yourselves that ye may attain this transcendent and most sublime station, the station that can insure the protection and security of all mankind. This goal excelleth every other goal, and this aspiration is the monarch of all aspirations.[3]

While visiting the West 'Abdu'l-Bahá repeatedly addressed this issue. An extract from a talk He gave in 1912 in Chicago at the Fourth Annual Conference of the National Association for the Advancement of Colored People explores the concept that humanity is created in the image of God:

Let us now discover more specifically how he [man] is the image and likeness of God and what is the standard or criterion by which he can be measured and estimated. This standard can be no other than the divine virtues which are revealed in him. Therefore, every man imbued with divine qualities, who reflects heavenly moralities and perfections, who is the expression of ideal and praiseworthy attributes, is, verily, in the image and likeness of God. If a man possesses wealth, can we call him an image and likeness of God? Or is human honor and notoriety the criterion of divine nearness? Can we apply the test of racial color and say that man of a certain hue—white, black, brown, yellow, red—is the true image of his Creator? We must conclude that color is not the standard and estimate of judgment and that it is of no importance, for color is accidental in nature. The spirit and intelligence of man is essential, and that is the manifestation of divine virtues, the merciful bestowals of God, the eternal life and baptism through the Holy Spirit. Therefore, be it known that color or race is of no importance. He who is the image and likeness of God, who is the manifestation of the bestowals of God, is acceptable at the threshold of God—whether his color be white, black or brown; it matters not. Man is not man simply because of bodily attributes. The standard of divine measure and judgment is his intelligence and spirit.

Therefore, let this be the only criterion and estimate, for this is the image and likeness of God. A man's heart may be pure and white though his outer skin be black; or his heart be dark and sinful though his racial color is white. The character and purity of the heart is of all importance. The heart illumined by the light of God is nearest and dearest to God, and inasmuch as God has endowed man with such favor that he is called the image of God, this is truly a supreme perfection of attainment, a divine station which is not to be sacrificed by the mere accident of color.[4]

On other occasions 'Abdu'l-Bahá likened humanity to a flower garden in which different hues and colors combine in a scene of wondrous beauty, or to different notes in musical chords designed to blend in perfect harmony. In this way He demonstrated that each group has a legitimate contribution to make to the beauty of the whole and that the overall variety enhances, in turn, the beauty of each constituent part.

One of the principles Bahá'u'lláh teaches is that an individual's words should not exceed his deeds. There are plenty of people who profess high ideals but whose deeds are found wanting. Many make an outward show of piety or philanthropy, hoping thereby to increase their reputations. Jesus Christ condemned the hypocrisy of such people. Bahá'u'lláh states that the proof of a person's sincerity lies in action, not words.

'Abdu'l-Bahá, observing that prejudice is one of the great barriers to peace, emphasized that freedom from prejudice must be more than just an ideal—it must be translated into practice to such an extent that it influences all of our interactions with others.

As 'Abdu'l-Bahá traveled throughout the United States in 1912, He readily acknowledged the many material and social accomplishments of the American people and praised their high ideals. Yet He was also clear-eyed and uncompromising in His assessment that America fell far short of its vision for equal rights and justice. In particular, He pointed out the injustices perpetrated by whites against blacks, who, decades after gaining freedom from slavery, still suffered from severe bigotry, discrimination, and frequent violence. 'Abdu'l-Bahá publicly warned the people of America that blood would run in the streets of its cities if the issue of racial prejudice were not dealt with—a prediction that has come true many times over.

'Abdu'l-Bahá enjoined the Bahá'ís to strive to remove prejudice from their own hearts and to manifest love for all humanity in their individual and collective activities. This was very challenging for the believers, many of whom struggled against a lifetime of attitudes and assumptions that were at variance with Bahá'í principles. 'Abdu'l-Bahá was loving but very firm and insistent, placing clear responsibility on the Bahá'ís gradually to transform their attitudes and behaviors. Many of these individuals, out of love for Him and for Bahá'u'lláh, were able to transform their lives so as to bring them into conformity with the principle of the oneness of humanity. To this day it is a struggle in which every Bahá'í must engage if he or she is to be faithful to the teachings of Bahá'u'lláh.

In the very early days after the Bahá'í Faith was established in the United States, it was the custom in most cities for black believers and white believers to meet separately. There were only a few exceptions to this. For the majority of Bahá'ís this was natural because it was the standard practice of the day. However, 'Abdu'l-Bahá put a stop to this practice, and soon meetings became integrated. He also took advantage of every opportunity to demonstrate how love for all people should be the rule, no matter if it went against social convention.

A well-known story about 'Abdu'l-Bahá tells of a luncheon and reception that took place in Washington, D.C., at the home of a husband and wife who were Bahá'ís. The two were socially prominent and had invited a number of eminent guests to join them in honoring 'Abdu'l-Bahá. As it happened, He had given a talk at Howard University earlier that day and had invited an African-American believer to this home for an interview. When luncheon was announced, this person made ready to leave the house. Although he, like many of the guests, was a Bahá'í, he had not been invited to join the group. Noticing this person's absence at the table, 'Abdu'l-Bahá sent for someone to retrieve him. By the time he entered the dining area, 'Abdu'l-Bahá had rearranged the place-settings and indicated that he should sit at the place of honor, to 'Abdu'l-Bahá's immediate right. 'Abdu'l-Bahá then gave a talk on the oneness of humanity. Such an act was virtually unheard of in that day and time and brought home the point of Bahá'u'lláh's statement, "Let deeds, not words, be your adorning."[5]

'Abdu'l-Bahá went even further, encouraging Bahá'ís of different colors to intermarry:

"If it be possible, gather together these two races, black and white, into one assembly and put such love into their hearts that they shall not only unite but even intermarry. Be sure that the result of this will abolish differences and disputes between black and white. Moreover by the will of God, may it be so. This is a great service to the world of humanity."[6]

The same African-American believer who attended the reception, Louis Gregory, eventually married a white believer, Louisa Mathew. It was 'Abdu'l-Bahá Himself Who suggested the match. Although the two had not entertained the thought of marrying before, their love for 'Abdu'l-Bahá was so great, and their trust in Him so unshakable, that they soon agreed even though they were well aware of the difficulties that their union would present for themselves and others. This was a time when interracial marriage was illegal in most states, and the very thought of it was generally abhorred even in the most liberal circles. The two could not even travel together safely in certain regions of the country. Over the course of time Mr. Gregory emerged as one of the most outstanding Bahá'ís in the history of the Faith, a towering example of how to promote racial understanding with courage and with love. 'Abdu'l-Bahá once said of him, "'He is like unto pure gold. This is why he is acceptable in any market and is current in every country.'"[7] His long and loving relationship with his wife proved that racial prejudice is an illusion and demonstrated the potential for true unity and happiness that comes with adherence to God's will.

The Equality of Women and Men

Another aspect of the principle of the oneness of humanity is the equality of women and men. Bahá'u'lláh states that "Women and men have been and will always be equal in the sight of God."[8] In this age women are destined to take their place as full equals in every aspect of human endeavor.

Addressing an audience in Philadelphia, 'Abdu'l-Bahá elaborated upon this principle:

In proclaiming the oneness of mankind He [Bahá'u'lláh] taught that men and women are equal in the sight of God and that there is no distinction to be made between them. The only difference between them now is due to lack of education and training. If woman is given equal opportunity of education, distinction and estimate of inferiority will disappear. The world of humanity has two wings, as it were: One is the female; the other is the male. If one wing be defective, the strong perfect wing will not be capable of flight. The world of humanity has two hands. If one be imperfect, the capable hand is restricted and unable to perform its duties. God is the Creator of mankind. He has endowed both sexes with perfections and intelligence, given them physical members and organs of sense, without differentiation or distinction as to superiority; therefore, why should woman be considered inferior? This is not according to the plan and justice of God. He has created them equal; in His estimate there is no question of sex. The one whose heart is purest, whose deeds are most perfect, is acceptable to God, male or female. Often in history women have been the pride of humanity—for example, Mary, the mother of Jesus. She was the glory of mankind. Mary Magdalene, Ásíyih, daughter of Pharaoh, Sarah, wife of Abraham, and innumerable others have glorified the human race by their excellences. In this day there are women among the Bahá'ís who far outshine men. They are wise, talented, well-informed, progressive, most intelligent and the light of men. They surpass men in courage. When they speak in meetings, the men listen with great respect. Furthermore, the education of women is of greater importance than the education of men, for they are the mothers of the race, and mothers rear the children. The first teachers of children are the mothers. Therefore, they must be capably trained in order to educate both sons and daughters. There are many provisions in the words of Bahá'u'lláh in regard to this.[9]

'Abdu'l-Bahá further explains how women's participation in world affairs will help bring about a healthy balance:

"The world in the past has been ruled by force, and man has dominated over woman by reason of his more forceful and aggressive qualities both of body and mind. But the balance is already shifting; force is losing its dominance, and mental alertness, intuition, and the spiritual qualities of love and service, in which woman is strong, are gaining ascendancy. Hence the new age will be an age less masculine and more permeated with the feminine ideals, or, to speak more exactly, will be an age in which the masculine and feminine elements of civilization will be more balanced."[10]

In the mid-nineteenth century at the time of the Báb's declaration of His mission, the women of Persia, as in most parts of the world, suffered under severe restrictions. Some religious leaders of the time went so far as to argue that women did not even possess a soul. Women's rights were a thing virtually unknown. Women had no systematic access to education, generally did not enter into businesses or the professions, and took no part in public life. In the mosque and public meeting places they were segregated and attended only on rare occasions. Their lives centered completely in the home, and even in that setting they ate and socialized apart from the men, almost never interacting with males who were not their close relatives. It was extremely difficult for women to protest such confinement, because any breach of tradition might easily be considered an act of dishonor worthy of the severest retribution.

Nonetheless the Báb upheld a high station for women, and Bahá'u'lláh boldly proclaimed the equality of women and men during His ministry. For the people of that time this was a very challenging concept. In the minds of many this idea, with its implication of open association between members of the opposite sex, carried with it the automatic taint of sexual impropriety. Yet these teachings had an immediate impact within the community of the believers.

One of the first to believe in the Báb was a woman of exceptional intelligence and courage who was known as Qurratu'l-'Ayn, meaning "Solace of the Eyes." She was deeply learned in religion and philosophy to such a degree that even as a young girl she was regarded as a prodigy. Once she embraced the new religion, she set about immediately to live and proclaim its principles. 'Abdu'l-Bahá provides a description of her accomplishments:

"Amongst the women of our own time is Qurratu'l-'Ayn, the daughter of a Muḥammadan priest. At the time of the appearance of the Báb she showed such tremendous courage and power that all who heard her were astonished. She threw aside her veil despite the immemorial custom of the women of Persia, and although it was considered impolite to speak with men, this heroic woman carried on controversies with the most learned men, and in every meeting she vanquished them. The Persian Government took her prisoner; she was stoned in the streets, anathematized, exiled from town to town, threatened with death, but she never failed in her determination to work for the freedom of her sisters. She bore persecution and suffering with the greatest heroism; even in prison she gained converts. To a Minister of Persia, in whose house she was imprisoned, she said: 'You can kill me as soon as you like but you cannot stop the emancipation of women.' At last the end of her tragic life came; she was carried into a garden and strangled. She put on, however, her choicest robes as if she were going to join a bridal party. With such magnanimity and courage she gave her life, startling and thrilling all who saw her. She was truly a great heroine. Today in Persia, among the Bahá'ís, there are women who also show unflinching courage, and who are endowed with great poetic insight. They are most eloquent, and speak before large gatherings of people.

"Women must go on advancing; they must extend their knowledge of science, literature, history, for the perfection of humanity. Erelong they will receive their rights. Men will see women in earnest, bearing themselves with dignity, improving the civil and political life, opposed to warfare, demanding suffrage and equal opportunities. I expect to see you advance in all phases of life; then will your brows be crowned with the diadem of eternal glory."[11]

Two more spiritual giants of the Bahá'í Faith are Bahá'u'lláh's daughter, Bahíyyih Khánum, and His wife Ásíyih Khánum, also known as Navváb. Both shared all of His years of exile and imprisonment with extraordinary courage and patience. Bahíyyih Khánum has provided a description of her mother's lifelong care for the poor and oppressed to one of the early Western believers:

> Even in the early years of their married life, they, my father and mother, took part as little as possible in State functions, social ceremonies, and the luxurious habits of ordinary highly-placed and wealthy families in the land of Persia; she, and her noble-hearted husband, counted these worldly pleasures meaningless, and preferred rather to occupy themselves in caring for the poor, and for all who were unhappy, or in trouble.
>
> From our doors nobody was ever turned away; the hospitable board was spread for all comers.
>
> Constantly the poor women came to my mother, to whom they poured out their various stories of woe, to be comforted and consoled by her loving helpfulness.
>
> Whilst the people called my father "The Father of the Poor," they spoke of my mother as "The Mother of Consolation. . . ."[12]

Bahíyyih Khánum proved herself worthy of her mother's legacy, for she served the Faith of Bahá'u'lláh with a degree of devotion unsurpassed by any other woman.

Shoghi Effendi, who was her grand-nephew and Guardian of the Cause of God (about whom we shall hear more in a later chapter), described her life of service in this manner at the time of her death:

> This heavenly being, during all the turmoil of her days, did not rest for a moment, nor ever did she seek quiet and peace. From the beginning of her life, from her very childhood, she tasted sorrow's cup; she drank down the afflictions and calamities of the earliest years of the great Cause of God. In the tumult of the Year of Hin*, as a result of the sacking and plundering of

---

* The numerical value of the letters composing "Hin" indicates 1268 A.H. or A.D. 1851–52.

her glorious Father's wealth and holdings, she learned the bitterness of destitution and want. Then she shared the imprisonment, the grief, the banishment of the Abhá Beauty [Bahá'u'lláh], and in the storm which broke out in 'Iráq—because of the plotting and the treachery of the prime mover of mischief, the focal centre of hate—she bore, with complete resignation and acquiescence, uncounted ordeals. She forgot herself, did without her kin, turned aside from possessions, struck off at one blow the bonds of every worldly concern; and then, like a lovelorn moth, she circled day and night about the flame of the matchless Beauty of her Lord.

In the heaven of severance, she shone like the Morning Star, fair and bright, and through her character and all her ways, she shed upon kin and stranger, upon the learned, and the lowly, the radiance of Bahá'u'lláh's surpassing perfection.

. . . In captivating hearts and winning over souls, in destroying doubts and misgivings, she led the field. With the waters of her countless mercies, she brought thorny hearts to a blossoming of love from the All-Glorious, and with the influence of her pure loving-kindness, transformed the implacable, the unyielding, into impassioned lovers of the celestial Beauty's peerless Cause. . . .

O Liege Lady of the people of Bahá!
Broken is our circle by thy going—
Broken our circle, broken too, our hearts.[13]

Many other Persian Bahá'í women, in spite of the cultural restrictions of the time, performed outstanding services for the Faith. Taking to heart Bahá'u'lláh's injunction to educate girls as well as boys, the believers founded outstanding schools for girls. To this day women in many countries continue to endure horrible discrimination, and almost everywhere they face abuses and humiliations of various kinds. At present Bahá'ís around the world are involved in many projects designed to enhance the status of women, often in collaboration with like-minded groups.

The shining record of service achieved by the Bahá'í women of Persia was matched in the West, where, due to much more progressive circumstances, the early Bahá'í women distinguished themselves as the leading promoters of the Faith. Their accomplishments demonstrate the truth of the following words of 'Abdu'l-Bahá:

Know thou, O handmaid, that in the sight of Bahá [Bahá'u'lláh], women are accounted the same as men, and God hath created all humankind in His own image, and after His own likeness. That is, men and women alike are the revealers of His names and attributes, and from the spiritual viewpoint there is no difference between them. Whosoever draweth nearer to God, that one is the most favored, whether man or woman. How many a handmaid, ardent and devoted, hath, within the sheltering shade of Bahá, proved superior to the men, and surpassed the famous of the earth.[14]

CHAPTER 23

THE HARMONY OF RELIGION AND SCIENCE

We have seen how the principle of oneness applies to several aspects of reality: the oneness of God, the oneness of religion, and the oneness of humanity. All of creation is a reflection of that same principle. God created all of existence, so it is natural that religious truth and scientific truth should be in harmony.

It is not surprising that Bahá'u'lláh upholds the importance of religion. "Religion," He writes, "is verily the chief instrument for the establishment of order in the world and of tranquillity amongst its peoples. . . . The greater the decline of religion, the more grievous the waywardness of the ungodly. This cannot but lead in the end to chaos and confusion." Elsewhere He writes, "In truth, religion is a radiant light and an impregnable stronghold for the protection and welfare of the peoples of the world." "As the body of man," He also writes, "needeth a garment to clothe it, so the body of mankind must needs be adorned with the mantle of justice and wisdom. Its robe is the Revelation vouchsafed unto it by God."[1] He has written extensively about the positive effect of religion in past societies and civilizations.

Bahá'u'lláh lamented the gradual decline of religion in His own day, which He predicted would continue for some time into the future: "The face of the world hath altered. The way of God and the religion of God have ceased to be of any worth in the eyes of men." "The vitality of men's belief in God," He also wrote, "is dying out in every land. . . . The corrosion of ungodliness is eating into the vitals of human society."[2]

In other passages Bahá'u'lláh explains that religion and belief in God are indispensable prerequisites not only for individual salvation but also for true civilization. Yet He also acknowledges that tremendous cruelties and suffering have been inflicted on humanity in the name of religion. He warns humanity about the importance of eliminating religious prejudice: "Religious fanaticism and hatred are a world-devouring fire, whose violence none can quench." He commanded his own followers to "Consort with all men . . . in a spirit of friendliness and fellowship."[3]

'Abdu'l-Bahá also notes the prevalence of religious intolerance, saying that this is against the spirit of true religion:

> Divine religion is not a cause for discord and disagreement. If religion becomes the source of antagonism and strife, the absence of religion is to be preferred. Religion is meant to be the quickening life of the body politic; if it be the cause of death to humanity, its nonexistence would be a blessing and benefit to man.[4]

He attributes the decline of religion in large part to the endless disputes between the followers of different faiths:

> . . . materialists are advancing and aggressive while divine forces are waning and vanishing. Irreligion has conquered religion. The cause of the chaotic condition lies in the differences among the religions and finds its origin in the animosity and hatred existing between sects and denominations. The materialists have availed themselves of this dissension amongst the religions and are constantly attacking them, intending to uproot the tree of divine planting. Owing to strife and contention among themselves, the religions are being weakened and vanquished. If a commander is at variance with his army in the execution of military tactics, there is no doubt he will be defeated by the enemy. Today the religions are at variance; enmity, strife and recrimination prevail among them; they refuse to associate; nay, rather, if necessary they shed each other's blood. Read history and record to see what dreadful events have happened in the name of religion. . . .
>
> Imitation destroys the foundation of religion, extinguishes the spirituality of the human world, transforms heavenly illumination into darkness and deprives man of the knowledge of God. It is the cause of the victory of materialism and infidelity over religion; it is the denial of Divinity and the law of revelation; it refuses Prophethood and rejects the Kingdom of God. When materialists subject imitations to the intellectual analysis of reason, they find them to be mere superstitions; therefore, they deny religion.[5]

Bahá'u'lláh was careful to distinguish between true religion, as revealed by the Messengers of God, and religious superstition, which is the product of human ignorance and corruption. The latter is the very antithesis of reason, whereas true religion is rational and in harmony with science.

'Abdu'l-Bahá explains:

Among other principles of Bahá'u'lláh's teachings was the harmony of science and religion. Religion must stand the analysis of reason. It must agree with scientific fact and proof so that science will sanction religion and religion fortify science. Both are indissolubly welded and joined in reality. If statements and teachings of religion are found to be unreasonable and contrary to science, they are outcomes of superstition and imagination. Innumerable doctrines and beliefs of this character have arisen in the past ages. Consider the superstitions and mythology of the Romans, Greeks and Egyptians; all were contrary to religion and science. It is now evident that the beliefs of these nations were superstitions, but in those times they held to them most tenaciously. . . . Therefore, we must cast aside such beliefs and investigate reality. That which is found to be real and conformable to reason must be accepted, and whatever science and reason cannot support must be rejected as imitation and not reality. Then differences of belief will disappear. All will become as one family, one people, and the same susceptibility to the divine bounty and education will be witnessed among mankind.[6]

It might seem strange at first to realize that the Bahá'í Faith promotes the harmony of science and religion. To many people religion is the opposite of science, in the sense that it does not appear to be based on rationality, or at least on anything that can be proven empirically. After all, scientific discoveries have proven many ancient religious beliefs about the universe to be baseless. There has also been a tendency on the part of many religious people to reject the clear findings of science, thereby enhancing the sense that religion is, at heart, irrational.

But the Bahá'í writings state that the human soul is a rational entity and that the power of intellectual investigation is what distinguishes us as human beings. This power is the greatest of all God's blessings, for with it we are able to discover the secrets of reality. It is a power that we possess both in this world and the next.

Not only is science compatible with religion, it is lauded in its own right. 'Abdu'l-Bahá states,

All blessings are divine in origin, but none can be compared with this power of intellectual investigation and research, which is an eternal gift producing fruits of unending delight. Man is ever partaking of these fruits. All other blessings are temporary; this is an everlasting possession. Even sovereignty has its limitations and overthrow; this is a kingship and dominion which none may usurp or destroy. Briefly, it is an eternal blessing and divine bestowal, the supreme gift of God to man. Therefore, you should put forward your most earnest efforts toward the acquisition of science and arts. The greater your attainment, the higher your standard in the divine purpose. The man of science is perceiving and endowed with vision, whereas he who is ignorant and neglectful of this development is blind. The investigating mind is attentive, alive; the callous and indifferent mind is deaf and dead. A scientific man is a true index and representative of humanity, for through processes of inductive reasoning and research he is informed of all that appertains to humanity, its status, conditions and happenings. He studies the human body politic, understands social problems and weaves the web and texture of civilization. In fact, science may be likened to a mirror wherein the infinite forms and images of existing things are revealed and reflected. It is the very foundation of all individual and national development. Without this basis of investigation, development is impossible. Therefore, seek with diligent endeavor the knowledge and attainment of all that lies within the power of this wonderful bestowal.[7]

'Abdu'l-Bahá was asked many questions about specific scientific issues. For example, He was frequently asked for the Bahá'í position on human evolution, a topic that ignites controversy even today. He states that the world itself has evolved over the course of considerable time, explaining, "It is clear that this terrestrial globe in its present form did not come into existence all at once, but . . . gradually passed through different phases until it became adorned with its present perfection."[8]

He acknowledges that humanity has evolved physically over the course of time but also asserts that humankind did not emerge by chance. Rather, this was destined by God from the beginning.

What of the biblical story of creation? 'Abdu'l-Bahá once said,

If we take this story in its apparent meaning, according to the interpretation of the masses, it is indeed extraordinary. The intelligence cannot accept it, affirm it, or imagine it; for such arrangements, such details, such speeches and reproaches are far from being those of an intelligent man, how much less of the Divinity—that Divinity Who has organized this infinite universe in the most perfect form, and its innumerable inhabitants with absolute system, strength and perfection.

We must reflect a little: if the literal meaning of this story were attributed to a wise man, certainly all would logically deny that this arrangement, this invention, could have emanated from an intelligent being. Therefore, this story of Adam and Eve who ate from the tree, and their expulsion from Paradise, must be thought of simply as a symbol. It contains divine mysteries and universal meanings, and it is capable of marvelous explanations.[9]

Not only are religion and science complementary, they must also develop hand-in-hand if civilization is to prosper. Religion without science is superstition, but science without religion is materialism, which also has its dangers. It is very misguided to think that science alone, without the moderating influence of religion, can establish human prosperity and happiness. Strictly materialist approaches can lead to disaster, as events of the twentieth century have amply proven.

Bahá'u'lláh writes,

Consider the civilization of the West, how it hath agitated and alarmed the peoples of the world. An infernal engine hath been devised, and hath proved so cruel a weapon of destruction that its like none hath ever witnessed or heard. The purging of such deeply-rooted and overwhelming corruptions cannot be effected unless the peoples of the world unite in pursuit of one common aim and embrace one universal faith.[10]

In the same letter He adds this ominous warning:

Strange and astonishing things exist in the earth but they are hidden from the minds and the understanding of men. These things are capable of changing the whole atmosphere of the earth and their contamination would prove lethal.[11]

An interesting incident occurred while 'Abdu'l-Bahá was in Paris. In a conversation with the Japanese ambassador to Spain, Viscount Arawaka, He remarked,

Scientific discoveries have increased material civilization. There is in existence a stupendous force, as yet, happily, undiscovered by man. Let us supplicate God, the Beloved, that this force be not discovered by science until spiritual civilization shall dominate the human mind. In the hands of men of lower material nature, this power would be able to destroy the whole earth.[12]

Bahá'u'lláh explains that all human advancement has resulted from the spiritual energy released by the Manifestations of God. Thus the miraculous scientific advances of the modern age can be attributed to Bahá'u'lláh's appearance in the world. Humanity's material progress is the necessary complement to the spiritual progress it will also make as the result of the revelation of Bahá'u'lláh. Peace will finally be established when our material and spiritual pursuits are in complete harmony. 'Abdu'l-Bahá turns again to the analogy of a bird to describe this inter-dependency:

> For man two wings are necessary. One wing is physical power and mate-rial civilization; the other is spiritual power and divine civilization. With one wing only, flight is impossible. Two wings are essential. Therefore, no matter how much material civilization advances, it cannot attain to perfec-tion except through the uplift of spiritual civilization. [13]

Observing the proliferation of armaments, He once remarked,

> And among the teachings of Bahá'u'lláh is that although material civiliza-tion is one of the means for the progress of the world of mankind, yet until it becomes combined with Divine civilization, the desired result, which is the felicity of mankind, will not be attained. Consider! These battleships that reduce a city to ruins within the space of an hour are the result of material civilization; likewise the Krupp guns, the Mauser rifles, dynamite, submarines, torpedo boats, armed aircraft and bombers—all these weapons of war are the malignant fruits of material civilization. Had material civili-zation been combined with Divine civilization, these fiery weapons would never have been invented. Nay, rather, human energy would have been wholly devoted to useful inventions and would have been concentrated on praiseworthy discoveries. Material civilization is like a lamp-glass. Divine civilization is the lamp itself and the glass without the light is dark. Material civilization is like the body. No matter how infinitely graceful, elegant and beautiful it may be, it is dead. Divine civilization is like the spirit, and the body gets its life from the spirit, otherwise it becomes a corpse. It has thus been made evident that the world of mankind is in need of the breaths of the Holy Spirit. Without the spirit the world of mankind is lifeless, and without this light the world of mankind is in utter darkness. [14]

CHAPTER 24

MORE PRINCIPLES FOR WORLD PEACE

The Bahá'í writings state that humanity's recognition of the oneness of God, the oneness of religion, and the oneness of humanity are essential to the establishment of world peace. So, too, are the recognition of the equality of women and men and the harmony of science and religion. There are a number of other important principles related to the establishment of peace. Like those we have already covered, their purpose is to foster a condition wherein the dignity of each human being is upheld and honored. They prescribe the role of the individual in society and the obligations of society to the individual. They also provide for the best relationships between the nations and peoples of the world. All recognize the essentially spiritual nature of human beings and define true prosperity as a balance of material and spiritual aims.

The Independent Investigation of Truth

Among the fundamental principles of the Bahá'í Faith is the independent investigation of truth. As we have seen, Bahá'u'lláh places great responsibility on the individual to investigate truth in all matters. This is one of the fundamental characteristics of justice. While there is validity in some traditions, and while Bahá'u'lláh counsels us to seek out the opinions of wise and trustworthy people in all important matters, He warns us not to rely solely on these things. We must also think, search, and eventually reach conclusions for ourselves. In no area is this more vital than in matters of faith.

In the Book of Certitude Bahá'u'lláh points out that the human tendency to cling to false traditions has always been one of the main reasons for the rejection and persecution to which every Messenger of God has been subjected. In other texts, Bahá'u'lláh upbraids the rulers of His day for relying on the opinions of corrupt ministers rather than working to ensure justice themselves.

Bahá'u'lláh decrees that humanity no longer needs an ecclesiastical class to be responsible for the spiritual guidance of others. The only true intermediary is the Messenger of God. Hence there is no clergy in the Bahá'í Faith. In this age every human being is capable of recognizing the truth for himself or herself; thus we are all responsible before God for our own actions.

We have established that religious beliefs should be counted as superstition when they run counter to established scientific fact. What happens when science appears to contradict the most essential aspects of religion, such as the existence of God and the immortal soul?

'Abdu'l-Bahá faced a great deal of religious skepticism during the course of His travels in the West. In His day there were many who had renounced belief in God, and some had even pronounced religion and religious sentiments as positively harmful. Sigmund Freud had called religion a kind of neurosis and was but one of many scientists who confidently predicted that it would disappear once humanity had become sufficiently "civilized." That and similar opinions were quickly gaining ground just as 'Abdu'l-Bahá was promoting the vital importance of religion.

'Abdu'l-Bahá gave numerous talks in which He established the rational basis for belief in God and in the human soul. He also showed that the ideas of materialists were erroneous because they relied on a limited body of information to reach their conclusions. He maintained that any issue must stand a variety of tests before the truth can be known.

In reversal of what Freud and others believed a century ago, it is now common for scientists to acknowledge that science has neither proved nor disproved the existence of God and the soul. Many believe that recent discoveries about the nature of the cosmos point to the existence of a Creator. Many now acknowledge the limitations of science when it comes to investigating spiritual phenomena. By definition some matters may lie forever outside of our power of physical observation, but that in and of itself is not proof against their existence.

Universal Education

In the light of the previous discussions it can easily be understood why Bahá'u'lláh prized education and knowledge. "Knowledge," He writes, "is as wings to man's life, and a ladder for his ascent." He continues,

Its acquisition is incumbent upon everyone. The knowledge of such sciences, however, should be acquired as can profit the peoples of the earth, and not those which begin with words and end with words. Great indeed is the claim of scientists and craftsmen on the peoples of the world. . . . In truth, knowledge is a veritable treasure for man, and a source of glory, of bounty, of joy, of exaltation, of cheer and gladness unto him.[1]

Bahá'u'lláh calls upon all parents to educate their children. He also gives responsibility to society as a whole to ensure that every child receives educational instruction. In the following passage Bahá'u'lláh exhorts humanity to ensure education for all children:

We prescribe unto all men that which will lead to the exaltation of the Word of God amongst His servants, and likewise, to the advancement of the world of being and the uplift of souls. To this end, the greatest means is education of the child. To this must each and all hold fast. We have verily laid this charge upon you in manifold Tablets as well as in My Most Holy Book. Well is it with him who deferreth thereto.[2]

Bahá'u'lláh emphasizes that education has two aspects: spiritual and material. Both are necessary for human progress and prosperity:

As to the children: We have directed that in the beginning they should be trained in the observances and laws of religion; and thereafter, in such branches of knowledge as are of benefit, and in commercial pursuits that are distinguished for integrity, and in deeds that will further the victory of God's Cause or will attract some outcome which will draw the believer closer to his Lord.

We beg of God to assist the children of His loved ones and adorn them with wisdom, good conduct, integrity and righteousness.[3]

Commenting on the importance of children's education, 'Abdu'l-Bahá writes,

Every child is potentially the light of the world—and at the same time its darkness; wherefore must the question of education be accounted as of primary importance. From his infancy, the child must be nursed at the breast of God's love, and nurtured in the embrace of His knowledge, that he may radiate light, grow in spirituality, be filled with wisdom and learning, and take on the characteristics of the angelic host.[4]

Elimination of Extremes of Wealth and Poverty

Bahá'u'lláh declares that it is every person's responsibility to engage in some occupation and that every person has the right to a fair means of livelihood. To ensure this, society must guard against extremes of wealth and poverty, conditions that inevitably produce unfair advantages for some and deprivation for others. Bahá'u'lláh, as we have already seen, severely condemned the rulers of His day for ignoring the rights of the poor.

This does not mean that complete economic equality can be realized, nor that it is even desirable. However, extremes must be avoided so that none will suffer from dire want while others wallow in excess. This is to be accomplished through a combination of legislation and voluntary sharing. Both are necessary.

On the subject of economic legislation, 'Abdu'l-Bahá stated to a Paris audience:

We see amongst us men who are overburdened with riches on the one hand, and on the other those unfortunate ones who starve with nothing; those who possess several stately palaces, and those who have not where to lay their head. Some we find with numerous courses of costly and dainty food; whilst others can scarce find sufficient crusts to keep them alive. Whilst some are clothed in velvets, furs and fine linen, others have insufficient, poor and thin garments with which to protect them from the cold.

This condition of affairs is wrong, and must be remedied. Now the remedy must be carefully undertaken. It cannot be done by bringing to pass absolute equality between men. . . .

Certainly, some being enormously rich and others lamentably poor, an organization is necessary to control and improve this state of affairs. It is important to limit riches, as it is also of importance to limit poverty. Either extreme is not good. To be seated in the mean is most desirable. If it be right for a capitalist to possess a large fortune, it is equally just that his workman should have a sufficient means of existence. . . .

There must be special laws made, dealing with these extremes of riches and of want. The members of the Government should consider the laws of God when they are framing plans for the ruling of the people. The general rights of mankind must be guarded and preserved.[5]

Legal measures alone do not ensure social welfare. It is essential for people with abundance to give to others out of a true sense of loving compassion. Such voluntary sharing occurs when the members of a society have developed a high sense of their obligations to each other and also realize that in so doing they incur the good pleasure of God. Voluntary sharing of wealth in philanthropic and charitable causes is an important element of a healthy and prosperous society. 'Abdu'l-Bahá writes,

> Man reacheth perfection through good deeds, voluntarily performed, not through good deeds the doing of which was forced upon him. And sharing is a personally chosen righteous act: that is, the rich should extend assistance to the poor, they should expend their substance for the poor, but of their own free will, and not because the poor have gained this end by force. For the harvest of force is turmoil and the ruin of the social order. On the other hand voluntary sharing, the freely-chosen expending of one's substance, leadeth to society's comfort and peace. It lighteth up the world; it bestoweth honor upon humankind.[6]

It is important to emphasize yet again that wealth itself is not condemned:

> Wealth is praiseworthy in the highest degree, if it is acquired by an individual's own efforts and the grace of God, in commerce, agriculture, art and industry, and if it be expended for philanthropic purposes. Above all, if a judicious and resourceful individual should initiate measures which would universally enrich the masses of the people, there could be no undertaking greater than this, and it would rank in the sight of God as the supreme achievement, for such a benefactor would supply the needs and insure the comfort and well-being of a great multitude. Wealth is most commendable, provided the entire population is wealthy. If, however, a few have inordinate riches while the rest are impoverished, and no fruit or benefit accrues from that wealth, then it is only a liability to its possessor. If, on the other hand, it is expended for the promotion of knowledge, the founding of elementary and other schools, the encouragement of art and industry, the training of orphans and the poor—in brief, if it is dedicated to the welfare of society— its possessor will stand out before God and man as the most excellent of all who live on earth and will be accounted as one of the people of paradise.[7]

Universal Language

To facilitate international commerce, communication, and understanding, Bahá'u'lláh advocated the adoption of an international auxiliary language. Such a language would be chosen through a process of international consultation and agreement, thereby making the process itself an important bulwark of international harmony. The intent is not to suppress or replace existing languages, nor is it to allow any one culture to dominate others. The idea is to support international peace. Bahá'u'lláh explains:

> Among the things which are conducive to unity and concord and will cause the whole earth to be regarded as one country is that the divers languages be reduced to one language and in like manner the scripts used in the world be confined to a single script. It is incumbent upon all nations to appoint some men of understanding and erudition to convene a gathering and through joint consultation choose one language from among the varied existing languages, or create a new one, to be taught to the children in all the schools of the world.
>
> The day is approaching when all the peoples of the world will have adopted one universal language and one common script. When this is achieved, to whatsoever city a man may journey, it shall be as if he were entering his own home. These things are obligatory and absolutely essential. It is incumbent upon every man of insight and understanding to strive to translate that which hath been written into reality and action.[8]

Elsewhere the Bahá'í writings envisage the adoption of a universal currency and a universal system of weights and measures. Again, the motivation is to facilitate harmony among all peoples.

Other International Measures for Peace

Bahá'u'lláh frequently expresses in His writings deep sadness at humanity's incessant warfare and the untold sufferings that it brings. Knowing full well that the world's rejection of Him would only prolong such tragedy, He writes,

> How long will humanity persist in its waywardness? How long will injustice continue? How long is chaos and confusion to reign amongst men? How long will discord agitate the face of society? . . . The winds of despair are, alas, blowing from every direction, and the strife that divideth and afflicteth the human race is daily increasing. The signs of impending convulsions and chaos can now be discerned, inasmuch as the prevailing order appeareth to be lamentably defective.[9]

He calls upon humanity to think in terms of the needs of all of God's children and to liberate themselves from petty interests. "Let your vision be world-embracing," He writes, "rather than confined to your own self. . . . It is incumbent upon every man, in this Day, to hold fast unto whatsoever will promote the interests, and exalt the station, of all nations and just governments." And on another occasion He writes, "'It is not his to boast who loveth his country, but it is his who loveth the world.'"[10]

Bahá'u'lláh lauds those who arise to serve the interests of all humanity:

That one indeed is a man who, today, dedicateth himself to the service of the entire human race. The Great Being saith: Blessed and happy is he that ariseth to promote the best interests of the peoples and kindreds of the earth. In another passage He hath proclaimed: It is not for him to pride himself who loveth his own country, but rather for him who loveth the whole world. The earth is but one country, and mankind its citizens.[11]

The Bahá'í teachings state that the time has come for the nations of the earth to work together to establish peace and to regulate international affairs in such manner as to ensure justice for all of humanity. The era of unfettered national sovereignty must come to a close. Addressing "the concourse of the rulers of the earth," Bahá'u'lláh states,

Take ye counsel together, and let your concern be only for that which profiteth mankind and bettereth the condition thereof. . . . Regard the world as the human body which, though at its creation whole and perfect, hath been afflicted, through various causes, with grave disorders and maladies. Not for one day did it gain ease, nay its sickness waxed more severe, as it fell under the treatment of ignorant physicians, who gave full rein to their personal desires and have erred grievously. And if, at one time, through the care of an able physician, a member of that body was healed, the rest remained afflicted as before.[12]

Later He added:

O kings of the earth! We see you increasing every year your expenditures, and laying the burden thereof on your subjects. This, verily, is wholly and grossly unjust. Fear the sighs and tears of this Wronged One, and lay not excessive burdens on your peoples. . . .
. . . Be reconciled among yourselves, that ye may need no more armaments save in a measure to safeguard your territories and dominions. . . .
Be united, O kings of the earth, for thereby will the tempest of discord be stilled amongst you, and your peoples find rest. . . . Should any one among

you take up arms against another, rise ye all against him, for this is naught but manifest justice.[13]

Bahá'u'lláh advocates the establishment of an international body composed of representatives of all nations. Such a body will resolve disputes and deal with other matters necessary to international harmony. Among its guiding principles will be that of collective security, whereby the nations of the world will unitedly oppose renegade acts of aggression.

'Abdu'l-Bahá describes a world that is becoming increasingly interdependent. No longer are the nations able to operate in isolation. This stage is the end result of a long historic process of social evolution:

> In cycles gone by, though harmony was established, yet, owing to the absence of means, the unity of all mankind could not have been achieved. Continents remained widely divided, nay even among the peoples of one and the same continent association and interchange of thought were well-nigh impossible. Consequently intercourse, understanding and unity amongst all the peoples and kindreds of the earth were unattainable. In this day, however, means of communication have multiplied, and the five continents of the earth have virtually merged into one. And for everyone it is now easy to travel to any land, to associate and exchange views with its peoples, and to become familiar, through publications, with the conditions, the religious beliefs and the thoughts of all men. In like manner all the members of the human family, whether peoples or governments, cities or villages, have become increasingly interdependent. For none is self-sufficiency any longer possible, inasmuch as political ties unite all peoples and nations, and the bonds of trade and industry, of agriculture and education, are being strengthened every day. Hence the unity of all mankind can in this day be achieved. Verily this is none other but one of the wonders of this wondrous age, this glorious century. Of this past ages have been deprived, for this century—the century of light—hath been endowed with unique and unprecedented glory, power and illumination. Hence the miraculous unfolding of a fresh marvel every day. Eventually it will be seen how bright its candles will burn in the assemblage of man.[14]

'Abdu'l-Bahá also describes the functions of the international body heralded by Bahá'u'lláh:

> True civilization will unfurl its banner in the midmost heart of the world whenever a certain number of its distinguished and high-minded sover-

eigns—the shining exemplars of devotion and determination—shall, for the good and happiness of all mankind, arise, with firm resolve and clear vision, to establish the Cause of Universal Peace. They must make the Cause of Peace the object of general consultation, and seek by every means in their power to establish a Union of the nations of the world. They must conclude a binding treaty and establish a covenant, the provisions of which shall be sound, inviolable and definite. They must proclaim it to all the world and obtain for it the sanction of all the human race. This supreme and noble undertaking—the real source of the peace and well-being of all the world— should be regarded as sacred by all that dwell on earth. All the forces of humanity must be mobilized to ensure the stability and permanence of this Most Great Covenant. In this all-embracing Pact the limits and frontiers of each and every nation should be clearly fixed, the principles underlying the relations of governments towards one another definitely laid down, and all international agreements and obligations ascertained. In like manner, the size of the armaments of every government should be strictly limited, for if the preparations for war and the military forces of any nation should be allowed to increase, they will arouse the suspicion of others. The fundamental principle underlying this solemn Pact should be so fixed that if any government later violate any one of its provisions, all the governments on earth should arise to reduce it to utter submission, nay the human race as a whole should resolve, with every power at its disposal, to destroy that government. Should this greatest of all remedies be applied to the sick body of the world, it will assuredly recover from its ills and will remain eternally safe and secure.

Observe that if such a happy situation be forthcoming, no government would need continually to pile up the weapons of war, nor feel itself obliged to produce ever new military weapons with which to conquer the human race. A small force for the purposes of internal security, the correction of criminal and disorderly elements and the prevention of local disturbances, would be required—no more. In this way the entire population would, first of all, be relieved of the crushing burden of expenditure currently imposed for military purposes, and secondly, great numbers of people would cease to devote their time to the continual devising of new weapons of destruction— those testimonials of greed and bloodthirstiness, so inconsistent with the gift of life—and would instead bend their efforts to the production of whatever will foster human existence and peace and well-being, and would become the cause of universal development and prosperity. Then every nation on earth will reign in honor, and every people will be cradled in tranquillity and content.

A few, unaware of the power latent in human endeavor, consider this matter as highly impracticable, nay even beyond the scope of man's utmost efforts. Such is not the case, however. On the contrary, thanks to the unfailing grace of God, the loving-kindness of His favored ones, the unrivaled endeavors of wise and capable souls, and the thoughts and ideas of the peerless leaders of this age, nothing whatsoever can be regarded as unattainable. Endeavor, ceaseless endeavor, is required. Nothing short of an indomitable determination can possibly achieve it. Many a cause which past ages have regarded as purely visionary, yet in this day has become most easy and practicable. Why should this most great and lofty Cause—the daystar of the firmament of true civilization and the cause of the glory, the advancement, the well-being and the success of all humanity—be regarded as impossible of achievement? Surely the day will come when its beauteous light shall shed illumination upon the assemblage of man.[15]

Collective security and other such matters might seem at first not to be spiritual issues and may appear to lie outside of the sphere of religion. But justice is a fundamental law of God. On a world scale, people must now act to enforce justice for all. Occasionally there will be the need to resort to force in order to prevent greater evils from occurring; hence the principle of collective security.

"A rabid dog," 'Abdu'l-Bahá writes, "if given the chance, can kill a thousand animals and men. Therefore, compassion shown to wild and ravening beasts is cruelty to the peaceful ones—and so the harmful must be dealt with."

And similarly He explains, "Kindness cannot be shown the tyrant, the deceiver, or the thief, because, far from awakening them to the error of their ways, it maketh them to continue in their perversity as before."[16]

Bahá'u'lláh foresaw that the world will eventually unite as one political commonwealth but that the road to that unity will not be smooth. Subsequent history has seen the cause of international peace move forward in fits and starts, punctuated both by important steps forward and by disastrous setbacks. The first international body resembling that described by 'Abdu'l-Bahá was the League of Nations, formed at the end of World War I in the hope of preventing another destructive world conflict. But 'Abdu'l-Bahá Himself stated that the League of Nations would not succeed in establishing peace because the leaders of nations had not yet developed sufficient consciousness of the need for a universal body for international arbitration. He predicted that "in the future another war, fiercer than the last, will assuredly break out; verily, of this there is no doubt whatever."[17]

After a second world cataclysm, the United Nations was established in 1946. Although it has achieved many notable things, yet it has failed to become a decisive force for peace because its national members are still gripped to a great extent by narrow interests. The supreme tribunal of which Bahá'u'lláh spoke has yet to emerge. Whether it is to develop from the United Nations or a new body is to be established, it will, according to 'Abdu'l-Bahá, "fulfill this sacred task" of establishing universal peace "with the utmost might and power."[18]

As we move into the twenty-first century it can be seen that humanity is becoming increasingly conscious, if only dimly so, that the earth is the common homeland of all. More and more thoughtful people are recognizing the need for a new system of international relationships that will preserve peace and ensure prosperity for all citizens of the planet. The Bahá'í teachings emphasize that political arrangements in and of themselves will not ensure lasting peace. More than this is required, for humanity must also heed the message of Bahá'u'lláh and become spiritually transformed through the power of the Word of God. In a later chapter we shall return to the theme of world peace and the process whereby it will be established.

CHAPTER 25

LEADING A MORE MEANINGFUL LIFE

So far in this volume we have touched upon the major principles that constitute the keys to living a more meaningful life. These include the knowledge and love of God; the acceptance of His Manifestation for today; the refinement of character and spiritual life through prayer, meditation, and obedience to divine teachings; love for humanity and service to others; and the development of a world-embracing vision.

The path to true fulfillment requires day-to-day effort as we face the challenges of managing our private lives, our family relationships, our careers, our interests, and our interactions with others. The Bahá'í teachings shed light on all of these issues, helping us to obtain a correct and healthy perspective on life's complexity. The following teachings and principles can serve as essential guidance in our life-long spiritual growth.

True Wealth

Bahá'u'lláh teaches that all of creation exists for our benefit. During our sojourn in this physical existence we are to begin the process of developing spiritual qualities and investigating spiritual reality—a process that will continue in the next world. Everything in creation potentially serves this end.

'Abdu'l-Bahá says that everything in the universe has a counterpart in the spiritual world. He often uses analogies taken from the natural world to explain spiritual truths. For example, in this world all creatures depend upon the sun for heat and light. Without the sun, life would be impossible. The spiritual counterpart of the sun is the Manifestation of God, upon Whom we depend for spiritual life. Just as the physical universe has laws that govern its operation, so does the spiritual world. Just as we find order, relationships, grades of distinction, and so on in physical reality, so do we also in spiritual reality.

The Bahá'í writings contain many analogies and metaphors drawn from the physical world to describe spiritual laws and realities. The analogies and metaphors are not mere poetic inventions; rather, they are doorways to understanding profound spiritual truths. In the Book of Certitude Bahá'u'lláh describes the attainment of such spiritual insight as the result of sincere and determined effort to draw closer to God. When this is achieved, the seeker begins to look upon the things of this world with new eyes:

> Only when the lamp of search, of earnest striving, of longing desire, of passionate devotion, of fervid love, of rapture, and ecstasy, is kindled within the seeker's heart, and the breeze of His loving-kindness is wafted upon his soul, will the darkness of error be dispelled, the mists of doubts and misgivings be dissipated, and the lights of knowledge and certitude envelop his being. At that hour will the mystic Herald, bearing the joyful tidings of the Spirit, shine forth from the City of God resplendent as the morn, and, through the trumpet-blast of knowledge, will awaken the heart, the soul, and the spirit from the slumber of negligence. Then will the manifold favors and outpouring grace of the holy and everlasting Spirit confer such new life upon the seeker that he will find himself endowed with a new eye, a new ear, a new heart, and a new mind. He will contemplate the manifest signs of the universe, and will penetrate the hidden mysteries of the soul. Gazing with the eye of God, he will perceive within every atom a door that leadeth him to the stations of absolute certitude. He will discover in all things the mysteries of divine Revelation and the evidences of an everlasting manifestation.[1]

While living in Baghdad in 1854 Bahá'u'lláh revealed a treatise that describes in metaphorical language the stages of progress in the journey of the soul towards God. That book, the Seven Valleys, was addressed to a follower of Ṣúfí mysticism. As the title implies, Bahá'u'lláh employs the metaphor of a wayfarer who must traverse seven valleys, each leading closer to the goal. In one, the valley of knowledge, the wayfarer progresses to the point where the signs of God's love are evident in all created things.

It is clear from many passages in the Bahá'í scriptures that the material world is not intrinsically evil, but good. God desires us to enjoy the material benefits of this life, which to some degree are necessary for happiness.

The problem comes if we allow material things to come between ourselves and God. If we become preoccupied with material pursuits, we forget God and neglect our spiritual side. The result is selfishness and a lack of spiritual awareness, the consequences of which affect not only ourselves but others as well.

The key, then, is not to become so attached to material things that they become more important to us than spiritual things. Bahá'u'lláh describes such attachments as "veils" or "barriers" between the human heart and God. It is essential to remember that material things are only temporary, whereas the things of the spirit are eternal. True wealth consists in the attainment of spiritual virtues, including love and the knowledge of God. 'Abdu'l-Bahá writes, "the happiness and greatness, the rank and station, the pleasure and peace, of an individual have never consisted in his personal wealth, but rather in his excellent character, his high resolve, the breadth of his learning, and his ability to solve difficult problems."[2]

Bahá'u'lláh teaches that there are many kinds of barriers, in addition to material possessions, that can prevent us from drawing near to God. Excessive pursuit of pleasure can be a barrier. Other potential barriers are excessive pride in one's own knowledge or attachment to tradition, both of which can prevent one from recognizing and accepting the Manifestation of God. Such attitudes are also a form of materialism, for they are founded upon human judgment rather than divine knowledge. This kind of lower attachment, according to Bahá'u'lláh, is especially dangerous, and He warns people not to allow themselves to be deceived by their own illusory notions.

The Principle of Moderation

This is not to say that pleasure and knowledge are bad. We have already seen that Bahá'u'lláh praises knowledge and also desires for us to be happy in this life. Nor is it wrong to possess material things. Wealth is good and necessary, but it must be based upon true knowledge of ourselves; that is to say, awareness of our spiritual reality.

Bahá'u'lláh writes, "In all matters moderation is desirable."[3] This crucial principle helps us to understand many of His laws and teachings, which guard us against extremes of behavior that are spiritually self-defeating. For example, while Bahá'u'lláh warns us not to become attached to our possessions, He also forbids asceticism, self-denial, and other such practices, which can actually retard spiritual progress.

'Abdu'l-Bahá advises us not to waste our lives in the pursuit of material treasures, yet this does not mean that the things of this life are not to be enjoyed:

"All that has been created is for man, who is at the apex of creation, and he must be thankful for the divine bestowals. All material things are for us, so that through our gratitude we may learn to understand life as a divine benefit. If we are disgusted with life we are ingrates, for our material and spiritual existence are the outward evidences of the divine mercy. Therefore we must be happy and spend our time in praises, appreciating all things."[4]

The rule of moderation applies to other aspects of life as well. For example, the Bahá'í teachings lay great emphasis on chastity. By this is meant, on the one hand, complete abstinence from sexual activity except between a husband and wife. On the other hand, it means purity in both thought and action. But this does not mean that the sexual impulse is considered evil or that sexual intercourse is wrong. On the contrary, it is intended to be one of the most fulfilling of human experiences and is considered a blessing from God. But it requires regulation and control, both for our own benefit and for the benefit of society.

The Law of God

We have referred several times to the laws of Bahá'u'lláh. Bahá'u'lláh revealed many laws and ordinances designed for the individual and for society. These laws are revealed in a spirit of love for humanity with the aim to promote its best interests. Moreover, the laws are divine in origin and are, therefore, in a category quite apart from the laws of man.

Bahá'u'lláh strongly advocates human freedom, which is essential to individual dignity and happiness. In particular, He emphasizes freedom of conscience, which permits a person to follow his chosen religion. But this is not license to do whatever we please. One can easily see that any good thing carried to an extreme is injurious to the individual and to society. The laws of Bahá'u'lláh are designed to provide humanity with the kind of freedom that ensures true happiness.

It is essential to understand that God's law is the only sure safeguard for the human soul and for the prosperity of all humanity. In the opening paragraphs of the Most Holy Book Bahá'u'lláh writes,

They whom God hath endued with insight will readily recognize that the precepts laid down by God constitute the highest means for the maintenance of order in the world and the security of its peoples. He that turneth away from them is accounted among the abject and foolish. We, verily, have commanded you to refuse the dictates of your evil passions and corrupt desires, and not to transgress the bounds which the Pen of the Most High hath fixed, for these are the breath of life unto all created things. . . .

O ye peoples of the world! Know assuredly that My commandments are the lamps of My loving providence among My servants, and the keys of My mercy for My creatures. Thus hath it been sent down from the heaven of the Will of your Lord, the Lord of Revelation. Were any man to taste the sweetness of the words which the lips of the All-Merciful have willed to utter, he would, though the treasures of the earth be in his possession, renounce them one and all, that he might vindicate the truth of even one of His commandments, shining above the Dayspring of His bountiful care and loving-kindness.[5]

To accept God's Messenger implies that we also accept that all of His teachings are for our benefit. This is similar to the relationship between parent and child. The loving parent must lay down rules and restrictions to protect the child and ensure its proper development. The child may not understand the wisdom of such rules for many years, but will certainly come to appreciate it in the fullness of time. The same is true for the laws that come down from our heavenly Father. We must trust that their value will eventually become evident in the course of time, even if at first we do not fully understand them.

Work and Service

Throughout Bahá'u'lláh's ministry He exhorted people to engage in a profession of some kind. In the Hidden Words He makes the following statement:

O MY SERVANT!
The best of men are they that earn a livelihood by their calling and spend upon themselves and upon their kindred for the love of God, the Lord of all worlds.[6]

Bahá'u'lláh has elevated work to the level of worship of God:

It is enjoined upon every one of you to engage in some form of occupation, such as crafts, trades and the like. We have graciously exalted your engagement in such work to the rank of worship unto God, the True One. Ponder ye in your hearts the grace and the blessings of God and render thanks unto Him at eventide and at dawn. Waste not your time in idleness and sloth. Occupy yourselves with that which profiteth yourselves and others. Thus hath it been decreed in this Tablet from whose horizon the daystar of wisdom and utterance shineth resplendent.

The most despised of men in the sight of God are those who sit idly and beg. Hold ye fast unto the cord of material means, placing your whole trust in God, the Provider of all means. When anyone occupieth himself in a craft or trade, such occupation itself is regarded in the estimation of God as an act of worship; and this is naught but a token of His infinite and all-pervasive bounty.[7]

The specific occupation is not important, so long as it is done in the spirit of service. 'Abdu'l-Bahá explains:

In the Bahá'í Cause arts, sciences and all crafts are (counted as) worship. The man who makes a piece of notepaper to the best of his ability, conscientiously, concentrating all his forces on perfecting it, is giving praise to God. Briefly, all effort and exertion put forth by man from the fullness of his heart is worship, if it is prompted by the highest motives and the will to do service to humanity. This is worship: to serve mankind and to minister to the needs of the people. Service is prayer. A physician ministering to the sick, gently, tenderly, free from prejudice and believing in the solidarity of the human race, he is giving praise.[8]

Elsewhere 'Abdu'l-Bahá writes, "Service to the friends [the Bahá'ís] is service to the Kingdom of God."[9] Extolling those who devote their lives for the benefit of others, He writes,

Every imperfect soul is self-centered and thinketh only of his own good. But as his thoughts expand a little he will begin to think of the welfare and comfort of his family. If his ideas still more widen, his concern will be the felicity of his fellow citizens; and if still they widen, he will be thinking of the glory of his land and of his race. But when ideas and views reach the utmost degree of expansion and attain the stage of perfection, then will he be interested in the exaltation of humankind. He will then be the well-wisher of all men and the seeker of the weal and prosperity of all lands. This is indicative of perfection.[10]

Again, there are those famed and accomplished men of learning, possessed of praiseworthy qualities and vast erudition, who lay hold on the strong handle of the fear of God and keep to the ways of salvation. In the mirror of their minds the forms of transcendent realities are reflected, and the lamp of their inner vision derives its light from the sun of universal knowledge. They are busy by night and by day with meticulous research into such sciences as are profitable to mankind, and they devote themselves to the training of students of capacity. It is certain that to their discerning taste, the proffered treasures of kings would not compare with a single drop of the waters of knowledge, and mountains of gold and silver could not outweigh the successful solution of a difficult problem. To them, the delights that lie outside their work are only toys for children, and the cumbersome load of unnecessary possessions is only good for the ignorant and base. Content, like the birds, they give thanks for a handful of seeds, and the song of their wisdom dazzles the minds of the world's most wise.[11]

Finally, 'Abdu'l-Bahá describes such service to humanity as the highest source of happiness:

And the honor and distinction of the individual consist in this, that he among all the world's multitudes should become a source of social good. Is any larger bounty conceivable than this, that an individual, looking within himself, should find that by the confirming grace of God he has become the cause of peace and well-being, of happiness and advantage to his fellow men? No, by the one true God, there is no greater bliss, no more complete delight.[12]

Marriage and Family

Bahá'u'lláh makes it clear that individual spiritual progress cannot occur if one deliberately chooses to live apart from society. One must serve others, cultivate human relationships, and work for the benefit of humanity. For this reason asceticism is not allowed. While chastity is expected, taking vows of celibacy for religious purposes is not a part of the Bahá'í teachings.

The Bahá'í Faith recognizes the family unit as the basic building block of society. Thus Bahá'u'lláh strongly encourages marriage, but it is not obligatory. Only monogamy is permissible, and only between members of the opposite sex.

'Abdu'l-Bahá describes Bahá'í marriage in the following terms:

Marriage, among the mass of the people, is a physical bond, and this union can only be temporary, since it is foredoomed to a physical separation at the close.

Among the people of Bahá [Bahá'ís], however, marriage must be a union of the body and of the spirit as well, for here both husband and wife are aglow with the same wine, both are enamored of the same matchless Face, both live and move through the same spirit, both are illumined by the same glory. This connection between them is a spiritual one, hence it is a bond that will abide forever. Likewise do they enjoy strong and lasting ties in the physical world as well, for if the marriage is based both on the spirit and the body, that union is a true one, hence it will endure. If, however, the bond is physical and nothing more, it is sure to be only temporary, and must inexorably end in separation.

When, therefore, the people of Bahá undertake to marry, the union must be a true relationship, a spiritual coming together as well as a physical one, so that throughout every phase of life, and in all the worlds of God, their union will endure; for this real oneness is a gleaming out of the love of God.[13]

The Bahá'í Faith does not allow for arranged marriages. Instead, husband and wife should both freely choose each other, then seek the permission of their parents to marry. Bahá'ís are free to marry outside of their religion; the most important issue to consider when choosing a mate is character. 'Abdu'l-Bahá advises the believers to choose their mates with care:

Bahá'í marriage is union and cordial affection between the two parties. They must, however, exercise the utmost care and become acquainted with each other's character. This eternal bond should be made secure by a firm covenant, and the intention should be to foster harmony, fellowship and unity and to attain everlasting life. . . .[14]

Divorce is strongly discouraged, but it is permissible in cases where aversion and differences are insurmountable, provided that there has been a sincere attempt on the part of both husband and wife to reconcile. Husband and wife are expected to strive to repair their union for at least one full year after separation before divorce is finalized.

Bahá'u'lláh places great emphasis upon the unity of the family and the mutual support of its members. Children should be obedient to their parents. Parents are obliged to ensure character training and education for their children and must provide for their material needs until they become self-sufficient.

True marriage—the physical and spiritual union of two people with the aim of serving God and humanity—is one of the most rewarding and joyous aspects of life. Such a union is described by Bahá'u'lláh as "a fortress for well-being and salvation."[15]

Health and Healing

The soul is the only part of a person that is eternal. However, the body is the vehicle through which we experience this world, and for that reason it deserves care and attention. Moreover, the soul and body have a close connection; each affects the other in important ways. Physical health and cleanliness have a powerful impact upon the quality of our spiritual lives, and our spiritual health influences our physical well-being.

The Bahá'í teachings enjoin complete abstinence from drugs and alcohol, except when prescribed by a competent physician, and encourage moderation in diet and regular exercise. Just as purity of heart and mind are conducive to happiness, so is physical cleanliness:

> . . . in every aspect of life, purity and holiness, cleanliness and refinement, exalt the human condition and further the development of man's inner reality. Even in the physical realm, cleanliness will conduce to spirituality, as the Holy Writings clearly state. And although bodily cleanliness is a physical thing, it hath, nevertheless, a powerful influence on the life of the spirit. It is even as a voice wondrously sweet, or a melody played: although sounds are but vibrations in the air which affect the ear's auditory nerve, and these vibrations are but chance phenomena carried along through the air, even so, see how they move the heart. A wondrous melody is wings for the spirit, and maketh the soul to tremble for joy. The purport is that physical cleanliness doth also exert its effect upon the human soul.[16]

Healing is to be sought by both material and spiritual means:

> There are two ways of healing sickness, material means and spiritual means. The first is by the treatment of physicians; the second consisteth in prayers offered by the spiritual ones to God and in turning to Him. Both means should be used and practiced.
> . . . they are not contradictory. Therefore thou shouldst also accept physical remedies inasmuch as these too have come from the mercy and favor of God, Who hath revealed and made manifest medical science so that His servants may profit from this kind of treatment also.[17]

In times of illness Bahá'ís are told to seek out the advice and assistance of competent physicians. Physicians themselves are advised not only to rely on their medical knowledge, but also to ask God for assistance in healing patients.

The Bahá'í writings state that the spiritual and emotional dimensions can exert a powerful influence on one's health. Many today are aware of the positive health effects of good attitude, a sense of purpose, a general feeling of well-being, of loving others and feeling loved. In addition to these we are assured of the power of prayer and the Holy Spirit to bring about good results. Many of us know of cases that were deemed hopeless, yet the patients recovered, due apparently to such influences.

Prayer does not necessarily guarantee the outcome we desire. This is dependent upon God's will. 'Abdu'l-Bahá explains that we often do not understand the reasons for this in the short term, but that they are made known to us eventually. In one instance He also reminded a believer about the proper use of physical health:

"If the health and well-being of the body be expended in the path of the Kingdom, this is very acceptable and praiseworthy; and if it be expended to the benefit of the human world in general—even though it be to their material benefit—and be a means of doing good, that is also acceptable. But if the health and welfare of man be spent in sensual desires, in a life on the animal plane, and in devilish pursuits—then disease were better than such health; nay, death itself were preferable to such a life. If thou art desirous of health, wish thou health for serving the Kingdom. I hope that thou mayest attain perfect insight, inflexible resolution, complete health, and spiritual and physical strength in order that thou mayest drink from the fountain of eternal life and be assisted by the spirit of divine confirmation."[18]

Music and the Arts

We have seen that the Bahá'í teachings endorse a high degree of refinement in morals, intellectual pursuits, and physical cleanliness. The same is true of artistic pursuits. Music and the arts give expression to the human spirit and are thus very important to the individual and society, provided they reflect spiritual refinement.

Bahá'u'lláh refers to music as a "ladder" for human souls, "a means whereby they may be lifted up unto the realm on high." But He warns that it should not be used "as wings to self and passion," nor should it "overstep the bounds of propriety and dignity."[19]

Music, drama, visual arts, architecture, poetry, and other art forms, when born of love for God and a spirit of service to humanity, are all encouraged as essential elements of civilized life and stimulants to spiritual and social progress. 'Abdu'l-Bahá is reported to have said,

> "All Art is a gift of the Holy Spirit. When this light shines through the mind of a musician, it manifests itself in beautiful harmonies. Again, shining through the mind of a poet, it is seen in fine poetry and poetic prose. When the Light of the Sun of Truth inspires the mind of a painter, he produces marvellous pictures. These gifts are fulfilling their highest purpose, when showing forth the praise of God."[20]

In a talk given at a children's reception in 1912, 'Abdu'l-Bahá also encouraged musical education for children:

> The art of music is divine and effective. It is the food of the soul and spirit. Through the power and charm of music the spirit of man is uplifted. It has wonderful sway and effect in the hearts of children, for their hearts are pure, and melodies have great influence in them. The latent talents with which the hearts of these children are endowed will find expression through the medium of music. Therefore, you must exert yourselves to make them proficient; teach them to sing with excellence and effect. It is incumbent upon each child to know something of music, for without knowledge of this art the melodies of instrument and voice cannot be rightly enjoyed. Likewise, it is necessary that the schools teach it in order that the souls and hearts of the pupils may become vivified and exhilarated and their lives be brightened with enjoyment.[21]

Music and the arts are prominent features of Bahá'í life, yet at this time there is nothing that can be considered "Bahá'í art." However, Bahá'ís look forward to a time in the future when a new world civilization based upon Bahá'í principles will inspire new artistic expressions wholly in keeping with Bahá'u'lláh's world-embracing vision.

CHAPTER 26

UNDERSTANDING TESTS AND AFFLICTIONS

One of the issues that humanity has always faced is how to reconcile the notion of a benevolent God with the reality of human suffering. Only a viewpoint that takes into consideration the existence of an afterlife can possibly explain both the terrible afflictions that human beings are sometimes made to endure in this world and the loving concern of God for His children.

Bahá'u'lláh teaches that tests and afflictions are sent by God to help us turn to Him. Although they sometimes seem harsh, they are necessary and beneficial:

O SON OF MAN!
My calamity is My providence, outwardly it is fire and vengeance, but inwardly it is light and mercy. Hasten thereunto that thou mayest become an eternal light and an immortal spirit. This is My command unto thee, do thou observe it.[1]

'Abdu'l-Bahá explains the concept of suffering as follows:

The trials of man are of two kinds. (a) The consequences of his own actions. If a man eats too much, he ruins his digestion; if he takes poison he becomes ill or dies. If a person gambles he will lose his money; if he drinks too much he will lose his equilibrium. All these sufferings are caused by the man himself, it is quite clear therefore that certain sorrows are the result of our own deeds.

(b) Other sufferings there are, which come upon the Faithful of God. Consider the great sorrows endured by Christ and by His apostles!

Those who suffer most, attain to the greatest perfection.

Those who declare a wish to suffer much for Christ's sake must prove their sincerity; those who proclaim their longing to make great sacrifices can only prove their truth by their deeds. Job proved the fidelity of his love for God by being faithful through his great adversity, as well as during the prosperity of his life. The apostles of Christ who steadfastly bore all their trials and sufferings—did they not prove their faithfulness? Was not their endurance the best proof?

These griefs are now ended.

Caiaphas lived a comfortable and happy life while Peter's life was full of sorrow and trial; which of these two is the more enviable? Assuredly we should choose the present state of Peter, for he possesses immortal life whilst Caiaphas has won eternal shame. The trials of Peter tested his fidelity. Tests are benefits from God, for which we should thank Him. Grief and sorrow do not come to us by chance, they are sent to us by the Divine Mercy for our own perfecting.

While a man is happy he may forget his God; but when grief comes and sorrows overwhelm him, then will he remember his Father who is in Heaven, and who is able to deliver him from his humiliations.

Men who suffer not, attain no perfection. The plant most pruned by the gardeners is that one which, when the summer comes, will have the most beautiful blossoms and the most abundant fruit.

The labourer cuts up the earth with his plough, and from that earth comes the rich and plentiful harvest. The more a man is chastened, the greater is the harvest of spiritual virtues shown forth by him. A soldier is no good General until he has been in the front of the fiercest battle and has received the deepest wounds.[2]

What about those whose lives are taken prematurely due to accidents or other causes? What happens to such victims?

Shortly after 'Abdu'l-Bahá arrived in America in 1912, news came of the sinking of the *Titanic*. Interestingly, some Bahá'ís had offered to secure His passage to New York on the ship's maiden voyage, but He had chosen another vessel instead. He made the following remarks about the disaster:

Within the last few days a terrible event has happened in the world, an event saddening to every heart and grieving every spirit. I refer to the *Titanic* disaster, in which many of our fellow human beings were drowned, a number of beautiful souls passed beyond this earthly life. Although such an event is indeed regrettable, we must realize that everything which happens is due to some wisdom and that nothing happens without a reason. Therein is a mystery; but whatever the reason and mystery, it was a very sad occurrence, one which brought tears to many eyes and distress to many souls. I was greatly affected by this disaster. Some of those who were lost voyaged on the *Cedric* with us as far as Naples and afterward sailed upon the other ship. When I think of them, I am very sad indeed. But when I consider this calamity in another aspect, I am consoled by the realization that the worlds of God are infinite; that though they were deprived of this existence, they have other opportunities in the life beyond, even as Christ has said, "In my Father's house are many mansions." They were called away from the temporary and transferred to the eternal; they abandoned this material existence and entered the portals of the spiritual world. Foregoing the pleasures and comforts of the earthly, they now partake of a joy and happiness far more abiding and real, for they have hastened to the Kingdom of God. The mercy of God is infinite, and it is our duty to remember these departed souls in our prayers and supplications that they may draw nearer and nearer to the Source itself.

. . .

Furthermore, these events have deeper reasons. Their object and purpose is to teach man certain lessons. We are living in a day of reliance upon material conditions. Men imagine that the great size and strength of a ship, the perfection of machinery or the skill of a navigator will ensure safety, but these disasters sometimes take place that men may know that God is the real Protector. If it be the will of God to protect man, a little ship may escape destruction, whereas the greatest and most perfectly constructed vessel with the best and most skillful navigator may not survive a danger such as was present on the ocean. The purpose is that the people of the world may turn to God, the One Protector; that human souls may rely upon His preservation and know that He is the real safety. These events happen in order that man's faith may be increased and strengthened. Therefore, although we feel sad and disheartened, we must supplicate God to turn our hearts to the Kingdom and pray for these departed souls with faith in His infinite mercy so that, although they have been deprived of this earthly life, they may enjoy a new existence in the supreme mansions of the Heavenly Father.

Let no one imagine that these words imply that man should not be thorough and careful in his undertakings. God has endowed man with intelligence so that he may safeguard and protect himself. Therefore, he must provide and surround himself with all that scientific skill can produce. He must be deliberate, thoughtful and thorough in his purposes, build the best ship and provide the most experienced captain; yet, withal, let him rely upon God and consider God as the one Keeper. If God protects, nothing can imperil man's safety; and if it be not His will to safeguard, no amount of preparation and precaution will avail.[3]

On another occasion 'Abdu'l-Bahá wrote to two believers, explaining that those whose lives are cut short still receive divine mercies:

> The inscrutable divine wisdom underlieth such heartrending occurrences. It is as if a kind gardener transferreth a fresh and tender shrub from a confined place to a wide open area. This transfer is not the cause of the withering, the lessening or the destruction of that shrub; nay, on the contrary, it maketh it to grow and thrive, acquire freshness and delicacy, become green and bear fruit. This hidden secret is well known to the gardener, but those souls who are unaware of this bounty suppose that the gardener, in his anger and wrath, hath uprooted the shrub. Yet to those who are aware, this concealed fact is manifest, and this predestined decree is considered a bounty. Do not feel grieved or disconsolate, therefore, at the ascension of that bird of faithfulness; nay, under all circumstances pray for that youth, supplicating for him forgiveness and the elevation of his station.[4]

By no means did 'Abdu'l-Bahá intend to encourage complacency about the suffering inflicted by oppressors. On the contrary, we have already seen how urgently both He and Bahá'u'lláh exhorted humanity to establish justice in the world. When we are in the midst of tests and afflictions it can be difficult to remember that their real purpose is to help us draw nearer to God and thereby find true happiness. Yet these very challenges can lead us to greater spiritual understanding, provided that we turn to Him. With the help of God, we can find the strength to rise above our challenges and become better and happier human beings.

CHAPTER 27

'ABDU'L-BAHÁ'S
FINAL YEARS

'Abdu'l-Bahá spent much of His time and energy encouraging the believers to live up to the teachings of Bahá'u'lláh and to share His message with others. A typical example is an address He gave in December 1912 to the American Bahá'ís at the very end of His visit to North America:

> The earth is one native land, one home; and all mankind are the children of one Father. God has created them, and they are the recipients of His compassion. Therefore, if anyone offends another, he offends God. It is the wish of our heavenly Father that every heart should rejoice and be filled with happiness, that we should live together in felicity and joy. The obstacle to human happiness is racial or religious prejudice, the competitive struggle for existence and inhumanity toward each other. . . .
>
> Beware lest ye offend any heart, lest ye speak against anyone in his absence, lest ye estrange yourselves from the servants of God. You must consider all His servants as your own family and relations. Direct your whole effort toward the happiness of those who are despondent, bestow food upon the hungry, clothe the needy, and glorify the humble. Be a helper to every helpless one, and manifest kindness to your fellow creatures in order that ye may attain the good pleasure of God. This is conducive to the illumination of the world of humanity and eternal felicity for yourselves. I seek from God everlasting glory in your behalf; therefore, this is my prayer and exhortation.
>
> . . . Your efforts must be lofty. Exert yourselves with heart and soul so that, perchance, through your efforts the light of universal peace may shine and this darkness of estrangement and enmity may be dispelled from amongst

men, that all men may become as one family and consort together in love
and kindness, that the East may assist the West and the West give help to the
East, for all are the inhabitants of one planet, the people of one original
native land and the flocks of one Shepherd.[1]

There can be no doubt that the effect of 'Abdu'l-Bahá's visit upon the early
believers was extremely profound. It was not limited to His words alone. His
deeds, His loving consideration for others, His spiritual power and majesty, all
combined to make an indelible impression on those who associated with Him.
Some were believers before His arrival in America, and others came to believe as
the result of meeting Him. Many people in both categories spent their remaining
years in service to the Bahá'í Faith.

Return to the Holy Land

Within a year of 'Abdu'l-Bahá's return to the Holy Land the world was engulfed in
an unprecedented crisis. Failing to heed His repeated warnings about the grave
dangers that loomed on the international horizon, and refusing to rise to the principles He had unceasingly called upon them to practice in their relations with
each other, the nations of the earth, led by the powers of Europe and America, fell
upon each other in a struggle the like of which had neither been witnessed nor
dreamed of until then.

World War I and its immediate aftermath were a period of horrific tragedy that
affected nations and territories around the entire globe. The Middle East was no
exception. For a time 'Abdu'l-Bahá was virtually cut off from the outside world.

The carnage created by the war caused 'Abdu'l-Bahá intense distress. Observers
recalled that He was agonized at the slaughter raging across the earth, decimating
entire populations through the combination of war, disease, and famine. And all
of it was due to humanity's failure to appreciate the very principles that He had
suffered for an entire lifetime to uphold.

Toward the end of the war it came to the attention of the Bahá'ís in Europe
that 'Abdu'l-Bahá was in great danger. The Turkish authorities had been aroused
against 'Abdu'l-Bahá by some of His old adversaries. So grave was the situation
that He had been openly threatened with crucifixion. This news was conveyed to
the British Foreign Office, which in turn instructed General Allenby, at that time
in Jerusalem in command of the British forces, to extend to 'Abdu'l-Bahá every
protection and consideration.

Soon British forces took Haifa, and immediately Allenby sent a cablegram to London which read: "'Have to-day taken Palestine. Notify the world that 'Abdu'l-Bahá is safe.'"[2]

Life returned to normal soon thereafter. Communications were reestablished, and a stream of visitors began to make their way to Haifa once again.

'Abdu'l-Bahá's life was filled with great events. At this juncture it is worth looking at the smaller events of His daily routine, which also demonstrate His profound attitude of loving service. Myron Phelps, a prominent New York attorney who was not a member of the Bahá'í Faith, visited Haifa for a month and recorded a typical scene in his book, *The Master in 'Akká*:

Imagine that we are in the ancient house of the still more ancient city of 'Akká, which was for a month my home. The room in which we are faces the opposite wall of a narrow paved street, which an active man might clear at a single bound. Above is the bright sun of Palestine; to the right a glimpse of the old sea-wall and the blue Mediterranean. As we sit we hear a singular sound rising from the pavement, thirty feet below—faint at first, and increasing. It is like the murmur of human voices. We open the window and look down. We see a crowd of human beings with patched and tattered garments. Let us descend to the street and see who these are.

It is a noteworthy gathering. Many of these men are blind; many more are pale, emaciated, or aged. . . . Most of the women are closely veiled, but enough are uncovered to cause us well to believe that, if the veils were lifted, more pain and misery would be seen. Some of them carry babes with pinched and sallow faces. There are perhaps a hundred in this gathering, and besides, many children. They are of all the races one meets in these streets—Syrians, Arabs, Ethiopians, and many others.

These people are ranged against the walls or seated on the ground, apparently in an attitude of expectation;—for what do they wait? Let us wait with them.

We have not to wait long. A door opens and a man comes out. He is of middle stature, strongly built. He wears flowing light-colored robes. On his head is a light buff fez with a white cloth wound about it. He is perhaps sixty years of age. His long grey hair rests on his shoulders. His forehead is broad, full, and high, his nose slightly aquiline, his moustaches and beard, the latter full though not heavy, nearly white. His eyes are grey and blue, large, and both soft and penetrating. His bearing is simple, but there is grace, dignity, and even majesty about his movements. He passes through the crowd, and as he goes utters words of salutation. We do not understand them, but we see the benignity and kindliness of his countenance. He stations himself at a narrow angle of the street and motions to the people to come towards him. They crowd up a little too insistently. He pushes them gently back and lets them pass him one by one. As they come they hold their hands extended. In each open palm he places some small coins. He knows them all. He caresses them with his hands on the face, on the shoulders, on the head. Some he stops and questions. An aged negro who hobbles up, he greets with some kindly inquiry; the old man's broad face breaks into a sunny smile, his white teeth glistening against his ebony skin as he replies. He stops a woman with a babe and fondly strokes the child. As they pass, some kiss his hand. To all he says, "Marḥabá, marḥabá"—"Well done, well done!"

So they all pass him. The children have been crowding around him with extended hands, but to them he has not given. However, at the end, as he turns to go, he throws a handful of coppers over his shoulder, for which they scramble. . . .

This scene you may see almost any day of the year in the streets of 'Akká. There are other scenes like it, which come only at the beginning of the winter season. In the cold weather which is approaching, the poor will suffer, for, as in all cities, they are thinly clad. Some day at this season, if you are advised of the place and time, you may see the poor of 'Akká gathered at one of the shops where clothes are sold, receiving cloaks from the Master. Upon many, especially the most infirm or crippled, he himself places the garment, adjusts it with his own hands, and strokes it approvingly, as if to say, "There! Now you will do well." There are five or six hundred poor in 'Akká, to all of whom he gives a warm garment each year.

On feast days he visits the poor at their homes. He chats with them, inquires into their health and comfort, mentions by name those who are absent, and leaves gifts for all.

Nor is it the beggars only that he remembers. Those respectable poor who cannot beg, but must suffer in silence—those whose daily labor will not support their families—to these he sends bread secretly. His left hand knoweth not what his right hand doeth.

All the people know him and love him—the rich and the poor, the young and the old—even the babe leaping in its mother's arms. If he hears of any one sick in the city—Muslim or Christian, or of any other sect, it matters not—he is each day at their bedside, or sends a trusty messenger. If a physician is needed, and the patient poor, he brings or sends one, and also the necessary medicine. If he finds a leaking roof or a broken window menacing health, he summons a workman, and waits himself to see the breach repaired. If any one is in trouble,—if a son or a brother is thrown into prison, or he is threatened at law, or falls into any difficulty too heavy for him,—it is to the Master that he straightway makes appeal for counsel or for aid. Indeed, for counsel all come to him, rich as well as poor. He is the kind father of all the people. . . .

For more than thirty-four years this man has been a prisoner at 'Akká. But his jailors have become his friends. The governor of the city, the commander of the Army Corps, respect and honor him as though he were their brother. No man's opinion or recommendation has greater weight with them. He is the beloved of all the city, high and low. And how could it be otherwise? For to this man it is the law, as it was to Jesus of Nazareth, to do good to those who injure him. Have we yet heard of any one in lands which boast the name of Christ who lived that life? . . .

This Master is as simple as his soul is great. He claims nothing for himself—neither comfort, nor honor, nor repose. Three or four hours of sleep suffice him; all the remainder of his time and all his strength are given to the succor of those who suffer, in spirit or in body. "I am," he says, "the servant of God."

Such is 'Abbás Effendi, the Master of 'Akká.[3]

Palestine became a British protectorate in the years immediately following the war. Many British soldiers and statesmen came to visit 'Abdu'l-Bahá during this time, and several left memorable accounts of these occasions. 'Abdu'l-Bahá was quickly recognized as one of the leading figures of the region, and His character and teachings were deeply admired. Moreover, the British came to learn of His humanitarian efforts during the war, which had benefited countless souls without regard to race, creed, or class. In 1920 the British government, in recognition of these services to humanity, invested 'Abdu'l-Bahá with the insignia of the Knighthood of the British Empire. 'Abdu'l-Bahá graciously accepted the honor but never used the title.

By this time His days on earth were rapidly coming to a close. Although His natural constitution was quite strong and resilient, years of suffering and trials were rapidly taking their toll. He passed away in the early morning hours of November 28, 1921.

The passing of 'Abdu'l-Bahá had the same effect on the Bahá'ís at that time as the death of His Father had nearly three decades before. They were plunged into grief.

And they were not alone. Expressions of grief and condolence poured in from friends and admirers throughout the Middle East and Europe. Throngs of people of every class and background attended His funeral. Eulogies, poems, and tributes were offered by leaders of all of the chief religions in Palestine—Jewish,

Christian, and Muslim. State officials attended and expressed their sorrow. They were joined by countless souls from every walk of life, who had forever lost their friend and faithful protector.

A noted Christian writer by the name of Ibráhím Naṣṣár offered one of the eulogies, which revealed the depth of the anguish felt by those who were present. His remarkable tribute to 'Abdu'l-Bahá follows:

"I weep for the world, in that my Lord hath died; others there are who, like unto me, weep the death of their Lord. . . . O bitter is the anguish caused by this heart-rending calamity! It is not only our country's loss but a world affliction. . . . He hath lived for well-nigh eighty years the life of the Messengers and Apostles of God. He hath educated the souls of men, hath been benevolent unto them, hath led them to the Way of Truth. Thus he raised his people to the pinnacle of glory, and great shall be his reward from God, the reward of the righteous! Hear me O people! 'Abbás is not dead, neither hath the light of Bahá been extinguished! Nay, nay! this light shall shine with everlasting splendor. The lamp of Bahá, 'Abbás, hath lived a goodly life, hath manifested in himself the true life of the Spirit. And now he is gathered to glory, a pure angel, richly robed in benevolent deeds, noble in his precious virtues. Fellow Christians! Truly ye are bearing the mortal remains of this ever lamented one to his last resting place, yet know of a certainty that your 'Abbás will live forever in spirit amongst you, through his deeds, his words, his virtues, and all the essence of his life. We say farewell to the material body of our 'Abbás, and his material body vanisheth from our gaze, but his reality, our spiritual 'Abbás, will never leave our minds, our thoughts, our hearts, our tongues.

"O great revered Sleeper! Thou hast been good to us, thou hast guided us, thou hast taught us, thou hast lived amongst us greatly, with the full meaning of greatness, thou hast made us proud of thy deeds and of thy words. Thou hast raised the Orient to the summit of glory, hast shown loving kindness to the people, trained them in righteousness, and hast striven to the end, till thou hast won the crown of glory. Rest thou happily under the shadow of the mercy of the Lord thy God, and He, verily, shall well reward thee."[4]

Surely there was never another occasion, in all the long and troubled history of the Holy Land, when such a large and diverse group laid aside their differences and came together in memory of a single person. How appropriate for one Who had worked every day of His life for one goal: that all peoples and faiths be reconciled.

For 'Abdu'l-Bahá, servitude to humanity was the highest station to which any soul could aspire. True service, as He exemplified it, was founded upon indiscriminate love for all people, regardless of race, creed, or class. This in turn was founded upon love for God and recognition of God's love for all creation. The path to individual happiness and fulfillment that He demonstrated was that of adherence to God's commandments and a spirit of sincere, selfless effort for the betterment of the world.

Let us turn once again to the memoirs of Howard Colby Ives, who describes in moving terms what 'Abdu'l-Bahá meant to those who knew and loved Him:

Here I saw a man who, outwardly, like myself, lived in the world of confusion, yet, inwardly, beyond the possibility of doubt, lived and worked in that higher and real world. All His concepts, all His motives, all His actions, derived their springs from that "World of Light." And, which is to me a most inspiring and encouraging fact, He took it for granted that you and I, the ordinary run-of-the-mill humanity, could enter into and live in that world if we would.[5]

PART 4

GOD'S PROMISES FULFILLED

CHAPTER 28

BUILDING A NEW WORLD

During the twenty-nine years of 'Abdu'l-Bahá's ministry the Bahá'í Faith spread to nations and territories around the globe. Groups of believers were established in several countries of Europe and in cities throughout North America. Existing Bahá'í communities in Persia, Egypt, India, Russia, Burma, and other areas grew and consolidated. New believers began to enter the Bahá'í Faith in certain islands of the Pacific, Japan, Australia, and elsewhere. These developments all took place under the guidance and inspiration of 'Abdu'l-Bahá, Who designed a plan for propagating the Faith throughout the world. He led the community of Bahá'ís to victory upon victory in spite of the vicious opposition and other extreme hardships described in previous chapters.

With 'Abdu'l-Bahá's passing in 1921, the Bahá'í Faith entered a new era in its evolution. In His Will and Testament 'Abdu'l-Bahá elaborated on the next stages of the development of the Covenant that Bahá'u'lláh had established to ensure the unity of the Faith. This included an elucidation of the basic features of the Faith's administrative order, which had been outlined earlier by Bahá'u'lláh, as well as steps for its accelerated development. The Will and Testament of 'Abdu'l-Bahá has since come to be considered one of the seminal documents of the Bahá'í Faith. Some of its main features merit review here.

In His Will and Testament 'Abdu'l-Bahá calls upon the believers to show love for each other and all humanity:

> Wherefore, O my loving friends! Consort with all the peoples, kindreds and religions of the world with the utmost truthfulness, uprightness, faithfulness, kindliness, good-will and friendliness, that all the world of being may be filled with the holy ecstasy of the grace of Bahá, that ignorance, enmity, hate and rancor may vanish from the world and the darkness of

estrangement amidst the peoples and kindreds of the world may give way to
the Light of Unity. Should other peoples and nations be unfaithful to you
show your fidelity unto them, should they be unjust toward you show justice
towards them, should they keep aloof from you attract them to yourselves,
should they show their enmity be friendly towards them, should they poison
your lives, sweeten their souls, should they inflict a wound upon you, be a
salve to their sores. Such are the attributes of the sincere! Such are the attributes of the truthful.[1]

'Abdu'l-Bahá also reviews the treacheries and assaults that He and Bahá'u'lláh
endured at the hands of Their enemies. This included not only external foes, but
also those enemies from within the Bahá'í Faith who had attempted to cause a
breach in its unity and to use the Cause of God for their own ends. Chief among
them during Bahá'u'lláh's lifetime was Azal. During 'Abdu'l-Bahá's ministry it was
his own half-brother Mírzá Muḥammad-'Alí. 'Abdu'l-Bahá refers in His Will and
Testament to the tremendous damage these people and their few followers did to
the prestige of the Bahá'í Faith as the result of their behavior, and He refers to the
grave dangers to which the Cause of God was thereby subjected.

'Abdu'l-Bahá calls upon the faithful to remain steadfast in their fidelity to the
Covenant of Bahá'u'lláh, the unique feature of the Bahá'í Faith that ensures its
doctrinal integrity and the unity of its followers. The Covenant provides the spiritual powers necessary for the Bahá'í Faith to accomplish its mission to unify the
world and to establish God's Kingdom on earth. In 'Abdu'l-Bahá's own lifetime
this meant that the believers should turn to Him as the sole interpreter and guide
of the community. In the Will and Testament He appoints His eldest grandson,
Shoghi Effendi, as Guardian of the Cause of God. The function of the Guardian
is to serve as "the expounder of the words of God"[2] and to oversee the affairs of the
Faith—roles in which he was the recipient of infallible divine guidance. 'Abdu'l-
Bahá also envisions the establishment of the supreme administrative institution of
the Bahá'í Faith—the Universal House of Justice—which serves a function complementary to that of the Guardian by helping to safeguard the Bahá'í Faith, guide
the Bahá'í community, and promote the Bahá'í teachings.

Shoghi Effendi was twenty-five years old when he became the Guardian of the
Cause of God. Before 'Abdu'l-Bahá's passing neither Shoghi Effendi nor anyone
else knew that this would happen; indeed, no one was aware that the Guardianship would even exist until the contents of the Will and Testament were read.

Over the years a few individuals had asked 'Abdu'l-Bahá whether someone would
be appointed to lead the Cause after His death. To one inquirer He answered,
"'know verily that this is a well-guarded secret. It is even as a gem concealed within

its shell. That it will be revealed is predestined. The time will come when its light will appear, when its evidences will be made manifest, and its secrets unraveled.'"[3]

To a Westerner who inquired about the meaning of Isaiah 11:6, "a little child shall lead them," He responded, "'Verily, that child is born and is alive and from him will appear wondrous things that thou wilt hear of in the future. . . . therefore forget this not as long as thou dost live inasmuch as ages and centuries will bear traces of him.'"[4]

Shoghi Effendi possessed rare qualities even as a young child. Many people observed this, and some left written descriptions of little episodes. Especially moving are those that recount his devotion to 'Abdu'l-Bahá even as a tiny child. But none imagined the future that was in store for him. It may be that 'Abdu'l-Bahá chose not to disclose Shoghi Effendi's future station out of concern for his safety. 'Abdu'l-Bahá Himself was not immune to the attempts of ill-wishers, who might have taken steps to harm the child had they suspected his future station.

Shoghi Effendi's remarkable capacities became apparent for all the world to see as he assumed the responsibilities of the Guardianship, guiding the Bahá'í community through a period that witnessed unprecedented expansion and the consolidation of its administrative system. Shoghi Effendi served as Guardian of the Cause of God for thirty-six years until his death in 1957.

The Plan of God

The Bahá'í teachings make clear that the vast changes the world has experienced in the modern age are aspects of God's plan for the unification of humanity. These changes have been stimulated by the appearance of Bahá'u'lláh and His new world order, which is now in the earliest embryonic stages of its development. "The world's equilibrium hath been upset," writes Bahá'u'lláh in the Most Holy Book, "through the vibrating influence of this most great, this new World Order. Mankind's ordered life hath been revolutionized through the agency of this unique, this wondrous System—the like of which mortal eyes have never witnessed."[5]

In other passages Bahá'u'lláh refers to the vast, mysterious forces that have been unleashed in the world as a direct result of His revelation. He laments that humanity as a whole seems oblivious to this reality: "A new life is, in this age, stirring within all the peoples of the earth; and yet none hath discovered its cause or perceived its motive."[6]

Bahá'u'lláh foresees that humanity's failure to recognize and accept Him—all the more tragic because His advent had been anticipated for so many centuries—will lead to grave and prolonged sufferings. He exhorts the peoples of the world to heed His call or face God's judgment: "Bestir yourselves, O people, in anticipation of the days of Divine Justice, for the promised hour is now come."[7]

Nonetheless, there are innumerable instances in which He speaks of the inevitable triumph of His Cause. In certain passages He indicates that the present state of affairs is but a prelude to a revolutionary turn of fortune:

"The whole earth is now in a state of pregnancy. The day is approaching when it will have yielded its noblest fruits, when from it will have sprung forth the loftiest trees, the most enchanting blossoms, the most heavenly blessings."[8]

"The time is approaching when every created thing will have cast its burden. Glorified be God Who hath vouchsafed this grace that encompasseth all things, whether seen or unseen!"[9]

"These great oppressions are preparing it for the advent of the Most Great Justice."[10]

In another place Bahá'u'lláh writes,

The world is in travail, and its agitation waxeth day by day. Its face is turned towards waywardness and unbelief. Such shall be its plight, that to disclose it now would not be meet and seemly. Its perversity will long continue. And when the appointed hour is come, there shall suddenly appear that which shall cause the limbs of mankind to quake. Then, and only then, will the Divine Standard be unfurled, and the Nightingale of Paradise warble its melody.[11]

Bahá'u'lláh envisioned a time in the future when the peoples of the world will live together in peace and unity as members of one faith. Universal justice will be established based on adherence to the law of God. A new civilization based on spiritual values will come into being. He referred to this as the Most Great Peace.

In His own time He called upon the rulers of the world to support His Cause and implied that had they done so, the Most Great Peace could have been established relatively quickly due to their leadership and influence. When they rejected Him, Bahá'u'lláh exhorted them to establish the "Lesser Peace"—a political unity of the nations that would be a prelude to the Most Great Peace.

Because they ignored His summons, Bahá'u'lláh predicted divine retribution for these rulers. In subsequent years each of the dynasties Bahá'u'lláh addressed was swept away, including those in France, Germany, Russia, Turkey, Iran, and

Austria. The only exceptions were Great Britain, whose government He praised for its constitution and representative government and for having abolished the slave trade, and the United States, which He indicated would play a special role in establishing justice in the world.

'Abdu'l-Bahá later explained that the Lesser Peace would be established over the course of time as the peoples of the world grow gradually more conscious that the world is our common homeland and that a system of international governance is indispensable for world stability. But He also made clear that political unity alone would not guarantee peace and prosperity in the long run. A higher level of unity must be achieved—one possible only through adherence to the spiritual verities taught by Bahá'u'lláh.

In the end, God's plan will not be thwarted. The Bahá'í writings explain that there will be three stages leading to the new divine civilization. First will be a period of great turmoil and suffering, which we are now witnessing. Then will come the Lesser Peace, which is the political unity of nations. After that will come the Most Great Peace.

Shoghi Effendi further explains that the spiritual forces released into the world through the revelation of Bahá'u'lláh have set into motion two simultaneous processes: the destruction of the old world order and the birth of the new world order. These processes interact upon each other and affect all of humanity:

> We are indeed living in an age which, if we would correctly appraise it, should be regarded as one which is witnessing a dual phenomenon. The first signalizes the death pangs of an order, effete and godless, that has stubbornly refused, despite the signs and portents of a century-old Revelation, to attune its processes to the precepts and ideals which that Heaven-sent Faith proffered it. The second proclaims the birth pangs of an Order, divine and redemptive, that will inevitably supplant the former, and within Whose administrative structure an embryonic civilization, incomparable and world-embracing, is imperceptibly maturing. The one is being rolled up, and is crashing in oppression, bloodshed, and ruin. The other opens up vistas of a justice, a unity, a peace, a culture, such as no age has ever seen. The former has spent its force, demonstrated its falsity and barrenness, lost irretrievably its opportunity, and is hurrying to its doom. The latter, virile and unconquerable, is plucking asunder its chains, and is vindicating its title to be the one refuge within which a sore-tried humanity, purged from its dross, can attain its destiny.

"Soon," Bahá'u'lláh Himself has prophesied, "will the present-day order be rolled up, and a new one spread out in its stead." And again: "By Myself! The day is approaching when We will have rolled up the world and all that is therein,

and spread out a new Order in its stead." "The day is approaching when God
will have raised up a people who will call to remembrance Our days, who will tell
the tale of Our trials, who will demand the restitution of Our rights, from them
who, without a tittle of evidence, have treated Us with manifest injustice." [12]

Although no definite time frame has been given for the consummation of these
twin processes, it is clear that both are well under way and are destined to converge in the fullness of time. "Such simultaneous processes of rise and of fall,"
writes Shoghi Effendi, "of integration and of disintegration, of order and chaos,
with their continuous and reciprocal reactions on each other, are but aspects of a
greater Plan, one and indivisible, whose Source is God, whose author is Bahá'u'lláh,
the theater of whose operations is the entire planet, and whose ultimate objectives
are the unity of the human race and the peace of all mankind." [13]

The Bahá'í Administrative Order

Bahá'u'lláh not only revealed principles and teachings for humanity—He went
even further by ordaining a system of governance that will ensure the successful
implementation of His laws. This system is the precursor and the nucleus and
pattern of a new world order that will emerge in the fullness of time.

As we have seen, Bahá'u'lláh established a new Covenant designed to provide
continuing guidance for the Bahá'í community after His passing. That Covenant
centers around the person of 'Abdu'l-Bahá. After Him, Shoghi Effendi became the
source of infallible guidance. After Shoghi Effendi's death, the Universal House of
Justice was brought into being. Today that body, consisting of nine members
elected by the world community of believers, continues to guide the affairs of the
Bahá'í Faith. The permanent seat of the Universal House of Justice is in Haifa,
Israel, in the precincts of the Shrine of the Báb on Mount Carmel.

The Universal House of Justice is empowered to legislate on all matters not
expressly covered in the Bahá'í writings. It has the authority to amend or abrogate
its own decisions as circumstances dictate. Thus the Bahá'í Faith now has not only
a firm, general framework for its future evolution as provided in its sacred scriptures, but also the necessary flexibility to adapt to changes that will surely be
dramatic over the course of the centuries to come.

Bahá'u'lláh Himself ordained the establishment of the Universal House of Justice. According to clear stipulations in His writings, that body is infallibly guided
by God. 'Abdu'l-Bahá in His Will and Testament states, "the guardian of the
Cause of God as well as the Universal House of Justice, to be universally elected
and established, are both under the care and protection of the Abhá Beauty

[Bahá'u'lláh], under the shelter and unerring guidance of His Holiness, the Exalted One [the Báb]. . . . Whatsoever they decide is of God."[14]

The administrative machinery of the Bahá'í Faith, designed to help ensure its unity and to promote its principles, also extends to the local level. In the Most Holy Book we find:

> The Lord hath ordained that in every city a House of Justice be established wherein shall gather counselors to the number of Bahá,* and should it exceed this number it doth not matter. They should consider themselves as entering the Court of the presence of God, the Exalted, the Most High, and as beholding Him Who is the Unseen. It behooveth them to be the trusted ones of the Merciful among men and to regard themselves as the guardians appointed of God for all that dwell on earth. It is incumbent upon them to take counsel together and to have regard for the interests of the servants of God, for His sake, even as they regard their own interests, and to choose that which is meet and seemly. Thus hath the Lord your God commanded you. Beware lest ye put away that which is clearly revealed in His Tablet. Fear God, O ye that perceive.[15]

Today the local governing bodies of the Bahá'í Faith are called Local Spiritual Assemblies. These institutions will evolve and mature over the course of time until they become the Houses of Justice envisioned by Bahá'u'lláh. The members of the Local Assemblies are elected annually by the adult members of the community in every town or locality where at least nine adult believers reside. Because there is no clergy, any adult believer resident in a particular locality is eligible to serve as a member of that community's Local Spiritual Assembly.

At the national level there are National Spiritual Assemblies, also elected once each year by the believers, and also consisting of nine members. In some cases these serve regions or territories rather than nations. Their responsibility is to oversee the affairs of the Faith in their respective countries. Though the Local Assemblies and National Assemblies are aided by the Spirit of God, only the Universal House of Justice is infallibly guided.

It may at first be difficult to appreciate how administrative matters could possibly be important in religion. Administration, as it is usually experienced and prac-

---

* According to the abjad system—an ancient Arabic system of assigning numerical value to letters of the alphabet so that letters may be represented by numbers and numbers by letters—the abjad numerical equivalent of "Bahá" is nine. "Bahá," meaning "Glory," is a form of Bahá'u'lláh's name.

ticed, is not a spiritual exercise. In the Bahá'í Faith, however, such is not the case. First of all, the administrative institutions of the Bahá'í Faith have been explicitly called into being by Bahá'u'lláh Himself, and they are invested by Him with spiritual powers and the necessary authority to ensure the successful realization of His teachings. The system is founded upon the recognition of the oneness of humanity, providing the means to safeguard the rights and privileges of all and stimulating the constant advancement of a world civilization inspired by the highest spiritual values.

Though it is beyond the scope of this volume to offer a thorough review of the Bahá'í administrative order, let us examine some of the distinctive characteristics of Bahá'í administration that help to shed light on this important reality.

Consultation

One of the most profound teachings of Bahá'u'lláh is the principle of consultation. Bahá'u'lláh writes,

> The Great Being saith: The heaven of divine wisdom is illumined with the two luminaries of consultation and compassion. Take ye counsel together in all matters, inasmuch as consultation is the lamp of guidance which leadeth the way, and is the bestower of understanding.[16]

By consultation is meant the dispassionate search for truth conducted in a spirit of true love and unity. Members of Spiritual Assemblies—indeed, all Bahá'ís— are expected to address important affairs in this manner, which is quite different from mere debate or intellectual discussion.

'Abdu'l-Bahá describes this distinction by contrasting it with an experience He had while visiting France in 1911:

> In this Cause consultation is of vital importance, but spiritual conference and not the mere voicing of personal views is intended. In France I was present at a session of the senate, but the experience was not impressive. Parliamentary procedure should have for its object the attainment of the light of truth upon questions presented and not furnish a battleground for opposition and self-opinion. Antagonism and contradiction are unfortunate and always destructive to truth. In the parliamentary meeting mentioned, altercation and useless quibbling were frequent; the result, mostly confusion and turmoil; even in one instance a physical encounter took place between two members. It was not consultation but comedy.

The purpose is to emphasize the statement that consultation must have for its object the investigation of truth. He who expresses an opinion should not voice it as correct and right but set it forth as a contribution to the consensus of opinion, for the light of reality becomes apparent when two opinions coincide. A spark is produced when flint and steel come together. Man should weigh his opinions with the utmost serenity, calmness and composure. Before expressing his own views he should carefully consider the views already advanced by others. If he finds that a previously expressed opinion is more true and worthy, he should accept it immediately and not willfully hold to an opinion of his own. By this excellent method he endeavors to arrive at unity and truth. Opposition and division are deplorable. It is better then to have the opinion of a wise, sagacious man; otherwise, contradiction and altercation, in which varied and divergent views are presented, will make it necessary for a judicial body to render decision upon the question. Even a majority opinion or consensus may be incorrect. A thousand people may hold to one view and be mistaken, whereas one sagacious person may be right. Therefore, true consultation is spiritual conference in the attitude and atmosphere of love. Members must love each other in the spirit of fellowship in order that good results may be forthcoming. Love and fellowship are the foundation.[17]

Elsewhere 'Abdu'l-Bahá writes,

The prime requisites for them that take counsel together are purity of motive, radiance of spirit, detachment from all else save God, attraction to His Divine Fragrances, humility and lowliness amongst His loved ones, patience and long-suffering in difficulties and servitude to His exalted Threshold. Should they be graciously aided to acquire these attributes, victory from the unseen Kingdom of Bahá shall be vouchsafed to them.[18]

Special emphasis is placed on the right of the individual to freedom of expression:

The members thereof [of the Assembly] must take counsel together in such wise that no occasion for ill-feeling or discord may arise. This can be attained when every member expresseth with absolute freedom his own opinion and setteth forth his argument. Should anyone oppose, he must on no account feel hurt for not until matters are fully discussed can the right way be revealed. The shining spark of truth cometh forth only after the clash of differing opinions.[19]

Duties of the Elected

Membership on Bahá'í administrative institutions is considered by the Bahá'ís to be a position of service. One's entire orientation should be to aid others and to promote spiritual principles. This requires an attitude of humility before God and deep respect for those whom the institutions serve. Shoghi Effendi explains,

> The duties of those whom the friends have freely and conscientiously elected as their representatives are no less vital and binding than the obligations of those who have chosen them. Their function is not to dictate, but to consult, and consult not only among themselves, but as much as possible with the friends whom they represent. . . . They should never be led to suppose that they are the central ornaments of the body of the Cause, intrinsically superior to others in capacity or merit, and sole promoters of its teachings and principles. They should approach their task with extreme humility, and endeavor, by their open-mindedness, their high sense of justice and duty, their candor, their modesty, their entire devotion to the welfare and interests of the friends, the Cause, and humanity, to win, not only the confidence and the genuine support and respect of those whom they serve, but also their esteem and real affection. They must, at all times, avoid the spirit of exclusiveness, the atmosphere of secrecy, free themselves from a domineering attitude, and banish all forms of prejudice and passion from their deliberations.[20]

> Let us also bear in mind that the keynote of the Cause of God is not dictatorial authority but humble fellowship, not arbitrary power, but the spirit of frank and loving consultation. Nothing short of the spirit of a true Bahá'í can hope to reconcile the principles of mercy and justice, of freedom and submission, of the sanctity of the right of the individual and of self-surrender, of vigilance, discretion and prudence on the one hand, and fellowship, candor, and courage on the other.[21]

Private Balloting/No Campaigning

Elections of Bahá'í administrative institutions occur by secret ballot in an atmosphere of prayer and reverence. Self-promotion, open discussion of possible members, canvassing, nominations, and campaigning of any kind are strictly forbidden. Each believer is completely free, after prayerful and private reflection, to vote for whomever he or she pleases, without interference. There is no notion of incumbency or tenure, meaning that serving members enjoy no special consideration in the voting process.

Shoghi Effendi, referring to the election of a National Spiritual Assembly, elucidates the qualifications for membership that believers should keep in mind as they cast their ballots. They should

> consider without the least trace of passion and prejudice, and irrespective of any material consideration, the names of only those who can best combine the necessary qualities of unquestioned loyalty, of selfless devotion, of a well-trained mind, of recognized ability and mature experience.[22]

The Duties of the Spiritual Assemblies

The Spiritual Assemblies are divine institutions, ordained by Bahá'u'lláh to ensure the betterment of the world. According to Shoghi Effendi,

> They must endeavor to promote amity and concord amongst the friends, efface every lingering trace of distrust, coolness and estrangement from every heart, and secure in its stead an active and whole-hearted cooperation for the service of the Cause.
>
> They must do their utmost to extend at all times the helping hand to the poor, the sick, the disabled, the orphan, the widow, irrespective of color, caste and creed.
>
> They must promote by every means in their power the material as well as the spiritual enlightenment of youth, the means for the education of children, institute, whenever possible, Bahá'í educational institutions, organize and supervise their work and provide the best means for their progress and development. . . .
>
> They must undertake the arrangement of the regular meetings of the friends, the feasts and the anniversaries, as well as the special gatherings designed to serve and promote the social, intellectual and spiritual interests of their fellow-men. . . .
>
> These rank among the most outstanding obligations of the members of every Spiritual Assembly.[23]

As important as administrative institutions are, they are only one aspect of Bahá'u'lláh's vision for community life. There are two other features of Bahá'í community life that deserve mention. We have seen that Bahá'u'lláh exhorted His followers to gather together for prayer and reading of the sacred scriptures. He also instituted a special gathering called the Feast, which is to be held regularly in each local community. This is a time for worship and fellowship and provides an important opportunity for members of the community to consult with each other about the affairs of the Faith. All Bahá'ís—children, youth, and adults—are called upon to attend the Feast once every nineteen days.

'Abdu'l-Bahá writes,

> You have asked as to the feast. . . . This feast is held to foster comradeship and love, to call God to mind and supplicate Him with contrite hearts, and to encourage benevolent pursuits.
>
> That is, the friends should there dwell upon God and glorify Him, read the prayers and holy verses, and treat one another with the utmost affection and love.[24]

In the Most Holy Book Bahá'u'lláh also calls for the establishment of houses of worship "throughout the lands." Bahá'í Houses of Worship are places for prayer and meditation, open to all people. Today there are seven of them—one each in North America, Central America, Africa, Australia, Europe, India, and Western Samoa—and one is being built in South America. Each is built on an ambitious scale, with nine sides, a dome, and decorative gardens. In the future such places will symbolize the spirit and genius of the new world civilization. They will exist in every city and will also be associated with humanitarian agencies such as schools, hospitals, and universities, thereby linking the worship of God and service to humanity in tangible form. 'Abdu'l-Bahá characterizes the Bahá'í House of Worship and its associated agencies as "one of the most vital institutions in the world."[25]

A New System of Governance

This has been a very brief overview, intended only as a starting point for further study. It must be emphasized that the administrative order ordained by Bahá'u'lláh is unique in concept and design, unlike anything the world has yet seen. Shoghi Effendi explains this in the following passage:

> A word should now be said regarding the theory on which this Adminis-trative Order is based and the principle that must govern the operation of its chief institutions. It would be utterly misleading to attempt a comparison between this unique, this divinely-conceived Order and any of the diverse systems which the minds of men, at various periods of their history, have contrived for the government of human institutions. . . . The divers and

ever-shifting systems of human polity, whether past or present, whether originating in the East or in the West, offer no adequate criterion wherewith to estimate the potency of its hidden virtues or to appraise the solidity of its foundations. . . .

This new-born Administrative Order incorporates within its structure certain elements which are to be found in each of the three recognized forms of secular government, without being in any sense a mere replica of any one of them, and without introducing within its machinery any of the objectionable features which they inherently possess. It blends and harmonizes, as no government fashioned by mortal hands has as yet accomplished, the salutary truths which each of these systems undoubtedly contains without vitiating the integrity of those God-given verities on which it is ultimately founded.[26]

The Bahá'í administrative order is designed to aid individuals and society as a whole to mirror increasingly God's own attributes of love, mercy, and justice. As time passes, the system itself will become more effective as more and more people embrace the Bahá'í Faith and endeavor to live up to its teachings, and then as world civilization gradually reflects the teachings of Bahá'u'lláh in their entirety.

In time, Bahá'u'lláh prophesies, the entire world will come to recognize His station as the Promised One of All Ages. The processes leading up to that day are twofold: first, the onward development of the Bahá'í community and its institutions; and second, the necessary changes in world society, involving both tests and triumphs, that will prepare humanity to accept His revelation. That day will mark the establishment of the Most Great Peace and the Golden Age of human history.

Unity in Diversity

Bahá'u'lláh's vision of unity does not imply cultural uniformity, nor does it involve the suppression of individual expression. On the contrary, a world united by basic moral and spiritual principles is one that can best guarantee personal fulfillment and ensure the unique contributions all societies and cultures can make to the whole. "Unity in diversity" is the guiding principle.

The Bahá'í vision for a new world order does not imply the destruction of legitimate loyalties, nor the assumption of centralized power by any entity. Shoghi Effendi writes,

Let there be no misgivings as to the animating purpose of the world-wide Law of Bahá'u'lláh. Far from aiming at the subversion of the existing foundations of society, it seeks to broaden its basis, to remold its institutions in a manner consonant with the needs of an ever-changing world. It can conflict with no legitimate allegiances, nor can it undermine essential loyalties. Its purpose is neither to stifle the flame of a sane and intelligent patriotism in men's hearts, nor to abolish the system of national autonomy so essential if the evils of excessive centralization are to be avoided. It does not ignore, nor does it attempt to suppress, the diversity of ethnical origins, of climate, of history, of language and tradition, of thought and habit, that differentiate the peoples and nations of the world. It calls for a wider loyalty, for a larger aspiration than any that has animated the human race. It insists upon the subordination of national impulses and interests to the imperative claims of a unified world. It repudiates excessive centralization on one hand, and disclaims all attempts at uniformity on the other. Its watchword is unity in diversity such as 'Abdu'l-Bahá Himself has explained:

"Consider the flowers of a garden. Though differing in kind, color, form and shape, yet, inasmuch as they are refreshed by the waters of one spring, revived by the breath of one wind, invigorated by the rays of one sun, this diversity increaseth their charm and addeth unto their beauty. How unpleasing to the eye if all the flowers and plants, the leaves and blossoms, the fruit, the branches and the trees of that garden were all of the same shape and color! Diversity of hues, form and shape enricheth and adorneth the garden, and heighteneth the effect thereof. In like manner, when divers shades of thought, temperament and character, are brought together under the power and influence of one central agency, the beauty and glory of human perfection will be revealed and made manifest. Naught but the celestial potency of the Word of God, which ruleth and transcendeth the realities of all things, is capable of harmonizing the divergent thoughts, sentiments, ideas and convictions of the children of men."

The call of Bahá'u'lláh is primarily directed against all forms of provincialism, all insularities and prejudices. If long-cherished ideals and time-honored institutions, if certain social assumptions and religious formulae have ceased to promote the welfare of the generality of mankind, if they no longer minister to the needs of a continually evolving humanity, let them be swept away and relegated to the limbo of obsolescent and forgotten doctrines. Why should these, in a world subject to the immutable law of change and decay, be exempt from the deterioration that must needs overtake every human institution? For legal standards, political and economic theories are solely designed to safeguard the interests of humanity as a whole, and not humanity to be crucified for the preservation of the integrity of any particular law or doctrine.[27]

The Bahá'í vision is not some utopian fantasy—it is the next inevitable stage in the long process of human social evolution:

Let there be no mistake. The principle of the Oneness of Mankind—the pivot round which all the teachings of Bahá'u'lláh revolve—is no mere outburst of ignorant emotionalism or an expression of vague and pious hope. Its appeal is not to be merely identified with a reawakening of the spirit of brotherhood and good-will among men, nor does it aim solely at the fostering of harmonious coöperation among individual peoples and nations. Its implications are deeper, its claims greater than any which the Prophets of old were allowed to advance. Its message is applicable not only to the individual, but concerns itself primarily with the nature of those essential relationships that must bind all the states and nations as members of one human family. It does not constitute merely the enunciation of an ideal, but stands inseparably associated with an institution adequate to embody its truth, demonstrate its validity, and perpetuate its influence. It implies an organic change in the structure of present-day society, a change such as the world has not yet experienced. It constitutes a challenge, at once bold and universal, to outworn shibboleths of national creeds—creeds that have had their day and which must, in the ordinary course of events as shaped and controlled by Providence, give way to a new gospel, fundamentally different from, and infinitely superior to, what the world has already conceived. It calls for no less than the reconstruction and the demilitarization of the whole civilized world—a world organically unified in all the essential aspects of its life, its political machinery, its spiritual aspiration, its trade and finance, its script and language, and yet infinite in the diversity of the national characteristics of its federated units.

It represents the consummation of human evolution—an evolution that has had its earliest beginnings in the birth of family life, its subsequent development in the achievement of tribal solidarity, leading in turn to the constitution of the city-state, and expanding later into the institution of independent and sovereign nations.

The principle of the Oneness of Mankind, as proclaimed by Bahá'u'lláh, carries with it no more and no less than a solemn assertion that attainment to this final stage in this stupendous evolution is not only necessary but inevitable, that its realization is fast approaching, and that nothing short of a power that is born of God can succeed in establishing it.[28]

What are the features of the civilization that will come about as the result of these changes? Shoghi Effendi makes clear that as yet we can only dimly visualize them. It stands to reason that such a civilization will be far different from what we now have, or from what we have ever experienced. Who, living a century ago, could have imagined the changes that have already taken place in the world as the result of advances in technology and the forces of social change? Shoghi Effendi writes,

> The long ages of infancy and childhood, through which the human race had to pass, have receded into the background. Humanity is now experiencing the commotions invariably associated with the most turbulent stage of its evolution, the stage of adolescence, when the impetuosity of youth and its vehemence reach their climax, and must gradually be superseded by the calmness, the wisdom, and the maturity that characterize the stage of manhood. Then will the human race reach that stature of ripeness which will enable it to acquire all the powers and capacities upon which its ultimate development must depend.
>
> Unification of the whole of mankind is the hall-mark of the stage which human society is now approaching. Unity of family, of tribe, of city-state, and nation have been successively attempted and fully established. World unity is the goal towards which a harassed humanity is striving. Nation-building has come to an end. The anarchy inherent in state sovereignty is moving towards a climax. A world, growing to maturity, must abandon this fetish, recognize the oneness and wholeness of human relationships, and establish once for all the machinery that can best incarnate this fundamental principle of its life. . . .
>
> The unity of the human race, as envisaged by Bahá'u'lláh, implies the establishment of a world commonwealth in which all nations, races, creeds and classes are closely and permanently united, and in which the autonomy of its state members and the personal freedom and initiative of the individuals that compose them are definitely and completely safeguarded. This commonwealth must, as far as we can visualize it, consist of a world legislature, whose members will, as the trustees of the whole of mankind, ultimately control the entire resources of all the component nations, and will enact such laws as shall be required to regulate the life, satisfy the needs and adjust the relationships of all races and peoples. A world executive, backed by an international Force, will carry out the decisions arrived at, and apply the laws enacted by, this world legislature, and will safeguard the organic unity of the whole commonwealth. A world tribunal will adjudicate and deliver its compulsory and final verdict in all and any disputes that may arise between the various elements constituting this universal system. A mechanism of world inter-communication will be devised, embracing the whole planet,

freed from national hindrances and restrictions, and functioning with marvellous swiftness and perfect regularity. A world metropolis will act as the nerve center of a world civilization, the focus towards which the unifying forces of life will converge and from which its energizing influences will radiate. A world language will either be invented or chosen from among the existing languages and will be taught in the schools of all the federated nations as an auxiliary to their mother tongue. A world script, a world literature, a uniform and universal system of currency, of weights and measures, will simplify and facilitate intercourse and understanding among the nations and races of mankind. In such a world society, science and religion, the two most potent forces in human life, will be reconciled, will coöperate, and will harmoniously develop. The press will, under such a system, while giving full scope to the expression of the diversified views and convictions of mankind, cease to be mischievously manipulated by vested interests, whether private or public, and will be liberated from the influence of contending governments and peoples. The economic resources of the world will be organized, its sources of raw materials will be tapped and fully utilized, its markets will be coördinated and developed, and the distribution of its products will be equitably regulated.

National rivalries, hatreds, and intrigues will cease, and racial animosity and prejudice will be replaced by racial amity, understanding and coöperation. The causes of religious strife will be permanently removed, economic barriers and restrictions will be completely abolished, and the inordinate distinction between classes will be obliterated. Destitution on the one hand, and gross accumulation of ownership on the other, will disappear. The enormous energy dissipated and wasted on war, whether economic or political, will be consecrated to such ends as will extend the range of human inventions and technical development, to the increase of the productivity of mankind, to the extermination of disease, to the extension of scientific research, to the raising of the standard of physical health, to the sharpening and refinement of the human brain, to the exploitation of the unused and unsuspected resources of the planet, to the prolongation of human life, and to the furtherance of any other agency that can stimulate the intellectual, the moral, and spiritual life of the entire human race.

A world federal system, ruling the whole earth and exercising unchallengeable authority over its unimaginably vast resources, blending and embodying the ideals of both the East and the West, liberated from the curse of war and its miseries, and bent on the exploitation of all the available sources of energy on the surface of the planet, a system in which Force is made the servant of Justice, whose life is sustained by its universal recognition of one

God and by its allegiance to one common Revelation—such is the goal towards which humanity, impelled by the unifying forces of life, is moving.[29]

The above passage might strike some readers as a naïve, unachievable dream. To Bahá'ís, however, it represents the fulfillment of God's purpose for humanity and is the goal toward which we are heading. This is not to say that the objective is an easy one. It will require conscientious, concentrated effort. The road ahead may very well be a long one. There may be many setbacks and reverses, but the ultimate destination will be attained because this is our destiny.

CHAPTER 29

THE NEW JERUSALEM

So far in this volume we have discussed the history and the essential teachings of the Bahá'í Faith. Let us now examine its relationship to the prophetic expectations of other religions. For the sake of brevity we will limit our focus primarily to the New Testament and Christian prophecy.*

Bahá'u'lláh writes, "This is the changeless Faith of God, eternal in the past, eternal in the future."[1] With this statement He affirms the continuity of the Cause of God, which has been revealed through a line of Prophets stretching from the dawn of history to the present day. Although Bahá'u'lláh's revelation represents the fulfillment of the prophetic statements of all previous Messengers, it shares much in common with earlier revelations. God's manner of interaction with humanity has not altered over time. The means whereby He sends His teachings to humanity, the essential spiritual truths that those teachings convey, and His expectations of us are the same now as they have always been.

To illustrate this process, we will turn to the example of Christ, but first it is important to reaffirm what the Bahá'í writings have to say about Him and about Christianity. Shoghi Effendi writes,

> As to the position of Christianity, let it be stated without any hesitation or equivocation that its divine origin is unconditionally acknowledged, that the Sonship and Divinity of Jesus Christ are fearlessly asserted, that the

---

* For more information on how the prophecies of other religions are fulfilled by Bahá'u'lláh, the reader may wish to consult the following books: Moojan Momen, *Islam and the Bahá'í Faith;* Moojan Momen, *Hinduism and the Bahá'í Faith;* Moojan Momen, *Buddhism and the Bahá'í Faith;* and Jamshed Fozdar, *Buddha Maitrya-Amitabha Has Appeared.*

divine inspiration of the Gospel is fully recognized, that the reality of the mystery of the Immaculacy of the Virgin Mary is confessed, and the primacy of Peter, the Prince of the Apostles, is upheld and defended. The Founder of the Christian Faith is designated by Bahá'u'lláh as the *"Spirit of God,"* is proclaimed as the One Who *"appeared out of the breath of the Holy Ghost,"* and is even extolled as the *"Essence of the Spirit."* His mother is described as *"that veiled and immortal, that most beauteous, countenance,"* and the station of her Son eulogized as a *"station which hath been exalted above the imaginings of all that dwell on earth,"* whilst Peter is recognized as one whom God has caused *"the mysteries of wisdom and of utterance to flow out of his mouth."*[2]

Abundant references to Christ are found in the writings of Bahá'u'lláh. On the subject of Christ's sacrifice, He writes,

Know thou that when the Son of Man yielded up His breath to God, the whole creation wept with a great weeping. By sacrificing Himself, however, a fresh capacity was infused into all created things. Its evidences, as witnessed in all the peoples of the earth, are now manifest before thee. The deepest wisdom which the sages have uttered, the profoundest learning which any mind hath unfolded, the arts which the ablest hands have produced, the influence exerted by the most potent of rulers, are but manifestations of the quickening power released by His transcendent, His all-pervasive, and resplendent Spirit.

We testify that when He came into the world, He shed the splendor of His glory upon all created things. Through Him the leper recovered from the leprosy of perversity and ignorance. Through Him the unchaste and wayward were healed. Through His power, born of Almighty God, the eyes of the blind were opened, and the soul of the sinner sanctified.

. . . He it is Who purified the world. Blessed is the man who, with a face beaming with light, hath turned towards Him.[3]

Bahá'u'lláh frequently defended the Bible to His Muslim audiences. Although Islam recognizes Jesus as a Messenger of God, many Muslims believe that the Bible (both the Old and New Testaments) has been corrupted and cannot, therefore, be regarded as the authentic repository of the Word of God. Bahá'u'lláh challenges this belief on two grounds: First, He asserts that the followers of Islam who hold this view have misunderstood certain statements in the Koran that actually mean that the followers of the Bible have misinterpreted it, not that the Bible itself is corrupt; second, He asserts that God, in His justice, would never hold people accountable for obeying His Word if they did not actually possess it. Bahá'u'lláh writes,

> We have also heard a number of the foolish of the earth assert that the genuine text of the heavenly Gospel doth not exist among the Christians. . . . How grievously they have erred! How oblivious of the fact that such a statement imputeth the gravest injustice and tyranny to a gracious and loving Providence![4]

'Abdu'l-Bahá makes this beautiful statement about the Bible:

> This book is the Holy Book of God, of celestial Inspiration. It is the Bible of Salvation, the Noble Gospel.[5]

From these statements it is clear that Bahá'u'lláh and His followers love and revere both Christ and the Bible.

The Ministry of Christ

Jesus of Nazareth lived at a time of intense expectation among the Jewish people. The great civilization that had been founded upon the Law of Moses and had reached its height in the days of King David and King Solomon had suffered severe decline as the result of a series of foreign conquests. Yet the people cherished its memory, and a succession of prophets had foretold a time to come when God would once again exalt His people. For many, expectation centered on a "Messiah" (meaning in Hebrew literally "anointed") who would one day appear. This person, God's chosen king, would exalt the Law of Moses, establish God's Kingdom, and deliver them from oppression.

As powerful as the Roman Empire was, some Jews believed that God would reverse their situation as effectively as He had before, when they had suffered under the yoke of slavery in Egypt and, in a later age, when they had endured captivity in Babylon. Many believed that in these times the signs of prophetic fulfillment could be discerned, and in some quarters anticipation of the expected Messiah reached a fever pitch.

Jesus Christ declared Himself to be that Messiah and consequently suffered rejection, torment, and death. As far as the vast majority of people were concerned, and particularly in the opinion of their leaders, He was an impostor. To them His humiliating crucifixion proved it, for they believed God would never have allowed such a thing to happen to the "real" Messiah.

In many respects Christ affirmed the essential teachings of Judaism: monotheistic belief in one God, in atonement and redemption, and basic issues of morality. He Himself stated that He had come not to destroy the Law of Moses, but to fulfill it. Yet Christ also challenged current understandings of the scriptures. Many saw this as a threat to the established religion, but a few saw it as the fulfillment of ancient hopes.

For example, His claim to be the Messiah did not correspond with deeply held beliefs as to how the Messiah would appear. He was a carpenter of questionable birth in the eyes of His generation, and He was most certainly not a king in any political sense. Furthermore, He taught not only that the Kingdom of God would be manifested on the earth in due course but also that its essential reality is spiritual, existing within the hearts of the people.

Other teachings of Jesus also challenged prevailing views and practices. He chastised religious leaders for their hypocrisy and for superficial interpretations of scripture that ignored deeper spiritual meanings. He challenged people's understanding of the Sabbath, provoking such ire that some wanted to kill Him. He condemned the greed and immorality that He saw everywhere, including at the temple in Jerusalem.

He also shed light on the real meaning of the Law of Moses and of religion, emphasizing God's compassion and love for His children. He emphasized the need for individuals to be born again through the Holy Spirit and thereby attain salvation, and He laid out new ethical precepts that stressed the need for love, mercy, and forgiveness.

'Abdu'l-Bahá writes of these issues:

> When Christ appeared, twenty centuries ago, although the Jews were eagerly awaiting His Coming, and prayed every day, with tears, saying: "O God, hasten the Revelation of the Messiah," yet when the Sun of Truth dawned, they denied Him and rose against Him with the greatest enmity, and eventually crucified that divine Spirit, the Word of God, and named Him Beelzebub, the evil one, as is recorded in the Gospel. The reason for this was that they said: "The Revelation of Christ, according to the clear text of the Torah, will be attested by certain signs, and so long as these signs have not appeared, whoso layeth claim to be a Messiah is an impostor. Among these signs is this, that the Messiah should come from an unknown place, yet we all know this man's house in Nazareth, and can any good thing come out of Nazareth? The second sign is that He shall rule with a rod of iron, that is, He must act with the sword, but this Messiah has not even a wooden staff. Another of the conditions and signs is this: He must sit upon the throne of David and establish David's sovereignty. Now, far from being en-

throned, this man has not even a mat to sit on. Another of the conditions is this: the promulgation of all the laws of the Torah; yet this man has abrogated these laws, and has even broken the sabbath day, although it is the clear text of the Torah that whosoever layeth claim to prophethood and revealeth miracles and breaketh the sabbath day, must be put to death. Another of the signs is this, that in His reign justice will be so advanced that righteousness and well-doing will extend from the human even to the animal world—the snake and the mouse will share one hole, and the eagle and the partridge one nest, the lion and the gazelle shall dwell in one pasture, and the wolf and the kid shall drink from one fountain. Yet now, injustice and tyranny have waxed so great in His time that they have crucified Him! Another of the conditions is this, that in the days of the Messiah the Jews will prosper and triumph over all the peoples of the world, but now they are living in the utmost abasement and servitude in the empire of the Romans. Then how can this be the Messiah promised in the Torah?"

In this wise did they object to that Sun of Truth, although that Spirit of God was indeed the One promised in the Torah. But as they did not understand the meaning of these signs, they crucified the Word of God. Now the Bahá'ís hold that the recorded signs did come to pass in the Manifestation of Christ, although not in the sense which the Jews understood, the description in the Torah being allegorical. For instance, among the signs is that of sovereignty. For Bahá'ís say that the sovereignty of Christ was a heavenly, divine, everlasting sovereignty, not a Napoleonic sovereignty that vanisheth in a short time. For well nigh two thousand years this sovereignty of Christ hath been established, and until now it endureth, and to all eternity that Holy Being will be exalted upon an everlasting throne.[6]

Jesus, and later the authors of the Gospels, explained many of the events of His ministry in terms of prophetic fulfillment. These explanations made clear that the prophecies were fulfilled in a symbolic, or spiritual, sense and were not to be taken literally. For example, many Jews expected not only the advent of a Messiah, but also the return of the prophet Elijah, or Elias, as he is called in the New Testament.* John the Baptist denied that he was Elias when asked; but Jesus, referring to John, said, "And if ye will receive it, this is Elias, which was for to come. He that hath ears to hear, let him hear."[7] If we interpret the "return" of Elias as a

---

* Elias was among the most revered of all Jewish prophets. He is the main figure in the book of Kings in the Bible. It was he who, according to that narrative, was taken up to heaven in a chariot of fire. He was famed for championing the one true God of Israel.

spiritual reality—meaning the return of the same qualities and attributes but not of the selfsame individual—then both statements can be considered true.

Another expectation was that all of the people would physically witness the Messiah and that the very mountains would be brought low. In the Gospel of Luke we find that this prophecy was considered to have been fulfilled, even though it is clear that not every human being literally witnessed it and that the mountains did not crumble: "As it is written in the book of the words of Esaias the prophet, saying, The voice of one crying in the wilderness, Prepare ye the way of the Lord, make his paths straight. Every valley shall be filled, and every mountain and hill shall be brought low; and the crooked shall be made straight, and the rough ways shall be made smooth; And all flesh shall see the salvation of God."[8] Again, a symbolic interpretation is clearly intended, for no such physical marvels occurred at Christ's appearance.

Jesus frequently used parables and metaphors to convey His teachings. Often His own disciples took them too literally or otherwise failed to grasp their meaning, requiring Him to explain again. He explained His own station in unfamiliar terms that seemed blasphemous to the people. He said, "He that hath seen me hath seen the Father," also "I and my Father are one," and "I am in the Father, and the Father in me."[9]

The Advent of God's Kingdom

Jesus knew it was His destiny to be rejected and killed. But He said that His death itself would be a sacrifice that would allow humanity to attain salvation. He also told of a second advent, when God's Kingdom will indeed be established on earth:

> . . . I go away, and come again unto you.[10]

> And I will pray the Father, and he shall give you another Comforter, that he may abide with you for ever. . . .[11]

Jesus and the book of Revelation also give signs of Christ's second coming:

> . . . the stars shall fall from heaven . . . then shall all the tribes of the earth mourn, and they shall see the Son of man coming in the clouds. . . .[12]

. . . every eye shall see him. . . .[13]

In the Bible we also find that Christ's followers will be given a "new name."[14]

Christians are advised to be watchful, for ". . . the day of the Lord will come as a thief in the night. . . ." Christ admonishes, "Be ye therefore ready also: for the Son of man cometh at an hour when ye think not." And in another place He says, "Watch ye therefore, and pray always, that ye may be accounted worthy to escape all these things that shall come to pass, and to stand before the Son of man."[15]

The Bible offers specific instructions as to how to identify a true Prophet. One qualification is that the Prophet must be able to disclose things to come. For example, we read, "Who hath declared from the beginning, that we may know? and beforetime, that we may say, He is righteous?" And in another place it is written, "Remember the former things of old: for I am God, and there is none else; I am God, and there is none like me, Declaring the end from the beginning, and from ancient times the things that are not yet done. . . ."[16]

In 1 John we find another test that a "true spirit" must pass:

Beloved, believe not every spirit, but try the spirits whether they are of God: because many false prophets are gone out into the world. Hereby know ye the Spirit of God: Every spirit that confesseth that Jesus Christ is come in the flesh is of God: And every spirit that confesseth not that Jesus Christ is come in the flesh is not of God. . . .[17]

And Jesus declares that true Prophets can be distinguished from false prophets by their "fruits":

Ye shall know them by their fruits. Do men gather grapes of thorns, or figs of thistles? Even so every good tree bringeth forth good fruit; but a corrupt tree bringeth forth evil fruit. A good tree cannot bring forth evil fruit, neither can a corrupt tree bring forth good fruit. Every tree that bringeth not forth good fruit is hewn down, and cast into the fire. Wherefore by their fruits ye shall know them.[18]

The Bible also indicates that the mysteries of the establishment of God's Kingdom will not entirely be understood until after the advent actually occurs. In the book of Daniel we find that God bids Daniel to "seal up the vision and prophecy."[19]

Christ's Triumph

From the perspective of two millennia it is easy to appreciate the achievements of Jesus Christ. Today there are hundreds of millions of people who turn to Him as their Lord and Savior. The growth and spread of Christianity is taken by many today as evidence of Christ's divine power, a belief confirmed in the Bahá'í writings. 'Abdu'l-Bahá writes,

> Recollect that Christ, solitary and alone, without a helper or protector, without armies and legions, and under the greatest oppression, uplifted the standard of God before all the people of the world, and withstood them, and finally conquered all, although outwardly He was crucified. Now this is a veritable miracle which can never be denied. There is no need of any other proof of the truth of Christ.[20]

Today Christians readily accept a set of beliefs that were extremely challenging when Christ first taught them. It is important to appreciate that He not only fulfilled the prophecies of the Old Testament but also reinterpreted them, opening the door to new spiritual understandings.

How Bahá'u'lláh Fulfilled Prophecy

Bahá'u'lláh's claims must be approached in a manner similar to that with which we approach Christ's teachings. Christ and Bahá'u'lláh both appeared in the world during times of great expectation; but both, for very similar reasons, experienced persecution rather than general acceptance. Like Christ, Bahá'u'lláh not only claimed to have fulfilled prophecies, but He also explained their true meaning, which was far different from conventional interpretations, thereby opening for all to see and understand the "vision and prophecy" referred to in Daniel 9:24. Neither Bahá'u'lláh nor Christ ever said or implied that the scriptures of earlier Manifestations of God were untrue, but both redefined certain spiritual concepts and revealed new concepts, challenging the prevailing understandings of the scriptures.

Bahá'u'lláh clarified prophecies largely by interpreting prophetic passages from the Bible and the Koran in allegorical terms. For example, we have already mentioned that in the Book of Certitude He explains that the concept of "return" is symbolic, meaning the return of the same spiritual qualities. Bahá'u'lláh is thus the return of Christ in the sense that He is also the Manifestation of God's attributes, although clearly He is not the same individual as Jesus. As we have seen, this interpretation of the concept of "return" has precedent in Christ's own explanation of the return of Elias in the person of John the Baptist. By this Jesus clearly did not mean that the two were one and the same individual.

Other signs of truth given in the Bible allow a believer to "test" the truth of any claim of Prophethood. Earlier in this chapter, we mentioned that there are several ways to identify a true Prophet. To be of God, a spirit must confess that "Jesus Christ is come in the flesh," must be able to clearly foretell future events, and should embody "fruits" that are in accord with what is good, and not evil.

Bahá'u'lláh asserts in unequivocal terms His belief in Christ. As we have seen, He clearly foresaw the events that eventually overtook the dominions of those rulers who rejected His announcement; and He told about a lethal force that would be discovered in the years to come, foreshadowing the discovery of nuclear power.

The fruits of Bahá'u'lláh's revelation can be seen in His life, in His teachings, and in their impact upon His followers. Each individual must decide for himself or herself whether these live up to the standard set by Christ.

In the Book of Certitude Bahá'u'lláh also gives many "proofs" of Prophethood. Among them is the rejection of the Prophet's message by the people, and especially by religious leaders. He returns to this theme in other writings, saying that the greatest proof of His station is His own person in the sense that He is the embodiment of divine qualities, and that the second greatest proof is the body of His written teachings.

Jesus as a Manifestation of God

Bahá'u'lláh's assertion that Christ was a Manifestation of God might seem at first to contradict the Bible. But this is not the case at all. Indeed, Bahá'u'lláh's assertion is completely compatible with scripture.

Bahá'u'lláh maintains that God could never incarnate His own essence. God, the Creator, is infinitely exalted above His creation, and such an act is, therefore, an impossibility. Instead, God reveals Himself through His Manifestations, Who are the perfect reflections of His qualities and attributes.

Bahá'u'lláh uses the metaphor of the sun and a mirror to explain this concept. The sun can never descend to earth in its full glory, for the world would be incapable of sustaining such an event. But the sun can be seen in the reflection of a mirror. The Manifestations of God are like perfect mirrors reflecting the image of the sun. To see the reflection of the sun in the mirror is, for all intents and purposes, the same as seeing the sun itself.

In this way it is possible for a Manifestation of God to say, "I am God," and at another time to assert that God is greater than He and that He is but a man. It also explains how one Manifestation of God can be understood to be the return of a previous One, for They all reflect God's glory.

In the Bible, we find Jesus made various statements that can be understood in the light of this metaphor. He says, "I and my Father are one." Yet He also says, "I do nothing of myself; but as my Father hath taught me, I speak these things." We also find a statement referring to Him as the "image of the invisible God."[21]

A further point is that the Holy Spirit revealed by the Manifestations of God is like the rays of the sun, which enlighten the world and bring life to those who turn to it.

With these understandings, 'Abdu'l-Bahá sheds new light on the concept of the Trinity:

> So the Reality of Christ was a clear and polished mirror of the greatest purity and fineness. The Sun of Reality, the Essence of Divinity, reflected itself in this mirror and manifested its light and heat in it; but from the exaltation of its holiness, and the heaven of its sanctity, the Sun did not descend to dwell and abide in the mirror. No, it continues to subsist in its exaltation and sublimity, while appearing and becoming manifest in the mirror in beauty and perfection.
>
> Now if we say that we have seen the Sun in two mirrors—one the Christ and one the Holy Spirit—that is to say, that we have seen three Suns, one in heaven and the two others on the earth, we speak truly. And if we say that there is one Sun, and it is pure singleness, and has no partner and equal, we again speak truly.
>
> The epitome of the discourse is that the Reality of Christ was a clear mirror, and the Sun of Reality—that is to say, the Essence of Oneness, with its infinite perfections and attributes—became visible in the mirror. The meaning is not that the Sun, which is the Essence of the Divinity, became divided and multiplied—for the Sun is one—but it appeared in the mirror. This is why Christ said, "The Father is in the Son," meaning that the Sun is visible and manifest in this mirror.
>
> The Holy Spirit is the Bounty of God which becomes visible and evident in the Reality of Christ. The Sonship station is the heart of Christ, and the Holy Spirit is the station of the spirit of Christ. Hence it has become certain

and proved that the Essence of Divinity is absolutely unique and has no equal, no likeness, no equivalent.

This is the signification of the Three Persons of the Trinity. If it were otherwise, the foundations of the Religion of God would rest upon an illogical proposition which the mind could never conceive, and how can the mind be forced to believe a thing which it cannot conceive? A thing cannot be grasped by the intelligence except when it is clothed in an intelligible form; otherwise, it is but an effort of the imagination.

It has now become clear, from this explanation, what is the meaning of the Three Persons of the Trinity. The Oneness of God is also proved.[22]

The Bahá'í writings confirm many teachings found in the Bible. For example, on the issue of rebirth we find that ". . . man must be born again. As the babe is born into the light of this physical world, so must the physical and intellectual man be born into the light of the world of Divinity." Regarding baptism, 'Abdu'l-Bahá says, "Man cannot free himself from the rage of the carnal passions except by the help of the Holy Spirit. That is why He [Christ] says baptism with the spirit, with water and with fire is necessary . . . that is to say, the spirit of divine bounty, the water of knowledge and life, and the fire of the love of God."[23]

Bahá'u'lláh did not agree with the church doctrine of original sin. On the contrary, He states that human beings are noble creations. At the moment they come into existence they are pure and free from sin. However, they are dependent on God's mercy and grace for their progress.

Bahá'u'lláh affirms the principle of grace in this way: "The tie . . . between the creature and the Creator, should in itself be regarded as a token of His gracious favor unto men, and not as an indication of any merit they may possess." He also emphasizes the need for repentance: ". . . return ye to God and repent, that He, through His grace, may have mercy upon you, may wash away your sins, and forgive your trespasses."[24]

A related concept is that of justification by faith. In the beginning of the Most Holy Book, Bahá'u'lláh states that it is man's duty to believe in and obey the Manifestation of God. Whoever fails to do so has gone astray, "though he be the author of every righteous deed."[25] This makes clear that good works alone do not suffice. Although good works are important, to be acceptable, they must be motivated by a spirit of true faith.

Bahá'u'lláh also affirms the concept of salvation:

> Blessed is the man that hath acknowledged his belief in God and in His signs, and recognized that "He shall not be asked of His doings."

. . . Such is the teaching which God bestoweth on you, a teaching that will deliver you from all manner of doubt and perplexity, and enable you to attain unto salvation both in this world and in the next.[26]

But sometimes some people, in their "doubt and perplexity," feel that the Manifestations of God must prove themselves to humanity. They ask the Prophets to perform "miracles."

Miracles

People often expect Prophets to perform miracles, and some contemporaries even request them to do so. Although Christ performed many miracles, He never did so when asked by the Pharisees and others whose intent was not sincere. He realized that such acts are not always appreciated even by those who witness them, as the incident of the ten lepers suggests.* The Pharisees ascribed Christ's miracles to satanic forces. He even warned His followers that miracles in and of themselves do not constitute decisive proof of Prophethood.[27]

Many miracles have been attributed to the Báb and to Bahá'u'lláh. Bahá'u'lláh was disinclined to mention them, however, explaining that the real miracle is the transformation of human hearts, which is something that only God can accomplish. On one occasion, which is described in chapter 7, Bahá'u'lláh did agree to produce a miracle for a group of clergy. But this offer was never fulfilled because those who requested it would not agree to His condition—their advance, written pledge to acknowledge the truth of the Bábí Faith if the miracle were successfully accomplished.

The Nature of Evil

Bahá'u'lláh redefined what constitutes a true miracle. He also redefined the nature of evil, explaining that it is not a force in its own right. Evil is the absence of good in the same sense that darkness is the absence of light. There are no such things as evil spirits or other sinister supernatural entities. Bahá'u'lláh taught that the name "Satan" is a symbol that refers to the lower instincts of human nature. It is this lower, or material, self against which we must struggle. In many sacred scriptures

---

* In Luke 17, Jesus is approached by ten lepers who beg Him to heal them. After being healed, only one of the ten offered thanks and praise to God. Jesus said, "Were not the ten cleansed? But where are the nine? There are not found that returned to give glory to God, save this stranger."

the "evil" aspect of human nature is often personified. This is true in the Bible, and it is also true in the writings of Bahá'u'lláh, Who often refers to "Satan" and "the Evil One." 'Abdu'l-Bahá explains,

. . . the evil spirit, Satan or whatever is interpreted as evil, refers to the lower nature in man. This baser nature is symbolized in various ways. In man there are two expressions: One is the expression of nature; the other, the expression of the spiritual realm.[28]

Divine Forgiveness

As the above passage implies, our growth depends upon moving towards the spiritual realm. It is a journey that takes a lifetime and even beyond. Just as a soul can progress in this life, the same is true in the life to come. After death, the human soul continues to advance, forever acquiring knowledge and perfections. "The wealth of the other world," says 'Abdu'l-Bahá, "is nearness to God."[29] Heaven and hell symbolize relative nearness to, or remoteness from, God.

This is not to say that there is no such thing as reward and punishment in the next life. These are realities that no wise person will ignore. Bahá'u'lláh states,

It is clear and evident that all men shall, after their physical death, estimate the worth of their deeds, and realize all that their hands have wrought. I swear by the Day Star that shineth above the horizon of Divine power! They that are the followers of the one true God shall, the moment they depart out of this life, experience such joy and gladness as would be impossible to describe, while they that live in error shall be seized with such fear and trembling, and shall be filled with such consternation, as nothing can exceed.[30]

The Bahá'í writings also state that divine forgiveness and mercy are possible in the life to come, especially when other people intercede and pray on one's behalf. Thus, although the deeds of this life profoundly influence an individual's progress in the next world, one is not necessarily consigned to eternal damnation for his or her sins:

It is even possible that the condition of those who have died in sin and unbelief may become changed—that is to say, they may become the object of pardon through the bounty of God, not through His justice—for bounty is giving without desert, and justice is giving what is deserved. As we have power to pray for these souls here, so likewise we shall possess the same power in the other world, which is the Kingdom of God. Are not all the people in that world the creatures of God? Therefore, in that world also they can make progress. As here they can receive light by their supplications, there also they can plead for forgiveness and receive light through entreaties and supplications. Thus as souls in this world, through the help of the supplications, the entreaties and the prayers of the holy ones, can acquire development, so is it the same after death. Through their own prayers and supplications they can also progress, more especially when they are the object of the intercession of the Holy Manifestations.[31]

Another essential principle is that the Bahá'í Faith does not automatically condemn "nonbelievers." The purpose of religion is to foster love of God, love for others, search for truth, and good works. Naturally there are many people of all religions who live up to this standard. Bahá'u'lláh frequently praised the actions of outstanding individuals of other faiths. For example, in one of His writings He recounts the lives of several early Greek philosophers, praising them for their sincere desire to discover the truth and for their fearless defense of high principles. Among those He mentions are Empedocles, Socrates, Hippocrates, Plato, and Aristotle.*

An incident in Bahá'u'lláh's life sheds even more light on the subject. During His days in Baghdad He was the victim of many plots designed to end in His ruin or death. In one particular episode one of the religious leaders succeeded in convening a concourse of divines who had agreed to declare holy war against Bahá'u'lláh and the Bábís. Shoghi Effendi writes,

To their amazement and disappointment, however, they found that the leading mujtahid [religious doctor] amongst them, the celebrated Shaykh Murtaḍáy-i-Anṣárí, a man renowned for his tolerance, his wisdom, his undeviating justice, his piety and nobility of character, refused, when apprized of their designs, to pronounce the necessary sentence against the Bábís. . . . Pleading insufficient knowledge of the tenets of this community, and claiming to have witnessed no act on the part of its members at variance with the Qur'án, he, disregarding the remonstrances of his colleagues, abruptly left the gathering, and returned to Najaf, after having expressed, through a messenger, his regret to Bahá'u'lláh for what had happened, and his devout wish for His protection.[32]

---

* See Bahá'u'lláh's Tablet of Wisdom in *Tablets of Bahá'u'lláh*, pp. 145–47.

Bahá'u'lláh later extols this person as among "Those doctors who have indeed drunk of the cup of renunciation" and "never interfered with [Him.]" 'Abdu'l-Bahá refers to him as "'the illustrious and erudite doctor, the noble and celebrated scholar, the seal of seekers after truth.'"[33]

Many other examples that contrast starkly with the attitude of intolerance displayed by so many adherents of religion can be found in Bahá'í scripture. "Those souls," writes 'Abdu'l-Bahá, "who during the war have served the poor and have been in the Red Cross Mission work, their services are accepted at the Kingdom of God and are the cause of their everlasting life." Bahá'u'lláh writes, "Every soul that walketh humbly with its God, in this Day, and cleaveth unto Him, shall find itself invested with the honor and glory of all goodly names and stations."[34]

The Unity of Religions

It can be very challenging at first to reconcile Bahá'u'lláh's assertion of the unity of religions with the apparent variations between them. Bahá'u'lláh attributes the differences between the divinely revealed religions to two essential causes.

First, each Manifestation of God, while affirming certain basic truths already revealed by other Manifestations of God, also brings specific laws and teachings that are necessary for the time in which He lives.

School provides an analogy that is useful for explaining this process. Humanity, progressing from one grade to the next, receives different Teachers who deliver different lessons. Each grade, or stage of progress, rests upon the previous one, thereby affirming what has already been learned. Yet new lessons are also introduced that might seem to differ from what was taught before. In one grade it might be necessary for the pupils to undertake specific exercises and drills, whereas at a later time they are no longer necessary.

Second, the followers of previous religions, either through ignorance or corruption, have always misunderstood to some extent the meanings of the past teachings. Rituals, superstitions, and spurious beliefs are added to the religions, thereby enhancing their apparent differences. This problem is compounded by strong attachments to tradition that prevent people from investigating the truth of matters.

It is relatively easy to imagine Judaism, Christianity, Islam, and the Bahá'í Faith as part of a continuum, because their principles and cultures of origin are so similar. Other religions, such as Buddhism and Hinduism, whose original Founders were also Manifestations of God, pose a bigger challenge. These religions seem to teach messages that differ vastly both from each other and from those of Judaism, Christianity, Islam, and the Bahá'í Faith. However, it is probable that Buddhism

and Hinduism have become so altered over the years that they have lost some of
their original concepts. Consideration must also be given to the fact that the
Founders of Buddhism and Hinduism appeared in vastly different cultural mi-
lieus that may have required different points of emphasis.

Also, major segments of the Eastern religions, like the Judeo-Christian-Islamic
traditions, anticipate a World Redeemer and an era of peace. Shoghi Effendi states:

> To His Dispensation the sacred books of the followers of Zoroaster had
> referred as that in which the sun must needs be brought to a standstill for no
> less than one whole month. To Him Zoroaster must have alluded when,
> according to tradition, He foretold that a period of three thousand years of
> conflict and contention must needs precede the advent of the World-Savior
> Sháh-Bahrám, Who would triumph over Ahriman and usher in an era of
> blessedness and peace.
>
> He alone is meant by the prophecy attributed to Gautama Buddha Him-
> self, that *"a Buddha named Maitreye, the Buddha of universal fellowship"* should,
> in the fullness of time, arise and reveal *"His boundless glory."* To Him the
> Bhagavad-Gita of the Hindus had referred as the *"Most Great Spirit,"* the
> *"Tenth Avatar,"* the *"Immaculate Manifestation of Krishna."* [35]

'Abdu'l-Bahá emphasizes that the religions are all fundamentally in agreement,
yet differences have arisen due to human limitations and not the inherent truths
that these religions contain:

> Therefore, if the religions investigate reality and seek the essential truth
> of their own foundations, they will agree and no difference will be found.
> But inasmuch as religions are submerged in dogmatic imitations, forsaking
> the original foundations, and as imitations differ widely, therefore, the reli-
> gions are divergent and antagonistic. These imitations may be likened to
> clouds which obscure the sunrise; but reality is the sun. If the clouds dis-
> perse, the Sun of Reality shines upon all, and no difference of vision will
> exist. The religions will then agree, for fundamentally they are the same. The
> subject is one, but predicates are many. [36]

The Day of Judgment

A concept that one finds in some form or another in the world's major religions
concerns the manner in which human history will be consummated. In the Judeo-
Christian-Islamic traditions there are references to the Day of Judgment. This is

commonly interpreted as a time when God will judge between the righteous and the wicked, when good will triumph over evil, and the faithful will be rewarded. Many among the Christians and Muslims take this to mean that the physical earth will be destroyed. History as we know it will come to an end, while the righteous continue to exist in heaven and the damned suffer in eternal hell.

The Bahá'í writings explain that the Day of Judgment is a reality that operates on several levels. Whenever a Manifestation of God appears in the world, that time is a "Day of Judgment" in the sense that humanity is faced with the test of either accepting or rejecting Him. By the same token, the Manifestation of God abrogates old laws and brings new teachings, which are also a form of "judgment" establishing a new era in human society. In other words, old concepts and practices are judged to be outdated and are replaced with new ones more suited to the new level of human development.

In this day the concept of divine judgment still applies. This is the era in which God's Manifestation has abrogated the old world order and inaugurated a new one. This particular "Day of Judgment" has been the focus of prophetic expectations because it marks the realization of the long-cherished hope of peace, justice, and happiness for all.

The Kingdom of God

A concept often linked with the Day of Judgment is that of the establishment of God's Kingdom. The Bahá'í concept of the means by which God's Kingdom will be established is certainly at variance with the expectations of many people. There are at least three important differences:

First, the establishment of the Kingdom of God is not a sudden event accompanied by physical marvels. The physical sun, stars, and heavens will not be destroyed. A new Jerusalem will not come down from heaven in the literal sense. These and some other signs are to be taken symbolically. Some are literal, however—for example, the notion of the special destiny of the Holy Land. Usually it is clear from context when it is necessary to choose a literal interpretation. As we have seen in the case of both Christ and Bahá'u'lláh, the Manifestations of God also offer explanations that help us to discern the difference between literal and symbolic meanings.

Second, the Kingdom of God will be built through the agency of human beings who have been inspired by the teachings of Bahá'u'lláh and who will also be aided by Him through the assistance of the Holy Spirit. This is precisely how Christianity spread; that is, through the efforts of the early Christian believers in spreading the gifts of the Holy Spirit to others.

Third, the building of the Kingdom is a gradual process that will continue forever. Eventually a day will come when war ends and peace and justice are established, but civilization will continue to evolve beyond that point. More Manifestations of God will appear in future ages to continue guiding humanity forward.

We might well ask why the process is a gradual one. Bahá'u'lláh explains that it is necessary in every Dispensation for the full powers of divine revelation to appear in stages. Otherwise humanity would be incapable of sustaining its force:

> Know of a certainty that in every Dispensation the light of Divine Revelation hath been vouchsafed unto men in direct proportion to their spiritual capacity. Consider the sun. How feeble its rays the moment it appeareth above the horizon. How gradually its warmth and potency increase as it approacheth its zenith, enabling meanwhile all created things to adapt themselves to the growing intensity of its light. How steadily it declineth until it reacheth its setting point. Were it, all of a sudden, to manifest the energies latent within it, it would, no doubt, cause injury to all created things. . . . In like manner, if the Sun of Truth were suddenly to reveal, at the earliest stages of its manifestation, the full measure of the potencies which the providence of the Almighty hath bestowed upon it, the earth of human understanding would waste away and be consumed; for men's hearts would neither sustain the intensity of its revelation, nor be able to mirror forth the radiance of its light. Dismayed and overpowered, they would cease to exist.[37]

Today the center of guidance for humanity, responsible for leading the vast enterprise of building God's Kingdom, is the Universal House of Justice. Its seat is on Mount Carmel, across the Bay of Haifa from the scene of Bahá'u'lláh's final imprisonment and in the shadow of the shrine of His Prophet-Herald, the Báb.

Although Bahá'u'lláh did not fulfill popular expectations, His advent represents the fulfillment of God's ancient promise conveyed in such passages as the following verse from the Old Testament:

> And many people shall go and say, Come ye, and let us go up to the mountain of the Lord, to the house of the God of Jacob; and he will teach us of his ways, and we will walk in his paths: for out of Zion shall go forth the law, and the word of the Lord from Jerusalem.
>
> And he shall judge among the nations, and shall rebuke many people: and they shall beat their swords into plowshares, and their spears into pruninghooks: nation shall not lift up sword against nation, neither shall they learn war any more.[38]

In the New Testament we find this passage in Revelation 21:1–4:

And I saw a new heaven and a new earth: for the first heaven and the first earth were passed away; and there was no more sea.

And I John saw the holy city, new Jerusalem, coming down from God out of heaven, prepared as a bride adorned for her husband.

And I heard a great voice out of heaven saying, Behold, the tabernacle of God is with men, and he will dwell with them, and they shall be his people, and God himself shall be with them, and be their God.

And God shall wipe away all tears from their eyes; and there shall be no more death, neither sorrow, nor crying, neither shall there be any more pain: for the former things are passed away.[39]

A Challenge for Further Study

In this chapter we have reviewed some ways in which Bahá'u'lláh addresses the prophetic expectations of the Bible. We have also seen how He explains certain important elements of biblical doctrine. A thorough examination of these issues is beyond the scope of this book. The discussion here is meant simply to be a start-ing point for further study. Other volumes have been written on this subject. There are also books that deal with Islamic prophecies and others that explore Hindu and Buddhist expectations. It is for the reader to decide whether to pursue these themes further.

Bahá'u'lláh's announcement that He is the Promised One is addressed to all peoples of every background. The following passages, although addressed to the Christian peoples of the world, can apply to anyone who wishes to know the character of Bahá'u'lláh's claims and the response He expects from humanity:

O followers of the Son! Have ye shut out yourselves from Me by reason of My Name? Wherefore ponder ye not in your hearts? Day and night ye have been calling upon your Lord, the Omnipotent, but when He came from the heaven of eternity in His great glory, ye turned aside from Him and re-mained sunk in heedlessness.

Consider those who rejected the Spirit [Jesus] when He came unto them with manifest dominion. How numerous the Pharisees who had secluded themselves in synagogues in His name, lamenting over their separation from Him, and yet when the portals of reunion were flung open and the divine Luminary shone resplendent from the Dayspring of Beauty, they disbelieved in God, the Exalted, the Mighty. They failed to attain His presence, notwithstanding that His advent had been promised them in the Book of Isaiah as well as in the Books of the Prophets and the Messengers. No one from among them turned his face towards the Dayspring of divine bounty except such as were destitute of any power amongst men. And yet, today, every man endowed with power and invested with sovereignty prideth himself on His Name. Moreover, call thou to mind the one who sentenced Jesus to death. He was the most learned of his age in his own country, whilst he who was only a fisherman believed in Him. Take good heed and be of them that observe the warning.

Consider likewise, how numerous at this time are the monks who have secluded themselves in their churches, calling upon the Spirit, but when He appeared through the power of Truth, they failed to draw nigh unto Him and are numbered with those that have gone far astray. Happy are they that have abandoned them and set their faces towards Him Who is the Desire of all that are in the heavens and all that are on the earth.

They read the Evangel and yet refuse to acknowledge the All-Glorious Lord, notwithstanding that He hath come through the potency of His exalted, His mighty and gracious dominion. We, verily, have come for your sakes, and have borne the misfortunes of the world for your salvation. Flee ye the One Who hath sacrificed His life that ye may be quickened? Fear God, O followers of the Spirit, and walk not in the footsteps of every divine that hath gone far astray. Do ye imagine that He seeketh His own interests, when He hath, at all times, been threatened by the swords of the enemies; or that He seeketh the vanities of the world, after He hath been imprisoned in the most desolate of cities? Be fair in your judgement and follow not the footsteps of the unjust.

Open the doors of your hearts. He Who is the Spirit verily standeth before them. Wherefore keep ye afar from Him Who hath purposed to draw you nigh unto a Resplendent Spot? Say: We, in truth, have opened unto you the gates of the Kingdom. Will ye bar the doors of your houses in My face? This indeed is naught but a grievous error. He, verily, hath again come down from heaven, even as He came down from it the first time. Beware lest ye dispute that which He proclaimeth, even as the people before you disputed His utterances. Thus instructeth you the True One, could ye but perceive it.[40]

CHAPTER 30

THE CALL OF THE PROMISED ONE

This volume offers a summary of the life and teachings of Bahá'u'lláh. At the heart of His Faith is the claim that He is God's latest Messenger and that His appearance represents the fulfillment of expectations cherished by peoples around the world. Bahá'u'lláh had this to say about His own station:

> Verily I say, this is the Day in which mankind can behold the Face, and hear the Voice, of the Promised One. The Call of God hath been raised, and the light of His countenance hath been lifted up upon men. It behoveth every man to blot out the trace of every idle word from the tablet of his heart, and to gaze, with an open and unbiased mind, on the signs of His Revelation, the proofs of His Mission, and the tokens of His glory.
>
> Great indeed is this Day! The allusions made to it in all the sacred Scriptures as the Day of God attest its greatness. The soul of every Prophet of God, of every Divine Messenger, hath thirsted for this wondrous Day. All the divers kindreds of the earth have, likewise, yearned to attain it. No sooner, however, had the Day Star of His Revelation manifested itself in the heaven of God's Will, than all, except those whom the Almighty was pleased to guide, were found dumbfounded and heedless.[1]

'Abdu'l-Bahá summarizes the life of Bahá'u'lláh in the following passage, describing the motivation that transformed a comfortable existence into a life of suffering and exile:

[Bahá'u'lláh] Himself—may the spirit of all existence be offered up for His loved ones—bore all manner of ordeals, and willingly accepted for Himself intense afflictions. No torment was there left that His sacred form was not subjected to, no suffering that did not descend upon Him. How many a night, when He was chained, did He go sleepless because of the weight of His iron collar; how many a day the burning pain of the stocks and fetters gave Him no moment's peace. From Níyávarán to Ṭihrán they made Him run—He, that embodied spirit, He Who had been accustomed to repose against cushions of ornamented silk—chained, shoeless, His head bared; and down under the earth, in the thick darkness of that narrow dungeon, they shut Him up with murderers, rebels and thieves. Ever and again they assailed Him with a new torment, and all were certain that from one moment to the next He would suffer a martyr's death. After some time they banished Him from His native land, and sent Him to countries alien and far away. During many a year in 'Iráq, no moment passed but the arrow of a new anguish struck His holy heart; with every breath a sword came down upon that sacred body, and He could hope for no moment of security and rest. From every side His enemies mounted their attack with unrelenting hate; and singly and alone He withstood them all. After all these tribulations, these body blows, they flung Him out of 'Iráq in the continent of Asia, to the continent of Europe, and in that place of bitter exile, of wretched hardships, to the wrongs that were heaped upon Him by the people of the Qur'án were now added the virulent persecutions, the powerful attacks, the plottings, the slanders, the continual hostilities, the hate and malice, of the people of the Bayán [the Bábís]. My pen is powerless to tell it all; but ye have surely been informed of it. Then, after twenty-four years in this, the Most Great Prison, in agony and sore affliction, His days drew to a close.

To sum it up, the Ancient Beauty was ever, during His sojourn in this transitory world, either a captive bound with chains, or living under a sword, or subjected to extreme suffering and torment, or held in the Most Great Prison. Because of His physical weakness, brought on by His afflictions, His blessed body was worn away to a breath; it was light as a cobweb from long grieving. And His reason for shouldering this heavy load and enduring all this anguish, which was even as an ocean that hurleth its waves to high heaven—His reason for putting on the heavy iron chains and for becoming the very embodiment of utter resignation and meekness, was to lead every soul on earth to concord, to fellow feeling, to oneness; to make known amongst all peoples the sign of the singleness of God, so that at last the primal oneness deposited at the heart of all created things would bear its destined fruit, and the splendor of "No difference canst thou see in the creation of the God of Mercy,"* would cast abroad its rays.[2]

The Day of World Unity

Bahá'u'lláh's aim was to establish world unity and peace and thus provide for the spiritual and material prosperity of all humanity. In countless passages of His writings He calls upon the peoples of the world to heed His call and arise to fulfill God's purpose for this age, which is to eliminate every source of strife from amongst His children:

> O contending peoples and kindreds of the earth! Set your faces towards unity, and let the radiance of its light shine upon you. Gather ye together, and for the sake of God resolve to root out whatever is the source of contention amongst you. Then will the effulgence of the world's great Luminary envelop the whole earth, and its inhabitants become the citizens of one city, and the occupants of one and the same throne. This wronged One hath, ever since the early days of His life, cherished none other desire but this, and will continue to entertain no wish except this wish. There can be no doubt whatever that the peoples of the world, of whatever race or religion, derive their inspiration from one heavenly Source, and are the subjects of one God.[3]

Bahá'u'lláh maintains that the only real and lasting solution to the ills of the present era is to turn to the Word of God, which alone has the power to transform human hearts and achieve the unity for which the world is increasingly desperate. 'Abdu'l-Bahá writes,

> . . . when divers shades of thought, temperament and character, are brought together under the power and influence of one central agency, the beauty and glory of human perfection will be revealed and made manifest. Naught but the celestial potency of the Word of God, which ruleth and transcendeth the realities of all things, is capable of harmonizing the divergent thoughts, sentiments, ideas, and convictions of the children of men. Verily, it is the penetrating power in all things, the mover of souls and the binder and regulator in the world of humanity.[4]

---

* Koran 67:3.

Being a Bahá'í

The call of Bahá'u'lláh is addressed to every individual who desires the joy and peace that come from recognition of God's Messenger for this day. To be a Bahá'í is not to abandon one's previous religion—rather it is to recognize the fulfillment of God's ancient promises as well as to acknowledge the spiritual journey of all humanity towards this long-awaited moment. To be a Bahá'í is to believe in humanity's divinely ordained destiny to live in universal peace and brotherhood.

Those who come to accept Bahá'u'lláh as God's Messenger for today are called upon to live up to the highest standards of conduct in every aspect of their private and public lives. Above all is His constant admonishment to make service to humanity the primary goal of one's life. He repeatedly counsels His followers to show forth love and to exercise wisdom in all dealings with others. A few passages from His writings will suffice to provide an example of the high standards the Bahá'ís are called to uphold:

> It is Our wish and desire that every one of you may become a source of all goodness unto men, and an example of uprightness to mankind. Beware lest ye prefer yourselves above your neighbors. Fix your gaze upon Him Who is the Temple of God amongst men. He, in truth, hath offered up His life as a ransom for the redemption of the world. He, verily, is the All-Bountiful, the Gracious, the Most High. If any differences arise amongst you, behold Me standing before your face, and overlook the faults of one another for My name's sake and as a token of your love for My manifest and resplendent Cause. We love to see you at all times consorting in amity and concord within the paradise of My good-pleasure, and to inhale from your acts the fragrance of friendliness and unity, of loving-kindness and fellowship. Thus counselleth you the All-Knowing, the Faithful. We shall always be with you; if We inhale the perfume of your fellowship, Our heart will assuredly rejoice, for naught else can satisfy Us. To this beareth witness every man of true understanding.[5]

In another place Bahá'u'lláh writes,

> O people of God! Do not busy yourselves in your own concerns; let your thoughts be fixed upon that which will rehabilitate the fortunes of mankind and sanctify the hearts and souls of men. This can best be achieved through pure and holy deeds, through a virtuous life and a goodly behaviour. Valiant acts will ensure the triumph of this Cause, and a saintly character will reinforce its power.[6]

In still another place He writes,

> O peoples of the world! Forsake all evil, hold fast that which is good. Strive to be shining examples unto all mankind, and true reminders of the virtues of God amidst men. He that riseth to serve My Cause should manifest My wisdom, and bend every effort to banish ignorance from the earth. Be united in counsel, be one in thought. Let each morn be better than its eve and each morrow richer than its yesterday. Man's merit lieth in service and virtue and not in the pageantry of wealth and riches. Take heed that your words be purged from idle fancies and worldly desires and your deeds be cleansed from craftiness and suspicion. Dissipate not the wealth of your precious lives in the pursuit of evil and corrupt affection, nor let your endeavours be spent in promoting your personal interest. Be generous in your days of plenty, and be patient in the hour of loss. Adversity is followed by success and rejoicings follow woe. Guard against idleness and sloth, and cling unto that which profiteth mankind, whether young or old, whether high or low. Beware lest ye sow tares of dissension among men or plant thorns of doubt in pure and radiant hearts.[7]

Transformation as a Process

Such standards as those taught by Bahá'u'lláh may seem impossible to achieve, but to become a Bahá'í does not require one to be perfect or morally superior to others. As we have already seen, the Bahá'í teachings emphasize that personal transformation is a neverending process. To become a Bahá'í is an important milestone in that process. It involves sincere effort—prayer, study of the sacred writings, and action—over the course of an entire lifetime. Indeed, even after this life we can continue to improve and develop our spiritual qualities as our souls progress in the other world. We are assured that a merciful God looks more to our faith and sincerity of effort than to the actual achievement of perfection.

Bahá'u'lláh envisions a world society that will increasingly come to abide by His teachings. To realize that goal, humanity needs to cultivate a world-embracing vision wherein each person strives not merely for his own benefit, but for the benefit of all. In the future we can imagine humanity as a whole attaining greater and greater spiritual capacity as centuries and ages unfold. Bahá'u'lláh assures us that God will continue to send Messengers in every age to guide humanity forward in its spiritual evolution.

The Spread of the Bahá'í Faith

Throughout His ministry Bahá'u'lláh urged His followers to share His teachings with others. He often elucidated how the Bahá'í Faith would spread across the globe. He abolished the concept of holy war and prohibited His followers from engaging in any contentious behavior. In particular He forbade sedition and involvement of any kind in partisan political activity. The Faith is not to be spread by force or argument of any kind, but through the power of example and utterance. He writes,

> "O peoples of the earth! Haste ye to do the pleasure of God, and war ye valiantly, as it behooveth you to war, for the sake of proclaiming His resistless and immovable Cause. We have decreed that war shall be waged in the path of God with the armies of wisdom and utterance, and of a goodly character and praiseworthy deeds. Thus hath it been decided by Him Who is the All-Powerful, the Almighty. There is no glory for him that committeth disorder on the earth after it hath been made so good. Fear God, O people, and be not of them that act unjustly."[8]

Bahá'ís are warned not to assume an attitude of superiority toward others; rather, to consider themselves as humble servants of humanity. At the heart of such exhortations is an abiding reverence for the right of each individual to investigate and determine the truth for himself or herself:

> Consort with all men, O people of Bahá, in a spirit of friendliness and fellowship. If ye be aware of a certain truth, if ye possess a jewel, of which others are deprived, share it with them in a language of utmost kindliness and goodwill. If it be accepted, if it fulfill its purpose, your object is attained. If anyone should refuse it, leave him unto himself, and beseech God to guide him. Beware lest ye deal unkindly with him. A kindly tongue is the lodestone of the hearts of men. It is the bread of the spirit, it clotheth the words with meaning, it is the fountain of the light of wisdom and understanding.[9]

Bahá'u'lláh also advises the Bahá'ís to use wisdom and moderation at all times and never to say more than people are ready or willing to hear. "The wise," He wrote, "are they who speak not unless they obtain a hearing."[10]

During Bahá'u'lláh's lifetime many Bahá'ís arose to teach their faith, often under extremely dangerous circumstances. On the whole they were careful to follow Bahá'u'lláh's counsel to share the Faith with caution. Nevertheless, they frequently provoked the wrath of the clergy and of the ignorant, and many met with suffering and even death. Notwithstanding such opposition, the Bahá'í Faith steadily gained in numbers and strength.

Ever since its inception the Bahá'í Faith has met with hostility and persecution from various quarters. This is still true today, especially in Iran. Bahá'u'lláh taught that such persecutions will not prevent the ultimate triumph of His Cause; indeed, there were many instances in His own life whereby such tribulations were transformed into astounding victories.

In the Most Holy Book Bahá'u'lláh anticipated the day when He would no longer be present to guide the affairs of the community. In that book and in other writings He makes provisions to ensure the unity and integrity of the Bahá'í Faith for all time. He also calls upon His followers to continue the work of spreading His teachings.

It has now been more than a century since Bahá'u'lláh passed away in 1892. In that time the Bahá'í Faith has spread to more than 190 countries and 46 territories of the globe. Its membership now numbers more than 5 million people of some 2,112 tribes, nationalities, and races. The worldwide Bahá'í community, with members in more than 116,000 localities, is engaged in a variety of local efforts, inspired by the words of Bahá'u'lláh, to achieve unity, peace, and social justice.[11] Such efforts are undertaken not only for the benefit of the Bahá'ís, but also for all humanity. As the Bahá'í Faith gains in numbers and resources, it will exercise an increasingly visible role in the process of world transformation now underway as the result of the revelation of Bahá'u'lláh.

It should be noted that the Bahá'í Faith accepts monetary contributions only from members of the religion. This guideline is not meant to discriminate against non-members but rather to reflect the belief of the Bahá'ís that the institutions they are building are "gifts from Bahá'u'lláh to the world" and can function best if they are built and supported only by "those who are fully conscious of, and unreservedly submissive to, the claims inherent in the Revelation of Bahá'u'lláh."[12]

The Universal House of Justice, the supreme governing body of the Bahá'í Faith, wrote a public statement that addressed the essential prerequisites for peace as taught by Bahá'u'lláh. In this document, entitled *The Promise of World Peace*, the Universal House of Justice points out that the hope of world unity is already substantiated in the progress that the Bahá'í Faith has made:

> The experience of the Bahá'í community may be seen as an example of this enlarging unity. It is a community of some three to four million* people

---

* When the statement was written in 1986, the worldwide Bahá'í population was estimated to be 3 to 4 million. Today, estimates place it at over 5 million.

drawn from many nations, cultures, classes and creeds, engaged in a wide range of activities serving the spiritual, social and economic needs of the peoples of many lands. It is a single social organism, representative of the diversity of the human family, conducting its affairs through a system of commonly accepted consultative principles, and cherishing equally all the great outpourings of divine guidance in human history. Its existence is yet another convincing proof of the practicality of its Founder's vision of a united world, another evidence that humanity can live as one global society, equal to whatever challenges its coming of age may entail. If the Bahá'í experience can contribute in whatever measure to reinforcing hope in the unity of the human race, we are happy to offer it as a model for study.[13]

Today, after a century of rapid growth, the Bahá'í community makes up only a small percentage of the human race. Yet 'Abdu'l-Bahá exhorted the Bahá'ís to take the long view, assuring them of the ultimate achievement of God's purpose:

Look ye not upon the present, fix your gaze upon the times to come. In the beginning, how small is the seed, yet in the end it is a mighty tree. Look ye not upon the seed, look ye upon the tree, and its blossoms, and its leaves and its fruits. Consider the days of Christ, when none but a small band followed Him; then observe what a mighty tree that seed became, behold ye its fruitage. And now shall come to pass even greater things than these, for this is the summons of the Lord of Hosts, this is the trumpet-call of the living Lord, this is the anthem of world peace, this is the standard of righteousness and trust and understanding raised up among all the variegated peoples of the globe; this is the splendor of the Sun of Truth, this is the holiness of the spirit of God Himself. This most powerful of dispensations will encompass all the earth, and beneath its banner will all peoples gather and be sheltered together.[14]

In the passage above, 'Abdu'l-Bahá draws a parallel between the spread of the Bahá'í Faith and that of Christianity. The biggest difference, which can already be seen, is that of scale; for whereas Christianity had only penetrated the Mediterranean world and parts of Asia Minor in some one hundred years, the Faith of Bahá'u'lláh has permeated nearly the entire globe in roughly the same time. According to *Encyclopaedia Britannica,* it is now second only to Christianity itself in the number of countries and territories where its followers can be found.[15] Such an unprecedented record of achievement is very much in keeping with the worldwide mission of the Bahá'í Faith and with Bahá'u'lláh's station as the Promised One of All Ages.

Prior reference has been made to the Covenant Bahá'u'lláh established to ensure that the religion remains one and indivisible. From time to time there have been attempts to cause a breach from within the ranks of the Bahá'ís. A few instances of this have been mentioned in this volume, and there have been others. Yet all have failed to achieve their end. After more than a century, the Bahá'í Faith remains undivided. This feat, unparalleled in religious history, constitutes yet another testimony to the divine power of its Author.

The Individual's Response to Bahá'u'lláh

Time and again Bahá'u'lláh announced the joyous news that the promises of God have been fulfilled in this day. Summoning the peoples of the world to investigate His Cause, He invites every sincere seeker after truth to experience the joy of reunion with the Beloved of the World. "The true seeker," He writes, "hunteth naught but the object of his quest, and the lover hath no desire save union with his beloved."[16] And elsewhere He writes,

My holy, My divinely ordained Revelation may be likened unto an ocean in whose depths are concealed innumerable pearls of great price, of surpassing luster. It is the duty of every seeker to bestir himself and strive to attain the shores of this ocean, so that he may, in proportion to the eagerness of his search and the efforts he hath exerted, partake of such benefits as have been pre-ordained in God's irrevocable and hidden Tablets.[17]

As we have seen, the Bahá'í writings emphasize that the search for spiritual truth is essentially personal in nature. Success depends upon sincerity of intent and freedom of spirit. 'Abdu'l-Bahá writes,

. . . the seeker must be endowed with certain qualities. First of all, he must be just and severed from all else save God; his heart must be entirely turned to the supreme horizon; he must be free from the bondage of self and passion, for all these are obstacles. Furthermore, he must be able to endure all hardships. He must be absolutely pure and sanctified, and free from the love or the hatred of the inhabitants of the world. Why? because the fact of his love for any person or thing might prevent him from recognizing the truth in another, and, in the same way, hatred for anything might be a hindrance in discerning truth. This is the condition of seeking, and the seeker must have these qualities and attributes. Until he reaches this condition, it is not possible for him to attain to the Sun of Reality.[18]

Bahá'u'lláh invites each individual to investigate his Cause. This is expressed here, in tones both poignant and joyous:

> Hear Me, ye mortal birds! In the Rose Garden of changeless splendor a Flower hath begun to bloom, compared to which every other flower is but a thorn, and before the brightness of Whose glory the very essence of beauty must pale and wither. Arise, therefore, and, with the whole enthusiasm of your hearts, with all the eagerness of your souls, the full fervor of your will, and the concentrated efforts of your entire being, strive to attain the paradise of His presence, and endeavor to inhale the fragrance of the incorruptible Flower, to breathe the sweet savors of holiness, and to obtain a portion of this perfume of celestial glory. Whoso followeth this counsel will break his chains asunder, will taste the abandonment of enraptured love, will attain unto his heart's desire, and will surrender his soul into the hands of his Beloved. Bursting through his cage, he will, even as the bird of the spirit, wing his flight to his holy and everlasting nest. . . .
>
> The everlasting Candle shineth in its naked glory. Behold how it hath consumed every mortal veil. O ye moth-like lovers of His light! Brave every danger, and consecrate your souls to its consuming flame. O ye that thirst after Him! Strip yourselves of every earthly affection, and hasten to embrace your Beloved. With a zest that none can equal make haste to attain unto Him. The Flower, thus far hidden from the sight of men, is unveiled to your eyes. In the open radiance of His glory He standeth before you. His voice summoneth all the holy and sanctified beings to come and be united with Him. Happy is he that turneth thereunto; well is it with him that hath attained, and gazed on the light of so wondrous a countenance.[19]

In the end, each of us must decide whether Bahá'u'lláh's claims are true. This book was written in that spirit by one of the many millions who believe that God has spoken again and that His Messenger is Bahá'u'lláh.

NOTES

Chapter 1

1. George Townshend, Introduction, in Nabíl-i-Aʻẓam, *The Dawn-Breakers,* pp. xxv–xxvi.
2. Lord Curzon, *Persia and the Persian Question,* quoted in Shoghi Effendi, Introduction, in Nabíl-i-Aʻẓam, *The Dawn-Breakers,* p. xxviii.
3. Lord Curzon, *Persia and the Persian Question,* quoted in Shoghi Effendi, Introduction, in Nabíl-i-Aʻẓam, *The Dawn-Breakers,* pp. lvi–lvii.
4. Lord Curzon, *Persia and the Persian Question,* quoted in Shoghi Effendi, Introduction, in Nabíl-i-Aʻẓam, *The Dawn-Breakers,* p. xxix.
5. Nabíl-i-Aʻẓam, *The Dawn-Breakers,* p. 52.
6. Ibid., pp. 52–55, 57, 61–63, 65.
7. Ḥájí Siyyid Javád-i-Karbilá'í, quoted in Nabíl-i-Aʻẓam, *The Dawn-Breakers,* p. 79.

Chapter 2

1. The Báb, quoted in Nabíl-i-Aʻẓam, *The Dawn-Breakers,* p. 96.
2. Lady Blomfield, *The Chosen Highway,* p. 40.
3. J. E. Esslemont, *Bahá'u'lláh and the New Era,* pp. 23–24, quoted in Nabíl-i-Aʻẓam, *The Dawn-Breakers,* p. 106 n.1.

Chapter 3

1. Nabíl-i-Aʻẓam, *The Dawn-Breakers,* p. 315.
2. The Báb, quoted in ibid., pp. 315–16.
3. Dr. Cormick, quoted in Shoghi Effendi, Introduction, in ibid., pp. xxxii–xxxiii.
4. Sám K͟hán, quoted in Nabíl-i-Aʻẓam, *The Dawn-Breakers,* p. 512.
5. The Báb, quoted in ibid., p. 522.
6. The Báb, quoted in ibid., p. 514.

Chapter 4

1. The Báb, quoted in Shoghi Effendi, *The World Order of Bahá'u'lláh,* p. 62.
2. The Báb, quoted in Bahá'u'llah, *Epistle to the Son of the Wolf,* p. 142.
3. The Báb, quoted in Shoghi Effendi, *God Passes By,* p. 25.
4. Bahá'u'lláh, *Epistle to the Son of the Wolf,* p. 20.
5. Bahá'u'lláh, quoted in Nabíl-i-A'ẓam, *The Dawn-Breakers,* pp. 607–08.
6. Bahá'u'lláh, *Epistle to the Son of the Wolf,* pp. 20–21.
7. Captain Alfred von Gumoens, letter dated 29 August 1852, quoted in Moojan Momen, ed., *The Bábí and Bahá'í Religions, 1844–1944,* pp. 132–34.
8. Bahá'u'lláh, quoted in Nabíl-i-A'ẓam, *The Dawn-Breakers,* pp. 631–32.
9. Bahá'u'lláh, quoted in Shoghi Effendi, *God Passes By,* pp. 101–02.

Chapter 5

1. Comte de Gobineau, "Les Religions et les Philosophies dans l'Asie Centrale," pp. 211–213, quoted in Périgord, *Translation of French Foot-Notes of the Dawn-Breakers,* pp. 57–58.
2. A. L. M. Nicolas, "Siyyid 'Alí-Muḥammad, dit le Báb," pp. 203–204, 376, quoted in ibid., pp. 60–61.
3. Bahá'u'lláh, quoted in Shoghi Effendi, *God Passes By,* p. 126.
4. Bahá'u'lláh, *The Hidden Words,* p. 3.
5. Bahá'u'lláh, *The Hidden Words,* Arabic, no. 3.
6. Ibid., Arabic, no. 4.
7. Ibid., Arabic, no. 1.
8. Ibid., Arabic, no. 2.
9. Ibid., Persian, no. 49.
10. Ibid., Persian, no. 64.
11. Ibid., Persian, no. 21.
12. Ibid., Persian, no. 7.
13. Nabíl, quoted in Shoghi Effendi, *God Passes By,* p. 152.
14. Nabíl, quoted in ibid., p. 137.
15. Nabíl, quoted in ibid., p. 137.
16. Bahá'u'lláh, quoted in ibid., p. 137.
17. Mullá Muḥammad-i-Qá'iní, quoted in Taherzadeh, *The Revelation of Bahá'u'lláh: Baghdád,* p. 94.
18. Zaynu'l-'Ábidín Khán, quoted in H. M. Balyuzi, *Bahá'u'lláh: The King of Glory,* p. 124.

Chapter 6

1. Bahá'u'lláh, *Kitáb-i-Íqán,* ¶104.
2. Ibid., ¶81.
3. Ibid., ¶15.
4. Ibid., ¶14.

5. Ibid., ¶24 (cf. Matt. 24:29–31).
6. Ibid., ¶2.

Chapter 7

1. 'Abdu'l-Bahá, *Some Answered Questions*, pp. 28–30.
2. Námiq Páshá, quoted by 'Abdu'l-Bahá in Shoghi Effendi, *God Passes By*, p. 150.

Chapter 8

1. Nabíl, quoted in Shoghi Effendi, *God Passes By*, p. 153.
2. Shoghi Effendi, *God Passes By*, p. 155.
3. Bahá'í International Community, *Bahá'u'lláh*, p. 29.
4. Matt. 24:27; Bahá'u'lláh, *Tablets of Bahá'u'lláh*, p. 13.

Chapter 9

1. Bahá'u'lláh, *Summons of the Lord of Hosts*, Súriy-i-Haykal, ¶192, ¶194.
2. Ibid., ¶265, ¶266, ¶268.
3. Ibid., Súriy-i-Mulúk, ¶59, ¶61, ¶64, ¶81–82.
4. Napoleon III, quoted in Shoghi Effendi, *Promised Day Is Come*, ¶124.
5. Bahá'u'lláh, *Summons of the Lord of Hosts*, Súriy-i-Haykal, ¶138.
6. Bahá'u'lláh, *Kitáb-i-Aqdas*, ¶86.
7. Ibid., ¶90.
8. Bahá'u'lláh, *Summons of the Lord of Hosts*, Súriy-i-Haykal, ¶106, ¶108, ¶112.
9. Ibid., ¶174–176.
10. Queen Victoria, quoted in Shoghi Effendi, *Promised Day Is Come*, ¶163.
11. Bahá'u'lláh, *Kitab-i-Aqdas*, ¶88.

Chapter 10

1. Bahá'u'lláh, quoted in Shoghi Effendi, *God Passes By*, p. 179
2. Áqá Ridá, quoted in ibid., p. 180.
3. Bahá'u'lláh, quoted in ibid., p. 186; Bahá'u'lláh, quoted in ibid., p. 187.
4. Bahá'u'lláh, quoted in ibid., p. 184.
5. Bahá'u'lláh, quoted in ibid., p. 185.
6. Isaiah 35:1–2.
7. Amos 1:2.
8. Micah 7:12.
9. Psalms 24:9–10.

10. Muḥammad, quoted in Shoghi Effendi, *God Passes By*, p. 184.
11. 'Abdu'l-Bahá, *Some Answered Questions*, p. 32.
12. Bahá'u'lláh, *Summons of the Lord of Hosts*, Súriy-i-Haykal, ¶140–41.
13. Bahá'u'lláh, *Gleanings*, pp. 99–100.

Chapter 11

1. Words of Bahá'u'lláh and Mírzá Mihdí as related by Áqá Ḥusayn-i-A<u>sh</u>chí in H. M. Balyuzi, *Bahá'u'lláh: The King of Glory*, pp. 311–12.
2. Bahá'u'lláh, *Gleanings*, pp. 117–18.
3. Bahá'u'lláh, *Epistle to the Son of the Wolf*, p. 23.
4. Bahá'u'lláh, *Gleanings*, pp. 100–01.
5. See H. M. Balyuzi, *Bahá'u'lláh: The King of Glory*, pp. 337–38.
6. Bahá'u'lláh, quoted in Shoghi Effendi, *God Passes By*, p. 215; Bahá'u'lláh, *Kitáb-i-Aqdas*, ¶99; Bahá'u'lláh, quoted in Shoghi Effendi, *God Passes By*, p. 216.
7. Bahá'u'lláh, quoted in J. E. Esslemont, *Bahá'u'lláh and the New Era*, p. 34.
8. J. E. Esslemont, *Bahá'u'lláh and the New Era*, p. 38.
9. Ḥájí Mírzá Ḥaydar-'Alí, quoted in Adib Taherzadeh, *Revelation of Bahá'u'lláh*, 3:248–49.
10. Ibid., p. 249.
11. Ḥájí Mírzá Ḥaydar-'Alí, quoted in Adib Taherzadeh, *Revelation of Bahá'u'lláh*, 4:135–36.

Chapter 12

1. Bahá'u'lláh, *Tablets of Bahá'u'lláh*, p. 149.
2. An eyewitness, quoted in Shoghi Effendi, *God Passes By*, pp. 170–71.
3. Shoghi Effendi, *God Passes By*, pp. 170–71.
4. Siyyid Asadu'lláh-i-Qumí, quoted in Adib Taherzadeh, *Revelation of Bahá'u'lláh*, 1:35–36.

Chapter 13

1. Bahá'u'lláh, *Epistle to the Son of the Wolf*, p. 118.
2. Bahá'u'lláh, *Gleanings*, pp. 46–47.
3. Ibid., p. 150.
4. Ibid., pp. 151–52.
5. Ibid., p. 177.
6. Ibid., p. 65.
7. Bahá'u'lláh, *Hidden Words*, Arabic, no. 3.
8. Bahá'u'lláh, *Gleanings*, pp. 47–48.
9. Bahá'u'lláh, *Tablets of Bahá'u'lláh*, p. 161.
10. Bahá'u'lláh, *Gleanings*, p. 74.
11. Ibid., p. 172.
12. Ibid., p. 217.

13. Ibid., p. 299.
14. Ibid., p. 213.
15. Bahá'u'lláh, *Tablets of Bahá'u'lláh*, p. 173.
16. Bahá'u'lláh, *Gleanings*, p. 142.
17. Ibid., p. 142.
18. Koran 5:73, John 6:40; Koran 20:100.
19. Bahá'u'lláh, *Gleanings*, p. 12–13.
20. Ibid., p. 11.
21. Ibid., p. 108.
22. Bahá'u'lláh, quoted in Shoghi Effendi, *Advent of Divine Justice*, p. 79.
23. Bahá'u'lláh, *Gleanings*, pp. 10–11.
24. Bahá'u'lláh, quoted in Shoghi Effendi, *World Order of Bahá'u'lláh*, p. 113.

Chapter 14

1. Bahá'u'lláh, *Gleanings*, p. 157.
2. Bahá'u'lláh, *Hidden Words*, Arabic, no. 32.
3. Bahá'u'lláh, *Gleanings*, pp. 153–54.
4. Ibid., pp. 155–56.
5. Ibid., p. 161.
6. Bahá'u'lláh, *Tablets of Bahá'u'lláh*, p. 118.

Chapter 15

1. Bahá'u'lláh, *Gleanings*, p. 149.
2. Ibid., pp. 156–57.
3. Bahá'u'lláh, *Kitáb-i-Aqdas*, ¶1.
4. Ibid., ¶2–3.
5. Ibid., ¶125.
6. Bahá'u'lláh, *Tablets of Bahá'u'lláh*, p. 35.
7. Bahá'u'lláh, *Gleanings*, p. 328.
8. Ibid., p. 138.
9. Ibid., p. 261.
10. Bahá'u'lláh, *Tablets of Bahá'u'lláh*, p. 24.
11. Bahá'u'lláh, *Gleanings*, p. 285.
12. Bahá'u'lláh, *Hidden Words*, Arabic, no. 2.
13. Bahá'u'lláh, *Kitáb-i-Aqdas*, ¶99.
14. Bahá'u'lláh, *Kitáb-i-Aqdas*, ¶78–79, ¶82–83.
15. Bahá'u'lláh, *Tablets of Bahá'u'lláh*, p. 84.
16. Bahá'u'lláh, quoted in Shoghi Effendi, *Advent of Divine Justice*, pp. 27–28.
17. Bahá'u'lláh, *Tablets of Bahá'u'lláh*, p. 164.
18. Ibid., p. 155.
19. Bahá'u'lláh, *Gleanings*, p. 171.

20. Bahá'u'lláh, *Epistle to the Son of the Wolf*, p. 27.
21. Bahá'u'lláh, *Gleanings*, p. 215.

Chapter 16

1. Bahá'u'lláh, *Gleanings*, pp. 308–10.
2. Edward Granville Browne, quoted in H. M. Balyuzi, *Edward Granville Browne and the Bahá'í Faith*, pp. 56–57.
3. Bahá'u'lláh, *Epistle to the Son of the Wolf*, p. 34.
4. Ibid., p. 104.
5. Shoghi Effendi, *God Passes By*, p. 222.
6. Nabíl, quoted in *God Passes By*, p. 222.

Chapter 17

1. Bahá'u'lláh, *Epistle to the Son of the Wolf*, p. 11.
2. Bahá'u'lláh, *Gleanings*, pp. 119–20.
3. Ibid., p. 307.
4. Bahá'u'lláh, *Kitáb-i-Aqdas*, ¶53.
5. Ibid., ¶101.

Chapter 18

1. Bahá'u'lláh, *Tablets of Bahá'u'lláh*, p. 219.
2. Ibid., p. 220.
3. Ibid., p. 223.
4. Bahá'u'lláh, *Kitáb-i-Aqdas*, ¶121.
5. H. M. Balyuzi, *'Abdu'l-Bahá*, p. 9.
6. Ibid., pp. 11–12.
7. Ibid., p. 4
8. See Shoghi Effendi, *World Order of Bahá'u'lláh*, p. 134.
9. 'Abdu'l-Bahá, quoted in Shoghi Effendi, *World Order of Bahá'u'lláh*, p. 139.

Chapter 20

1. P. A. Hearst, to O. M. Babcock, 5 December 1899, in Rev. Isaac Adams, M.D., *Persia by a Persian*, p. 289.
2. Howard Colby Ives, *Portals to Freedom*, pp. 115–16.
3. Lady Blomfield, *Chosen Highway*, pp. 149–50.
4. Reverend James T. Bixby, quoted in *Bábí and Bahá'í Religions, 1844–1944*, p. 329.

Chapter 21

1. 'Abdu'l-Bahá, *Selections from the Writings of 'Abdu'l-Bahá*, no. 12.1.
2. Bahá'u'lláh, *Hidden Words*, Arabic, no. 31.
3. Ibid., no. 5.
4. Bahá'u'lláh, *Hidden Words*, Arabic, no. 18.
5. Bahá'u'lláh, *Gleanings*, p. 295.
6. Bahá'u'lláh, *Kitáb-i-Aqdas*, ¶182.
7. Bahá'u'lláh, *Gleanings*, p. 175.
8. Bahá'u'lláh, in *Compilation of Compilations*, 1:no. 364.
9. Bahá'u'lláh, *Hidden Words*, Arabic, no. 1.
10. Bahá'u'lláh, *Gleanings*, p. 305.
11. Ibid., pp. 314–15.
12. Ibid., pp. 315–16.

Chapter 22

1. Bahá'u'lláh, *Gleanings*, p. 95.
2. Bahá'u'lláh, *Hidden Words*, Arabic, no. 68.
3. Bahá'u'lláh, *Epistle to the Son of the Wolf*, p. 14.
4. 'Abdu'l-Bahá, *Promulgation of Universal Peace*, p. 70.
5. Bahá'u'lláh, *Hidden Words*, Persian, no. 5.
6. 'Abdu'l-Bahá, quoted in Gayle Morrison, *To Move the World*, p. 46.
7. Ibid., p. 314.
8. Bahá'u'lláh, *Compilation of Compilations*, 2:no. 2145.
9. 'Abdu'l-Bahá, *Promulgation of Universal Peace*, pp. 174–75.
10. 'Abdu'l-Bahá, quoted in J.E. Esslemont, *Bahá'u'lláh and the New Era*, p. 149.
11. Ibid., pp. 148–49.
12. Bahíyyih Khánum, quoted in Lady Blomfield, *Chosen Highway*, p. 40.
13. Shoghi Effendi, in *Bahíyyih Khánum*, p. 26.
14. 'Abdu'l-Bahá, *Selections from the Writings of 'Abdu'l-Bahá*, no. 38.3.

Chapter 23

1. Bahá'u'lláh, *Tablets of Bahá'u'lláh*, pp. 63–64, 125; Bahá'u'lláh, *Gleanings*, p. 81.
2. Bahá'u'lláh, quoted in Shoghi Effendi, *The Promised Day Is Come*, ¶275.
3. Bahá'u'lláh, *Gleanings*, p. 288; Bahá'u'lláh, *Epistle to the Son of the Wolf*, p. 15.
4. 'Abdu'l-Bahá, *Promulgation of Universal Peace*, p. 117.
5. Ibid., 161.
6. Ibid., pp. 175–76.
7. Ibid., p. 50.
8. 'Abdu'l-Bahá, *Some Answered Questions*, p. 182.
9. 'Abdu'l-Bahá, *Some Answered Questions*, p. 123.

10. Bahá'u'lláh, *Tablets of Bahá'u'lláh*, p. 69.
11. Ibid.
12. 'Abdu'l-Bahá, *Japan Will Turn Ablaze!* p. 51.
13. 'Abdu'l-Bahá, *Promulgation of Universal Peace*, p. 12.
14. 'Abdu'l-Bahá, *Selections from the Writings of 'Abdu'l-Bahá*, no. 227.22.

Chapter 24

1. Bahá'u'lláh, *Tablets of Bahá'u'lláh*, p. 51.
2. Bahá'u'lláh, in *Compilation of Compilations*, 1:no. 557.
3. Ibid., 1:no. 575.
4. 'Abdu'l-Bahá, *Selections from the Writings of 'Abdu'l-Bahá*, no. 103.5.
5. 'Abdu'l-Bahá, *Paris Talks*, nos. 46.4–46.5, 46.10, 46.12.
6. 'Abdu'l-Bahá, *Selections from the Writings of 'Abdu'l-Bahá*, no. 79.3.
7. 'Abdu'l-Bahá, *Secret of Divine Civilization*, p. 24.
8. Bahá'u'lláh, *Tablets of Bahá'u'lláh*, pp. 165–66.
9. Bahá'u'lláh, *Gleanings*, p. 216.
10. Bahá'u'lláh, *Tablets of Bahá'u'lláh*, p. 87; Bahá'u'lláh, *Gleanings*, p. 95.
11. Bahá'u'lláh, *Gleanings*, p. 250.
12. Bahá'u'lláh, *Summons of the Lord of Hosts*, H174.
13. Ibid., H179, H181, H182.
14. 'Abdu'l-Bahá, *Selections from the Writings of 'Abdu'l-Bahá*, no. 15.6.
15. 'Abdu'l-Bahá, *Secret of Divine Civilization*, pp. 64–67.
16. 'Abdu'l-Bahá, *Selections from the Writings of 'Abdu'l-Bahá*, nos. 138.5, 138.1.
17. Ibid., ¶228.2.
18. Ibid., ¶227.31.

Chapter 25

1. Bahá'u'lláh, *Kitáb-i-Íqán*, ¶216.
2. 'Abdu'l-Bahá, *Secret of Divine Civilization*, pp. 23–24.
3. Bahá'u'lláh, *Tablets of Bahá'u'lláh*, p. 69.
4. 'Abdu'l-Bahá, quoted in J. E. Esslemont, *Bahá'u'lláh and the New Era*, p. 103.
5. Bahá'u'lláh, *Kitáb-i-Aqdas*, ¶2–3.
6. Bahá'u'lláh, *Hidden Words*, Persian, no. 82.
7. Bahá'u'lláh, *Tablets of Bahá'u'lláh*, p. 26.
8. 'Abdu'l-Bahá, *Paris Talks*, no. 55.1
9. 'Abdu'l-Bahá, *Selections from the Writings of 'Abdu'l-Bahá*, no. 11.1.
10. Ibid., no. 34.2.
11. 'Abdu'l-Bahá, *Secret of Divine Civilization*, p. 21.
12. Ibid., pp. 2–3.
13. 'Abdu'l-Bahá, *Selections from the Writings of 'Abdu'l-Bahá*, nos. 84.2–84.4.
14. 'Abdu'l-Bahá, quoted in J. E. Esslemont, *Bahá'u'lláh and the New Era*, p. 177.
15. Bahá'u'lláh, *Kitáb-i-Aqdas*, note 88.

16. 'Abdu'l-Bahá, *Selections from the Writings of 'Abdu'l-Bahá*, no. 129.4.
17. Ibid., nos. 133.1, 133.2.
18. 'Abdu'l-Bahá, quoted in J. E. Esslemont, *Bahá'u'lláh and the New Era*, pp. 114–15.
19. Bahá'u'lláh, *Kitáb-i-Aqdas*, ¶51.
20. 'Abdu'l-Bahá, quoted in Lady Blomfield, *Chosen Highway*, p. 167.
21. 'Abdu'l-Bahá, *Promulgation of Universal Peace*, p. 52.

Chapter 26

1. Bahá'u'lláh, *Hidden Words*, Arabic, no. 51.
2. 'Abdu'l-Bahá, *Paris Talks*, nos. 14.2–14.10.
3. 'Abdu'l-Bahá, *Promulgation of Universal Peace*, pp. 46–48.
4. 'Abdu'l-Bahá. *Selections from the Writings of 'Abdu'l-Bahá*, ¶169.2.

Chapter 27

1. 'Abdu'l-Bahá, *Promulgation of Universal Peace*, pp. 468, 469.
2. General Edmund Allenby, quoted in Lady Blomfield, *Chosen Highway*, p. 220.
3. Myron H. Phelps, *The Master in 'Akká*, pp. 2–6, 8, 10.
4. [Ibráhím Naṣṣár], quoted in *The Passing of 'Abdu'l-Bahá*, [comp. Shoghi Effendi and Lady Blomfield], pp. 21–22.
5. Howard Colby Ives, *Portals to Freedom*, p. 253.

Chapter 28

1. 'Abdu'l-Bahá, *Will and Testament*, p. 14.
2. 'Abdu'l-Bahá, *Will and Testament*, p. 11.
3. 'Abdu'l-Bahá, quoted in Shoghi Effendi, *World Order of Bahá'u'lláh*, p. 150.
4. 'Abdu'l-Bahá, quoted in Rúhíyyih Rabbani, *Priceless Pearl*, p. 2.
5. Bahá'u'lláh, Kitáb-i-Aqdas, ¶181.
6. Bahá'u'lláh, *Gleanings*, p. 195.
7. Ibid., p. 17.
8. Bahá'u'lláh, quoted in Shoghi Effendi, *World Order of Bahá'u'lláh*, p. 169.
9. Ibid.
10. Bahá'u'lláh, quoted in Shoghi Effendi, *Promised Day Is Come*, ¶8.
11. Bahá'u'lláh, *Gleanings*, pp. 118–19.
12. Shoghi Effendi, *Promised Day Is Come*, ¶33–34.
13. Shoghi Effendi, *Advent of Divine Justice*, pp. 72–73.
14. 'Abdu'l-Bahá, *Will and Testament*, p. 11.
15. Bahá'u'lláh, *Kitáb-i-Aqdas*, ¶30.
16. Bahá'u'lláh, *Tablets of Bahá'u'lláh*, p. 168.
17. 'Abdu'l-Bahá, *Promulgation of Universal Peace*, pp. 72–73.

18. 'Abdu'l-Bahá, *Selections from the Writings of 'Abdu'l-Bahá*, no. 43.1.

19. Ibid., no. 44.1.

20. Shoghi Effendi, *Bahá'í Administration*, p. 64.

21. Ibid., pp. 63–64.

22. Ibid., p. 88.

23. Ibid., pp. 38, 39.

24. 'Abdu'l-Bahá, *Selections from the Writings of 'Abdu'l-Bahá*, no. 50.

25. Bahá'u'lláh, *Kitáb-i-Aqdas*, ¶31; 'Abdu'l-Bahá, *Selections from the Writings of 'Abdu'l-Bahá*, no. 64.1.

26. Shoghi Effendi, *World Order of Bahá'u'lláh*, p. 152.

27. Ibid., 41–42.

28. Ibid., pp. 42–43.

29. Ibid., pp. 202–04.

Chapter 29

1. Bahá'u'lláh, *Gleanings*, p. 136.

2. Shoghi Effendi, *Promised Day Is Come*, ¶269.

3. Bahá'u'lláh, *Gleanings*, pp. 85–86.

4. Bahá'u'lláh, *Kitáb-i-Íqán*, ¶98.

5. 'Abdu'l-Bahá, *'Abdu'l-Bahá in London*, p. 18.

6. 'Abdu'l-Bahá, *Selections from the Writings of 'Abdu'l-Bahá*, nos. 20.1–20.2.

7. John 1:21; Matthew 11:14–15.

8. Luke 3:4–6.

9. John 14:9, 10:30, 14:11.

10. John 14:28.

11. John 14:16.

12. Matthew 24:29–30.

13. Revelation 1:7.

14. See Revelation 3:12.

15. 2 Peter 3:10; Luke 12:40, 21:36.

16. Isaiah 41:26, 46:9–10.

17. 1 John 4:1–4.

18. Matthew 7:16–20.

19. Daniel 9:24.

20. 'Abdu'l-Bahá, *Some Answered Questions*, p. 101.

21. John 10:30, 8:28; Colossians 1:15.

22. 'Abdu'l-Bahá, *Some Answered Questions*, pp. 114–15.

23. 'Abdu'l-Bahá, *Promulgation of Universal Peace*, p. 288; 'Abdu'l-Bahá, *Some Answered Questions*, p. 92.

24. Bahá'u'lláh, *Gleanings*, pp. 193–94, 130.

25. Bahá'u'lláh, *Kitáb-i-Aqdas*, ¶1.

26. Bahá'u'lláh, *Gleanings*, pp. 86, 87.

27. See John 17:12–18; see also Matthew 12:24, 24:24.

28. 'Abdu'l-Bahá, *Promulgation of Universal Peace*, pp. 294–95.

29. 'Abdu'l-Bahá, *Some Answered Questions*, p. 231.

30. Bahá'u'lláh, *Gleanings*, p. 171.

31. 'Abdu'l-Bahá, *Some Answered Questions*, p. 232.

32. Shoghi Effendi, *God Passes By*, p. 143.

33. Bahá'u'lláh, *Summons of the Lord of Hosts*, Súriy-i-Haykal, ¶234; 'Abdu'l-Bahá, quoted in Shoghi Effendi, *God Passes By*, p. 143.

34. 'Abdu'l-Bahá, *Selections from the Writings of 'Abdu'l-Bahá*, no. 81; Bahá'u'lláh, *Gleanings*, p. 159.

35. Shoghi Effendi, *God Passes By*, p. 95.

36. 'Abdu'l-Bahá, *Promulgation of Universal Peace*, p. 126.

37. Bahá'u'lláh, *Gleanings*, pp. 87–88.

38. Isaiah 2:3–4.

39. Revelation 21:1–4.

40. Bahá'u'lláh, *Tablets of Bahá'u'lláh*, pp. 9–11.

Chapter 30

1. Bahá'u'lláh, *Gleanings*, pp. 10–11.

2. 'Abdu'l-Bahá, *Selections from the Writings of 'Abdu'l-Bahá*, nos. 207.7–207.8.

3. Bahá'u'lláh, *Gleanings*, p. 217.

4. 'Abdu'l-Bahá, *Selections from the Writings of 'Abdu'l-Bahá*, no. 225.25.

5. Bahá'u'lláh, *Gleanings*, pp. 315–16.

6. Bahá'u'lláh, *Tablets of Bahá'u'lláh*, p. 86.

7. Ibid., p. 138.

8. Bahá'u'lláh, *Epistle to the Son of the Wolf*, p. 24.

9. Ibid., p. 15.

10. Bahá'u'lláh, *Hidden Words*, Persian, no. 36.

11. *Bahá'í World 2000–2001*, p. 277.

12. Shoghi Effendi, *Bahá'í Administration*, p. 182.

13. The Universal House of Justice, *Promise of World Peace*, pp. 36–37.

14. 'Abdu'l-Bahá, *Selections from the Writings of 'Abdu'l-Bahá*, no. 40.3.

15. "Worldwide Adherents of All Religions by Six Continental Areas, Mid-2002." *Encyclopaedia Britannica*. 2003. Encyclopaedia Britannica Premium Service. 16 Jul, 2003 <http://www.britannica.com/eb/article?eu=420485>.

16. Bahá'u'lláh, *The Seven Valleys and The Four Valleys*, p. 7.

17. Bahá'u'lláh, *Gleanings*, p. 326.

18. 'Abdu'l-Bahá, *Some Answered Questions*, pp. 38–39.

19. Bahá'u'lláh, *Gleanings*, pp. 320–22.

GLOSSARY

A

ABBASID DYNASTY Second great dynasty of the caliphate, the leadership of the Sunní branch of Islam. The 'Abbasids gained control of the caliphate in A.D. 750 and ruled until 1258, when their reign was destroyed by the invasion of the Mongols.

'ABDU'L-'AZÍZ (1830–76) Sultan of Turkey, 1861–76. He was responsible for Bahá'u'lláh's banishments to Contantinople, to Adrianople, and to the prison-fortress of 'Akká, Palestine. Willful and headstrong, 'Abdu'l-'Azíz was known for his lavish expenditures. Bahá'u'lláh stigmatizes him in the Kitáb-i-Aqdas as occupying the "throne of tyranny." His fall was prophesied in a Tablet (circa 1869) addressed to Fu'ád Páshá, Ottoman foreign minister while Bahá'u'lláh was imprisoned in 'Akká. As a result of public discontent, heightened by a crop failure in 1873 and a mounting public debt, he was deposed by his ministers in 1876.

'ABDU'L-BAHÁ *Servant of Bahá:* the title assumed by 'Abbás Effendi (23 May 1844–28 November 1921), eldest son and appointed successor of Bahá'u'lláh and the Center of His Covenant. Upon Bahá'u'lláh's ascension in 1892, 'Abdu'l-Bahá became Head of the Bahá'í Faith in accordance with provisions revealed by Bahá'u'lláh in the Kitáb-i-Aqdas and the Book of the Covenant. Among the titles by which He is known are the Center of the Covenant, the Mystery of God, the Master, and the Perfect Exemplar of Bahá'u'lláh's teachings.

'ABDU'L-ḤAMÍD II (1842–1918) Sultan of the Ottoman Empire, 1876–1909. He and his uncle, Sulṭán 'Abdu'l-'Azíz, who preceded him, were responsible for forty-six of 'Abdu'l-Bahá's fifty-six years of imprisonment and exile and for Bahá'u'lláh's banishments to Constantinople, Adrianople, and 'Akká. The Young Turks Rebellion in 1908 forced 'Abdu'l-Ḥamíd to reinstate the constitution he had suspended and to free all political and religious prisoners. As a result, 'Abdu'l-Bahá was released from house arrest in September 1908. 'Abdu'l-Ḥamíd was deposed the following year.

ABRAHAM Considered by Bahá'ís to be a Manifestation of God. He is also recognized as the founder of monotheism and the father of the Jewish and Arab people. According to the book of Genesis in the Bible, He left Ur, in Mesopotamia, because He was called by God to found a new nation (Canaan). He obeyed God without question, receiving repeated promises and a covenant that his seed would inherit the land. Muḥammad, the Báb, and Bahá'u'lláh are among His descendants. In Bahá'í texts He is often called the "Friend of God" and the "Father of the Faithful."

272

ADMINISTRATIVE ORDER The international system for administering the affairs of the Bahá'í community. Its prominent features, authority, and principles of operation are clearly set forth in the sacred texts of the Bahá'í Faith and their authorized interpretations. It consists, on the one hand, of a series of elected councils, universal, secondary and local, in which are vested legislative, executive and judicial powers over the Bahá'í community and, on the other, of eminent and devoted believers appointed to protect and propagate the Faith under the guidance of the Head of the Faith. The Administrative Order is the nucleus and pattern of the **new world order** Bahá'u'lláh has ushered in.

'AKKÁ (Acre, Akko) A four-thousand-year-old seaport and prison-city in northern Israel surrounded by fortress-like walls facing the sea. In the mid-1800s 'Akká became a penal colony to which the worst criminals of the Ottoman Empire were sent. In 1868 Bahá'u'lláh and His family and companions were banished to 'Akká by Sulṭán 'Abdu'l-'Azíz. Bahá'u'lláh was incarcerated within its barracks for two years, two months, and five days. Restrictions were gradually relaxed, and He lived in a series of houses within 'Akká until June 1877, when He moved outside the city walls. Bahá'u'lláh named 'Akká "the Most Great Prison."

ALEXANDRIAN AGE The period in which Alexander the Great reigned, 356–323 B.C.

'ALÍ-MUḤAMMAD Given name of the Báb.

ÁQÁ An honorific title, roughly equivalent to the English "sir" or "mister." Eg.: Mírzá Áqá Ján.

ÁQÁ JÁN, MÍRZÁ (1837–1901) Secretary of Bahá'u'lláh who accompanied Him throughout many parts of His exile.

AZAL (1831/2–1912) A half-brother of Bahá'u'lláh. His given name was Mírzá Yaḥyá. He was known later by the title Ṣubḥ-i-Azal (Morn of Eternity), or simply Azal. It was he who attempted a breach in the ranks of the Báb's followers after His death by rebelling against Bahá'u'lláh.

B

BÁB, THE *The Gate:* title assumed by Siyyid 'Alí-Muḥammad (20 October 1819–9 July 1850) after declaring His mission in Shíráz in 1844. The Báb's station is twofold: He is a Manifestation of God and the Founder of the Bábí Faith, and He is the Herald of Bahá'u'lláh.

BÁBÍ Follower of the Báb.

BAHÁ'U'LLÁH *The Glory of God:* title of Mírzá Ḥusayn-'Alí (12 November 1817–29 May 1892), Founder of the Bahá'í Faith. Bahá'ís refer to Him with a variety of titles, including the Promised One of All Ages, the Blessed Beauty, the Blessed Perfection, the Ancient Beauty.

BAHÍYYIH KHÁNUM *The Greatest Holy Leaf; the Most Exalted Leaf:* saintly daughter of Bahá'u'lláh and outstanding heroine of the Bahá'í Dispensation (1846–1932).

BAHJÍ *Delight, gladness, joy:* the name of the property north of 'Akká, Israel, where the Shrine of Bahá'u'lláh is situated and where Bahá'u'lláh lived from 1880 until His ascension in 1892.

BÁZÁR (bazaar) An Oriental market that usually consists of rows of shops or stalls where all kinds of goods are offered for sale.

BLACK PIT The subterranean dungeon in Tehran where Bahá'u'lláh was imprisoned from August through December 1852. Here, chained in darkness three flights of stairs underground, in the company of his fellow-Bábís and some 150 thieves and assassins, He received the first intimations of His world mission.

C

CAIAPHAS High priest of Jerusalem who governed the city during the time of Jesus.

CEDRIC, THE Steamship on which 'Abdu'l-Bahá journeyed to the United States in 1912.

COLLECTIVE SECURITY A principle taught by Bahá'u'lláh and elaborated by Shoghi Effendi that prescribes a system in which force is made to serve justice and which provides for the existence of an international peacekeeping force that will safeguard the organic unity of all nations.

COVENANT Generally, an agreement or contract between two or more people, usually formal, solemn, and binding. A religious covenant is a binding agreement between God and humankind, whereby God requires of humankind certain behavior in return for which He guarantees certain blessings, or whereby He gives humanity certain bounties in return for which He takes from those who accept them an effort to behave in a certain way. There are two types of religious covenant: The first is the Greater Covenant, which every Manifestation of God makes with His followers, promising that in the fullness of time a new Manifestation will be sent, and requiring that the followers will accept Him when this occurs. There is also the Lesser Covenant that a Manifestation of God makes with His followers that they will accept His appointed successor after Him.

D

DANIEL Biblical prophet of the Old Testament who predicted the appearance of Bahá'u'lláh in Daniel 12:6–7 and 12:11–12. 'Abdu'l-Bahá gives an explanation of these verses in *Some Answered Questions*, p. 43.

DAY OF GATHERING See **Day of Judgment.**

DAY OF JUDGMENT The time of the appearance of the Manifestation of God, when the true character of souls is judged according to their response to His revelation. Also known as the Day of Resurrection. Additionally, it can refer to the time after death when a soul stands before God and is called to account for its deeds in this life.

DISPENSATION The period of time during which the laws and teachings of a Prophet of God have spiritual authority. For example, the Dispensation of Jesus Christ lasted until the beginning of the Muḥammadan Dispensation, usually fixed at the year A.D. 622, when Muḥammad emigrated from Mecca to Medina. The Islamic Dispensation lasted until the advent of the Báb in 1844. The Dispensation of the Báb ended when Bahá'u'lláh experienced the intimation of His mission in the Black Pit, the subterranean dungeon in Tehran in which He was imprisoned between August and

December 1852. The Dispensation of Bahá'u'lláh will last until the advent of the next Manifestation of God, which Bahá'u'lláh asserts will occur in no less than one thousand years.

G

GENTILE A person of a non-Jewish nation or of non-Jewish faith.

GREATER COVENANT See **Covenant.**

GUARDIAN OF THE CAUSE OF GOD The institution, anticipated by Bahá'u'lláh in the Most Holy Book and established by 'Abdu'l-Bahá in His Will and Testament, to which **Shoghi Effendi** was appointed. The Guardianship and the **Universal House of Justice** are the twin successors of Bahá'u'lláh and 'Abdu'l-Bahá. The Guardian's chief functions are to interpret the writings of Bahá'u'lláh, the Báb, and 'Abdu'l-Bahá and to be the permanent head of the Universal House of Justice.

H

ḤUSAYN, MULLÁ (circa 1814–49) The first person to believe in the Báb.

ḤUSAYN-'ALÍ, MÍRZÁ See **Bahá'u'lláh.**

I

INTERNATIONAL AUXILIARY LANGUAGE A language that, according to Bahá'u'lláh, will be chosen in the future to improve communication between all the peoples of the world. It will not supplant or suppress existing native languages but will rather be used to facilitate harmony between the nations of the world.

J

JESUS (6–4 B.C.–A.D. 30) Recognized by Bahá'ís as a Manifestation of God and the Founder of Christianity. The Bahá'í writings often refer to Jesus as "the Spirit of God" and "the Son."

JOB The legendary figure featured in the book of Job in the Old Testament. He remained faithful to God despite appalling hardship and suffering.

K

KARBILÁ A city in central Iraq considered holy by Shí'ih Muslims. It was the site of the martyrdom of Imám Ḥusayn, the third Imam, and is the site of his shrine, making it a place of pilgrimage for Shí'ih Muslims.

KÁẒIM, SIYYID (1793–1843) Leader of the Shaykhí Islamic movement that predicted the imminent appearance of two figures in rapid succession who would establish God's reign on earth. He believed that the appointed time was very close at hand and, shortly before his death, called upon his followers to scatter far and wide in search of the first figure.

KORAN The holy book of Islam, regarded by Bahá'ís as divinely revealed scripture.

L

LESSER COVENANT See **Covenant.**

LESSER PEACE The first of two major stages in which Bahá'ís believe world peace will be established. The Lesser Peace is a political peace that will come about through a binding treaty among the nations for the political unification of the world. It will involve fixing every nation's boundaries, strictly limiting the size of their armaments, laying down the principles underlying the relations among governments, and ascertaining all international agreements and obligations. Its establishment will portend the coming of the second stage, the Most Great Peace, a condition of permanent, worldwide peace and prosperity that will be founded on the spirited principles and institutions of the World Order of Bahá'u'lláh. It will be the consequence of the spiritualization of the world and the fusion of all its races, creeds, classes, and nations into one human family and will represent the fulfillment of prophecies regarding the establishment of the Kingdom of God on earth.

LOCAL SPIRITUAL ASSEMBLY A Bahá'í administrative institution ordained in the writings of Bahá'u'lláh and composed of nine elected members operating at the local level. It is elected according to Bahá'í principles and is responsible for coordinating and directing the affairs of the Bahá'í community in its area of jurisdiction.

M

MANIFESTATION OF GOD Designation of a Prophet "endowed with constancy" Who is the Founder of a religious Dispensation, inasmuch as in His words, His person, and His actions He manifests the nature and purpose of God in accordance with the capacity and needs of the people to whom He comes.

MASTER, THE A title of 'Abdu'l-Bahá referring to the virtues He manifested and to His role as an enduring model for humanity to emulate.

MATERIALISTS Refers to those who do not believe in God and who seek to explain all matters on the basis of reason alone or to those who are excessively preoccupied with material pursuits such as wealth and power.

MECCA A city in Saudi Arabia that is the holy city of Islam and the birthplace of Muḥammad (A.D. 570). It is the principal place of pilgrimage for Muslims.

MEDINA A city in Saudi Arabia—Mecca's sister city to which Muḥammad and His followers fled in A.D. 622, marking the beginning of the Muslim calendar. It was home to the first Muslim community.

MESSIAH In Hebrew, literally "anointed." In Judaism, the term refers to the expected king and deliverer of the Jews. In Christianity, it refers to Jesus.

MIHDÍ, MÍRZÁ (1848–70) *The Purest Branch:* a son of Bahá'u'lláh and brother of 'Abdu'l-Bahá. He died at the age of twenty-two in 1870 when he fell through a skylight while engrossed in prayer on the roof of the prison barracks in 'Akká. He asked Bahá'u'lláh to accept his life as a ransom so that pilgrims prevented from attaining Bahá'u'lláh's presence would be enabled to do so.

MILLER, REVEREND WILLIAM (1782–1849) An American religious leader who in 1831 began preaching that the world would end around 1843. He based his predictions on a prophecy in the book of Daniel (8:13–14). His followers became known as "Millerites." After 1843 passed with no incident, some of his colleagues changed the time of the end to 1844—the year in which the Báb declared His mission.

MÍRZÁ A contraction of *Amír-Zádih,* meaning son of an amír (governor, lord, commander). When it follows a name, it signifies "prince"; when it precedes, it means simply "Mr."

MONGOL Refers to the invaders who looted Baghdad in A.D. 1258 and 1401.

MOSES (circa 1300 B.C.) Founder of Judaism, regarded by Bahá'ís as a Manifestation of God. The Bahá'í writings sometimes refer to Moses as "He who conversed with God."

MUḤAMMAD (circa A.D. 570–632) Founder of Islam, regarded by Bahá'ís as a Manifestation of God. He is often referred to in the Bahá'í writings as the "Friend of God," the "Prophet," and "the Apostle."

MULLÁ A Muslim trained in theology and Islamic jurisprudence; a Muslim theologian or cleric.

N

NAJAF A city in south central Iraq considered holy by Sh͟í'ih Muslims. It was the site of the martyrdom of the Imám 'Alí, the cousin of Muḥammad, making it a place of pilgrimage for Sh͟í'ih Muslims, who visit his shrine.

NÁṢIRI'D-DÍN-SH͟ÁH (1831–96) Notorious shah of Persia (now Iran) under whose reign the Báb was executed and Bahá'u'lláh was imprisoned and exiled. He was assassinated in 1896.

NATIONAL SPIRITUAL ASSEMBLY A Bahá'í administrative institution, established by 'Abdu'l-Bahá in His Will and Testament, that is responsible for coordinating and directing the affairs of a Bahá'í community at a nationwide level.

NAVVÁB (an honorific implying "Grace" or "Highness"); *the Most Exalted Leaf* (1820–86): wife of Bahá'u'lláh and mother of 'Abdu'l-Bahá, Bahíyyih K͟hánum, and Mírzá Mihdí. She was married to Bahá'u'lláh in 1835, accompanied Him in His exiles, and died in 1886.

NEW WORLD ORDER Bahá'u'lláh's scheme for worldwide solidarity that is destined to embrace all of humanity in the fullness of time. The current Bahá'í Administrative Order is its nucleus and pattern, providing the rudiments of a future all-enfolding Bahá'í commonwealth.

O

OLD WORLD ORDER The existing system of philosophies, beliefs, and political governance that Shoghi Effendi describes as "effete and godless, that has stubbornly refused, despite the signs and portents of a century-old Revelation, to attune its processes to the precepts and ideals which that Heaven-sent Faith proffered it." Bahá'u'lláh predicts that this system will eventually be "rolled up" and replaced by the **new world order.**

OTTOMAN EMPIRE The Turkish dynasty based in Constantinople (modern-day Istanbul) that ruled over Adrianople, 'Akká, and Baghdad during the time of Bahá'u'lláh. Its leaders, Sulṭán 'Abdu'l-'Azíz and Sulṭán 'Abdu'l-Ḥamíd II, were responsible for the imprisonment and banishment of Bahá'u'lláh and 'Abdu'l-Bahá in Constantinople, Adrianople, and 'Akká. Both leaders were eventually deposed.

P

PROMISED ONE See **Bahá'u'lláh.**

PROPHET Two types of prophets are mentioned in Bahá'í writings—the Lesser prophets and the Greater Prophets. Lesser prophets, such as Isaiah and Daniel, can predict future events and are followers of the Greater Prophets. Greater Prophets, such as Abraham, Moses, Jesus, Muḥammad, the Báb, and Bahá'u'lláh, are independent Manifestations of God who come to renew the Word of God and establish a new religion.

S

SHAH A king of Iran.

SHAYKH Title of respect given to elderly men, men of authority, elders, chiefs, professors, or superiors of a dervish order.

SHÍ'IH ISLAM One of the two major branches of Islam (the other being Sunní), distinguished by its belief in the Imamate as the rightful succession of religious authority in Islam after the death of Muḥammad. The dominant branch of Islam in Iran.

SHÍRÁZ / SHIRAZ The city in Iran where, in His home, the Báb declared His mission to Mullá Ḥusayn on 22 May 1844.

SHOGHI EFFENDI The title by which Shoghi Rabbání (1 March 1897–4 November 1957), great-grandson of Bahá'u'lláh and eldest grandson of 'Abdu'l-Bahá, is generally known to Bahá'ís. (*Shoghi* is an Arabic name meaning "the one who longs"; *Effendi* is a Turkish honorific signifying "sir" or "master.") He was appointed Guardian of the Bahá'í Faith by 'Abdu'l-Bahá in His Will and Testament and assumed the office upon 'Abdu'l-Bahá's passing in 1921.

SINAI Mountain situated where the Lord revealed the Ten Commandments to Moses.

SIYYID Literally *lord, chief, prince:* an honorific title denoting a descendant of the Prophet Muḥammad.

SUNNÍ ISLAM Branch of Islam that accepts the authority of the caliphs as leaders of Islam and rejects the claims of the hereditary imams.

T

TEHRAN / ṬIHRÁN Capital of present-day Iran and the site of Bahá'u'lláh's revelation in the underground dungeon known as the Black Pit, where He was falsely imprisoned after the attempted assassination of the shah in 1852.

U

UNIVERSAL HOUSE OF JUSTICE The supreme governing and legislative body of the Bahá'í Faith. The Guardianship and the Universal House of Justice are the twin, crowning institutions of the Bahá'í Administrative Order. Elected every five years at an international Bahá'í convention, the Universal House of Justice gives spiritual guidance to, and directs the administrative activities of, the worldwide Bahá'í community. It is the institution Bahá'u'lláh ordained as the agency invested with authority to legislate on matters not covered in His writings. In His Will and Testament 'Abdu'l-Bahá elaborates on its functions and affirms that it is infallibly guided.

V

VAḤÍD *Peerless:* Title given by the Báb to a leading Muslim clergyman who was assigned by the shah to investigate the Báb and His claims, and who, after conducting several interviews with Him, became one of His most ardent followers. He was later martyred for his beliefs.

W

WILL AND TESTAMENT OF 'ABDU'L-BAHÁ A document unique in the history of religion, the Will and Testament of 'Abdu'l-Bahá is the charter for the Bahá'í Administrative Order. Written, signed, and sealed by 'Abdu'l-Bahá, it—among other things—affirms the nature of the Báb's mission, discloses Bahá'u'lláh's station, declares the fundamental teachings of the Bahá'í Faith, establishes the institution of the Guardianship, and appoints Shoghi Effendi as Guardian of the Cause of God.

Y

YOUNG TURKS A group of insurgents who threatened to overthrow the Ottoman government in 1908. As a result of their demands, all political and religious prisoners—including 'Abdu'l-Bahá—were set free. In 1909 Sulṭán 'Abdu'l-Ḥamíd was deposed.

Z

ZOROASTER (660–583 B.C.) Accepted by Bahá'ís as an independent Manifestation of God and Founder of the Zoroastrian religion. Bahá'u'lláh is a descendant of Zoroaster. Zoroaster predicted the coming of a world redeemer named S̲h̲áh-Bahrám, who would create an era of world peace. Bahá'ís believe the figure referred to in this prophecy is Bahá'u'lláh.

BIBLIOGRAPHY

Works of Bahá'u'lláh

Epistle to the Son of the Wolf. Translated by Shoghi Effendi. 1st pocket-size ed. Wilmette, Ill.: Bahá'í Publishing Trust, 1988.

Gleanings from the Writings of Bahá'u'lláh. 1st pocket-size ed. Translated by Shoghi Effendi. Wilmette, Ill.: Bahá'í Publishing Trust, 1983.

The Hidden Words. Translated by Shoghi Effendi. Wilmette, Ill.: Bahá'í Publishing, 2002.

The Kitáb-i-Aqdas: The Most Holy Book. 1st pocket-size ed. Wilmette, Ill.: Bahá'í Publishing Trust, 1993.

The Kitáb-i-Íqán: The Book of Certitude. Translated by Shoghi Effendi. Wilmette, Ill.: Bahá'í Publishing, 2003.

The Seven Valleys and the Four Valleys. New ed. Translated by Marzieh Gail and Ali-Kuli Khan. Wilmette, Ill.: Bahá'í Publishing Trust, 1991.

The Summons of the Lord of Hosts: Tablets of Bahá'u'lláh. Haifa, Israel: Bahá'í World Centre, 2002.

Tablets of Bahá'u'lláh revealed after the Kitáb-i-Aqdas. Compiled by the Research Department of the Universal House of Justice. Translated by Habib Taherzadeh et al. Wilmette, Ill.: Bahá'í Publishing Trust, 1988.

Works of 'Abdu'l-Bahá

'Abdu'l-Bahá in London: Addresses and Notes of Conversations. [Compiled by Eric Hammond.] London: Longmans Green, 1912; reprinted Bahá'í Publishing Trust, 1982.

Paris Talks: Addresses Given by 'Abdu'l-Bahá in Paris in 1911. 12th ed. London: Bahá'í Publishing Trust, 1995.

The Promulgation of Universal Peace: Talks Delivered by 'Abdu'l-Bahá during His Visit to the United States and Canada in 1912. Compiled by Howard MacNutt. 2d ed. Wilmette, Ill.: Bahá'í Publishing Trust, 1982.

The Secret of Divine Civilization. 1st pocket-size ed. Translated by Marzieh Gail and Ali-Kuli Khan. Wilmette, Ill.: Bahá'í Publishing Trust, 1990.

Selections from the Writings of 'Abdu'l-Bahá. Compiled by the Research Department of the Universal House of Justice. Translated by a Committee at the Bahá'í World Center and Marzieh Gail. Wilmette, Ill.: Bahá'í Publishing Trust, 1997.

Some Answered Questions. Compiled and translated by Laura Clifford Barney. 1st pocket-size ed. Wilmette, Ill.: Bahá'í Publishing Trust, 1984.

Will and Testament of 'Abdu'l-Bahá. Wilmette, Ill.: Bahá'í Publishing Trust, 1944.

Works of Shoghi Effendi

The Advent of Divine Justice. 1st pocket-size ed. Wilmette, Ill.: Bahá'í Publishing Trust, 1990.
Bahá'í Administration: Selected Messages 1922–1932. 7th ed. Wilmette, Ill.: Bahá'í Publishing Trust, 1974.
God Passes By. New ed. Wilmette, Ill.: Bahá'í Publishing Trust, 1974.
The Promised Day Is Come. 3rd ed. Wilmette, Ill.: Bahá'í Publishing Trust, 1980.
The World Order of Bahá'u'lláh: Selected Letters. 1st pocket-size ed. Wilmette, Ill.: Bahá'í Publishing Trust, 1991.

Works of the Universal House of Justice

The Promise of World Peace: To the Peoples of the World. Wilmette, Ill.: Bahá'í Publishing Trust, 1985.

Compilations

Bahá'u'lláh, 'Abdu'l-Bahá, Shoghi Effendi, and Bahíyyih Khánum. *Bahíyyih Khánum: The Greatest Holy Leaf.* Compiled by the Research Department at the Bahá'í World Centre. Haifa: Bahá'í World Centre, 1982.
[Shoghi Effendi and Lady Blomfield, comp.]. *The Passing of 'Abdu'l-Bahá: A Compilation.* Los Angeles: Kalimát Press, 1991.
[National Spiritual Assembly of the Bahá'ís of Japan, comp.]. *Japan Will Turn Ablaze! Tablets of 'Abdu'l-Bahá, Letters of Shoghi Effendi and Historical Notes About Japan.* Japan: Bahá'í Publishing Trust, 1974.
The Bahá'í World: An International Record, 2000–2001. Compiled by the Universal House of Justice. Haifa: Bahá'í World Centre, 2002.
The Compilation of Compilations: Prepared by the Universal House of Justice 1963–1990. 2 vols. Australia: Bahá'í Publications Australia, 1991.

Other Works

Adams, Rev. Isaac. *Persia by a Persian: Personal Experiences, Manners, Customs, Habits, Religious and Social Life in Persia.* Washington, D.C.: Rev. Isaac Adams, 1900.
Bahá'í International Community Office of Public Information. *Bahá'u'lláh.* Wilmette, Ill.: Bahá'í Publishing Trust, 1991.
Balyuzi, H. M. *'Abdu'l-Bahá: The Centre of the Covenant of Bahá'u'lláh.* London: George Ronald, 1971.
Balyuzi, H. M. *Bahá'u'lláh: The King of Glory.* Oxford: George Ronald, 1980.
Balyuzi, H. M. *Edward Granville Browne and the Bahá'í Faith.* Oxford: George Ronald, 1970.
Blomfield, Lady [Sitárih Khánum], *The Chosen Highway.* Wilmette, Ill.: Bahá'í Publishing Trust, n.d.; reprinted 1975.
Curzon, Lord. *Persia and the Persian Question.* London: Longmans, Green and Co., 1892.
Esslemont, J. E. *Bahá'u'lláh and the New Era: An Introduction to the Bahá'í Faith.* 5th rev. ed. Wilmette, Ill.: Bahá'í Publishing Trust, 1980.
Ives, Howard Colby. *Portals to Freedom.* Rev. ed. Oxford: George Ronald, 1983.
Marks, Geoffry W. *Call to Remembrance: Connecting the Heart to Bahá'u'lláh.* Wilmette, Ill.: Bahá'í Publishing Trust, 1992.
Momen, Moojan, ed. *The Bábí and Bahá'í Religions, 1844–1944: Some Contemporary Western Accounts.* Oxford: George Ronald, 1981.

Morrison, Gayle. *To Move the World: Louis G. Gregory and the Advancement of Racial Unity in America.* Foreword by Glenford E. Mitchell. Wilmette, Ill.: Bahá'í Publishing Trust, 1982.

Nábil-i-A'zam [Muḥammad-i-Zarandí]. *The Dawn-Breakers: Nabíl's Narrative of the Early Days of the Bahá'í Revelation.* Translated and edited by Shoghi Effendi. Wilmette, Ill.: Bahá'í Publishing Trust, 1932.

Périgord, Emily McBride. *Translation of French Foot-Notes of the Dawn-Breakers.* Wilmette, Ill.: Bahá'í Publishing Trust, 1939.

Phelps, Myron H. *The Master in 'Akká.* Los Angeles: Kalimát Press, 1985.

Rabbaní, Rúḥíyyih. *The Priceless Pearl.* London: Bahá'í Publishing Trust, 1969.

Taherzadeh, Adib. *The Revelation of Bahá'u'lláh: Baghdád 1853–63.* Rev. ed. Oxford: George Ronald, 1976.

SUGGESTED READING

By Bahá'u'lláh

Epistle to the Son of the Wolf. Translated by Shoghi Effendi. 1st pocket-size ed. Wilmette, Ill.: Bahá'í
Publishing Trust, 1988.

Gleanings from the Writings of Bahá'u'lláh. 1st pocket-size ed. Translated by Shoghi Effendi. Wilmette, Ill.: Bahá'í Publishing Trust, 1983.

The Hidden Words. Translated by Shoghi Effendi. Wilmette, Ill.: Bahá'í Publishing, 2002.

The Kitáb-i-Aqdas: The Most Holy Book. 1st pocket-size ed. Wilmette, Ill.: Bahá'í Publishing Trust,
1993.

The Kitáb-i-Íqán: The Book of Certitude. Translated by Shoghi Effendi. Wilmette, Ill.: Bahá'í Publishing, 2003.

The Seven Valleys and The Four Valleys. New ed. Translated by Marzieh Gail and Ali-Kuli Khan.
Wilmette, Ill.: Bahá'í Publishing Trust, 1991.

Tablets of Bahá'u'lláh revealed after the Kitáb-i-Aqdas. Compiled by the Research Department of the
Universal House of Justice. Translated by Habib Taherzadeh et al. Wilmette, Ill.: Bahá'í
Publishing Trust, 1988.

By 'Abdu'l-Bahá

*The Promulgation of Universal Peace: Talks Delivered by 'Abdu'l-Bahá during His Visit to the United
States and Canada in 1912.* Compiled by Howard MacNutt. 2d ed. Wilmette, Ill.: Bahá'í
Publishing Trust, 1982.

Selections from the Writings of 'Abdu'l-Bahá. Compiled by the Research Department of the Universal
House of Justice. Translated by a Committee at the Bahá'í World Center and Marzieh
Gail. Wilmette, Ill.: Bahá'í Publishing Trust, 1997.

Some Answered Questions. Compiled and translated by Laura Clifford Barney. 1st pocket-size ed.
Wilmette, Ill.: Bahá'í Publishing Trust, 1984.

By Shoghi Effendi

God Passes By. New ed. Wilmette, Ill.: Bahá'í Publishing Trust, 1974.

The World Order of Bahá'u'lláh: Selected Letters. 1st pocket-size ed. Wilmette, Ill.: Bahá'í Publishing
Trust, 1991.

By the Universal House of Justice

The Promise of World Peace: To the Peoples of the World. Wilmette, Ill.: Bahá'í Publishing Trust, 1985.

Compilations of Bahá'í Writings

Bahá'u'lláh, the Báb, and 'Abdu'l-Bahá. *Bahá'í Prayers: A Selection of Prayers Revealed by Bahá'u'lláh, the Báb, and 'Abdu'l-Bahá.* New ed. Wilmette, Ill.: Bahá'í Publishing Trust, 2002.

Bahá'u'lláh, the Báb, 'Abdu'l-Bahá, Shoghi Effendi, the Universal House of Justice. *Bahá'í Marriage and Family Life: Selections from the Writings of the Bahá'í Faith.* [Compiled by the National Spiritual Assembly of the Bahá'ís of Canada.] N.p.: National Spiritual Assembly of the Bahá'ís of Canada, 1983.

Bahá'u'lláh, the Báb, 'Abdu'l-Bahá, and Shoghi Effendi. *Refresh and Gladden my Spirit: Prayers and Meditations from Bahá'í Scripture.* Compiled by Pam Brode. Wilmette, Ill.: Bahá'í Publishing Trust, 2002.

Bahá'u'lláh, 'Abdu'l-Bahá. *Waging Peace: Selections From the Bahá'í Writings on Universal Peace.* Los Angeles: Kalimat Press, 1985.

Other Works

Balyuzi, H. M. *'Abdu'l-Bahá: The Center of the Covenant of Bahá'u'lláh.* London: George Ronald, 1971.

Balyuzi, H. M. *Bahá'u'lláh: The King of Glory.* Oxford: George Ronald, 1980.

Esslemont, J. E. *Bahá'u'lláh and the New Era: An Introduction to the Bahá'í Faith.* 5th rev. ed. Wilmette, Ill.: Bahá'í Publishing Trust, 1980.

Hatcher, William S., and J. Douglas Martin. *The Bahá'í Faith: The Emerging Global Religion.* Wilmette, Ill.: Bahá'í Publishing Trust, 2002.

Khan, Janet A. and Peter J. Khan. *Advancement of Women: A Bahá'í Perspective.* Wilmette, Ill.: Bahá'í Publishing, 2003.

Matthews, Gary. *He Cometh with Clouds.* Oxford: George Ronald, 1996.

Matthews, Gary. *The Challenge of Bahá'u'lláh.* Oxford: George Ronald, 1993.

Momen, Moojan. *Hinduism and the Bahá'í Faith.* Oxford: George Ronald, 1990.

Nábil-i-A'zam [Muhammad-i-Zarandí]. *The Dawn-Breakers: Nabíl's Narrative of the Early Days of the Bahá'í Revelation.* Translated and edited by Shoghi Effendi. Wilmette, Ill.: Bahá'í Publishing Trust, 1932.

The National Spiritual Assembly of the Bahá'ís of the United States. *The Vision of Race Unity: America's Most Challenging Issue.* Wilmette, Ill.: Bahá'í Publishing Trust, 1991.

The National Spiritual Assembly of the Bahá'ís of the United States. *Two Wings of a Bird: The Equality of Women and Men.* Wilmette, Ill.: Bahá'í Publishing Trust, 1997.

Sears, William. *Thief in the Night: Or The Strange Case of the Missing Millennium.* Oxford: George Ronald, 1980.

Sheppherd, Joseph. *A Wayfarer's Guide to Bringing the Sacred Home.* Wilmette, Ill.: Bahá'í Publishing, 2002.

Smith, Peter. *A Concise Encyclopedia of the Bahá'í Faith.* Oxford: Oneworld Publications, 2000.

Smith, Peter. *A Short History of the Bahá'í Faith.* Oxford: Oneworld Publications, 1996.

Sours, Michael. *Prophecies of Jesus.* Oxford: Oneworld Publications, 1991.

Thompson, Thom. *Questions from Christians about Baha'u'llah and the Baha'i Faith.* [N.p.: Xlibris Corporation, 2001.

Townshend, George. *Christ and Bahá'u'lláh.* Rev. ed. Oxford: George Ronald, 1966.

Townshend, George. *The Heart of the Gospel.* 2d ed., rev. and enl. Oxford: George Ronald, 1951; Wilmette, Ill.: Bahá'í Publishing Trust, 1972.

INDEX

A

'Abbas Effendi. *See* 'Abdu'l-Bahá
Abbasid dynasty, 39
  glossary definition for, 272
'Abdu'l-'Azíz, Sulṭán (Ottoman sultan)
  Bahá'u'lláh's foresight about, 102
  Bahá'u'lláh writes to, 65–66
  glossary definition for, 272
'Abdu'l-Bahá (Servant of Bahá)
  in 'Akká, 141
  Bahá'u'lláh and, 79–80, 138–39
  as Bahá'u'lláh's successor, 136
  Black Pit and, 29, 137
  as the Center of the Covenant, 139
  character of, 138, 145, 147–48, 205–7,
    208–9
  as a child, 136–37
  freedom of, 143, 146
  glossary definition for, 272
  Knighthood of, 207
  passing of, 207–8
  physical description of, 138, 147, 205
  the poor and, 206
  power of presence of, 145–48, 204
  as prisoner, 141
  in social circles, 146–47
  Titanic and, 200–201
  titles of, 139–40
  in the West, 146–47, 159, 161, 173,
    203–4, 220
  Will and Testament of, 213–14, 279
  World War I and, 204–5
'Abdu'l-Ḥamíd II, Sulṭán, 125–26, 142–43
  glossary definition for, 272
Abraham, glossary definition for, 272
Abu Bakr, 135
Adam and Eve, 173
administrative order
  description of, 218–20
  glossary definition for, 273
  membership on institutions of, 222–23
  uniqueness of, 224–25
Adrianople, Bahá'u'lláh in, 59, 71–72
afflictions, purpose of, 199–202
afterlife, the soul and, 107–9, 243–45
'Akká (Acre, Accho)
  'Abdu'l-Bahá in, 141
  Bahá'u'lláh in, 72–76, 77–82, 126, 252
  glossary definition for, 273
  pilgrims journey to, 77
al-Amín (the Trusted One). *See* Muḥammad
    (the Prophet)
alcohol, 195
Alexander II (czar of Russia), 68
Alexandrian Age, 9
  glossary definition for, 273
'Alí, as Muḥammad's successor, 135
'Alí-Muḥammad
  glossary definition for, 273
  See also Báb, the

287

Allenby, General, 204–5
America
    'Abdu'l-Bahá in, 203–4
    racial prejudice in, 161
American republics, Bahá'u'lláh writes to
        rulers of, 69–70
Amos, 74
'Amú, Mullá Ḥasan, 54–55
Ancient Beauty. *See* Bahá'u'lláh
Áqá, glossary definition for, 273
Áqá Ján, Mírzá
    as Bahá'u'lláh's secretary, 90–91
    glossary definition for, 273
Arabic
    Bahá'u'lláh's mastery of, 89–90
    Hidden Words in, 40
    Most Holy Book in, 81
Aristotle, 244
arts, importance of, 196–97
asceticism, 193
Ásíyih Khánum (Navváb), 165, 277
attributes of God
    in humanity, 94–95, 158, 159–60
    in Prophets, 99, 239–40. 104
Azal (Mírzá Yaḥyá)
    campaigns against Bahá'u'lláh, 60–62,
        71, 77–78, 214
    glossary definition for, 273
    killing of followers of, 78
Azerbaijan, the Báb in, 22

B

Báb, the (Gate of God)
    in Azerbaijan, 22
    claims of, 16, 38
    foresight of, 38, 102
    glossary definition for, 273
    "He Whom God shall make manifest"
        and, 16, 27, 38
    influence of, 37
    in Isfahan, 21
    Jesus and, 36, 37–38
    in Máh-Kú, 22
    martyrdom of, 23–26, 27, 38
    ministry of, 16, 36, 38
    Mullá Ḥusayn and, 13–15

physical description of, 24
    as Promised One, 23
    prophecies of, 27
    remains of, at Shrine, 124
    as salvation for humanity, 38
    in Shiraz, 21
    in Tabriz, 23
    teachings of, 22
Bábís
    Bahá'u'lláh as leader of, 27–28, 39
    glossary definition for, 273
    persecution of, 23, 24, 30–31, 101–2
    youth attempt to kill shah, 28
Baghdad, Bahá'u'lláh in, 33, 39, 40, 55–56,
        57, 188, 244
Bahá, significance of, 219n
Bahá'í Faith
    being member of, 254–55
    investigation of, 259–60
    persecution of, 257
    spread of, 257–58
    teachings of, 5–6, 40–43
    vision of, 4–5
Bahá'í Houses of Worship, 224
Bahá'ís
    martyrdom of, 101–2
    meaning of name, 60
Bahá'u'lláh
    'Abdu'l-Bahá and, 138–39
    addresses rulers, 63–70, 117–18, 176,
        181–82, 216–17
    in Adrianople, 59, 71–72
    in 'Akká, 72–76, 77–82, 126, 252
    awareness of station, 100
    Azal campaigns against, 60–62, 71, 77–
        78, 214
    as Bábí leader, 27–28, 39
    background of, 17–19
    in Baghdad, 33, 39, 40, 55–56, 57, 188,
        244
    in Bahjí, 82–83
    in Black Pit, 28–29, 31–32
    in Constantinople, 58–59
    corresponds with followers, 121–22
    declaration of, 57, 60, 102
    education of, 18, 89–90
    foresight of, 102

Bahá'u'lláh *(continued)*
  glossary definition for, 273
  and God, relationship with, 104
  in Haifa, 124
  in Holy Land, 74–75
  imprisonment of, 73–76, 79
  miracles of, 54–55, 242
  at Mount Carmel, 82–83, 124
  murder attempts on, 53–54
  passing of, 125–26
  poisoning of, 61–62
  power of presence of, 43–45, 83–85,
    123–24
  as Promised One, 5, 249–50, 251
  prophecy and, 103, 105, 248–49
  as return of Christ, 238–39
  revelation of (*See* revelation of
    Bahá'u'lláh)
  as salvation for humanity, 76, 128, 133,
    154, 250, 252–53, 254
  shrine of, 126
  sufferings of, 76, 127–28, 252
  in Sulaymaniyyah, 40
  teachings of, 5–6, 40–43
  writings of (*See* writings of Bahá'u'lláh)
Bahíyyih Khánum
  character of, 165–66
  glossary definition for, 273
Bahjí
  atmosphere of, 123
  Bahá'u'lláh in, 82–83
  glossary definition for, 273
  shrine of Bahá'u'lláh at, 126
baptism, Bahá'í writings on, 241
Báqir-i-Shírází, Mírzá, 90–91
bázár, glossary definition for, 274
Bell, Alexander Graham, 146
Berlin, 67
Bhagavad-Gita, 246
Bible, 48–51, 232–33, 237–39
bird, analogy of, 162–63, 174
Bixby, Reverend James T., 148
Black Pit
  'Abdu'l-Bahá and, 29, 137
  Bahá'u'lláh in, 28–29, 31–32
  glossary definition for, 274
Blessed Beauty. *See* Bahá'u'lláh

Blessed Perfection. *See* Bahá'u'lláh
Blomfield, Sara Louisa, 147
body, connection with soul, 195–96
Book of Certitude, 47, 52, 175–76, 238–39
book of Revelation, 236–37
Book of the Covenant, 133–34
Browne, Edward Granville
  describes 'Abdu'l-Bahá, 138
  describes Bahá'u'lláh, 122–24
Buddhism, 245–46

C

Caiaphas, 200
  glossary definition for, 274
calling, 191–93
Canada, 'Abdu'l-Bahá in, 146
Carnegie, Andrew, 146
Catholicism, Roman, 135
Cave of Elijah, 124
Cedric, The
  'Abdu'l-Bahá and, 201
  glossary definition for, 274
celibacy, 193
Center of the Covenant, 139
character, good, 213–14
  importance of, 116–17, 203–4, 254–55
  spiritual growth and, 150, 153–54, 254
Chase, Thornton, 145
chastity, 190
Chicago, 'Abdu'l-Bahá in, 159
children
  education of, 177
  music and, 197
Christ. *See* Jesus Christ
Christianity
  Bahá'í Faith on, 231–33
  divisions in, 134–35
  spread of, 258
Christians, German, 74
civilization, material, 173–74
civilization, spiritual, 173–74, 217
cleanliness, 195
clergy, 176
"clouds" in New Testament, 48–49
collective security, 182
  glossary definition for, 274

communication, improvements in, 182
conduct, good. *See* character, good
Conference of the National Association for
        the Advancement of Colored
        People, 159
Constantinople, Bahá'u'lláh in, 58–59
consultation, 220–21
Cormick, Dr., 23–24
covenant
    glossary definition for, 274
    Greater and Lesser, 134, 136
    See also Covenant of Bahá'u'lláh
Covenant of Bahá'u'lláh (Lesser Covenant),
        134, 136
    attempts to breach, 259
    Center of, 139
    establishment of, 81, 218
    steadfastness to, 214
creation, story of, 172–73
currency, universal, 180, 229
Curzon, Lord, 10–11

D

Daniel (the prophet)
    book of, 237
    glossary definition for, 274
    Iran and, 9
David, King, 74
Day of God, 103, 251
    See also Day of Judgment
Day of Judgment
    explanation of, 103–4, 246–47
    glossary definition for, 274
Day of Resurrection, 103–4, 251
    See also Day of Judgment
death
    accounting for deeds after, 119, 150, 243
    praying for after, 243–44
    premature, 202
    the soul after, 107–9, 243–45
deeds
    accounting for, 119, 150, 243
    words and, 160, 161
de Gobineau, Comte, 36–37
departed, praying for, 243–44
detachment, 115–16

dispensation, glossary definition for, 274–75
divine civilization, 173–74, 217
divorce, 194
drugs, 195
Dublin, New Hampshire, 146

E

economic legislation, 178
Edirne, Turkey. *See* Adrianople
education
    of children, 177, 197
    of music, 197
    two aspects of, 177
    of women, 162–63, 164–65, 166
Egypt, 'Abdu'l-Bahá in, 146
Elias (Elijah), return of, 235–36, 239
Empedocles, 244
Epistle to the Son of the Wolf, 125
equality of men and women, 162–67, 164
Esslemont, Dr. John, 83
Europe, 'Abdu'l-Bahá in, 146
Eve, Adam and, 173
evil, 242–43
evolution, human. *See* human evolution

F

faith
    definition of, 114
    good works and, 241
    in laws of God, 112–13
family, unity of, 194
fasting, 152–53
fear of God, 118–19
Feast, 224
forgiveness, divine, 243–44
France, 'Abdu'l-Bahá in, 146, 173, 220
freedom
    of expression, 221
    obedience and, 113–14
Freud, Sigmund, 176

G

garden in Baghdad, 56, 57
gentile, glossary definition for, 275

German Christians, 74
Germany, Bahá'u'lláh's foresight about, 67, 102
God
    attributes of, in humanity, 94–95, 158, 159–60
    attributes of, in Prophets, 99, 104, 239–40
    fear of, 118–19
    love of, 41, 95, 115–16, 149–50, 158
    nature of, 47–48, 93–95
    nearness to (See nearness to God)
    oneness of, 93, 97, 157
    will of, 151
Golden Age, 225
Golden Rule, 158
good works, faith and, 241
government
    international body of, 182–85
    war and, 183
grace, Bahá'í writings on, 241
Great Britain
    'Abdu'l-Bahá in, 146–47
    Bahá'u'lláh praised, 217
Great Disappointment, the, 12
Greater Covenant, 134, 136
Greek Orthodox Church, 135
Guardian of the Cause of God
    glossary definition for, 275
    See also Shoghi Effendi

H

Haifa
    Bahá'u'lláh in, 124
    Universal House of Justice in, 218, 248
    See also Mount Carmel
happiness
    attainment of, 150, 189, 209
    freedom and, 113–14
    laws of God and, 42, 190, 209
    obstacle to, 203
    service as, 193
    in the spiritual world, 109
Haydar-'Alí, describes Bahá'u'lláh, 83–85
healing, 152, 195–96
health, 195–96
Hearst, Phoebe, 145

heaven, 109–10, 243
hell, 109–10, 243
Hidden Words, 40–43
Hinduism, 245–46
Hippocrates, 244
Holy Land, 74–75, 247
    See also 'Akká; Haifa; Mount Carmel
Holy Spirit, 247
holy war, 256
human beings, two natures of, 114–15
human evolution
    next stage in, 182, 227–30
    story of creation and, 172–73
humanity
    attributes of God in, 94–95, 158, 159–60
    evolution of, 172–73, 182, 227–30
    oneness of, 158–62, 203–4, 227–30
    sufferings of, 180–81
    testing of, 50, 51
    two wings of, 162–63, 174
    unity of, 182, 227–30, 253
Husayn, Mullá
    the Báb and, 13–15
    glossary definition for, 275
    martyrdom of, 27
    in Tehran, 17
Husayn-'Alí, Mírzá. See Bahá'u'lláh

I

Immaculate Manifestation of Krishna, 246
independent investigation of truth, 105, 175–76, 256, 259–60
international auxiliary language
    adoption of, 179–80, 229
    glossary definition for, 275
international governing body, 182–85
    See also world commonwealth
interracial marriage, 161–62
Iran (Persia), 9–11
    conditions of, 99
    women of, 163–64
Isfahan, the Báb in, 21
Islam
    the Bible and, 232–33
    Promised One of, 12
    sects of, 135

Islamic civilization, 98
Ismá'íl, 44
Ives, Howard Colby, 146–47, 209

J

Jesus Christ
    achievements of, 35, 238
    apostles of, 200
    the Báb and, 36, 37–38
    Bahá'í Faith on, 231–33
    crucifixion of, 37–38
    foresight of, 102
    glossary definition for, 275
    as Messiah, 51, 233–36, 238
    miracles of, 242
    power of, 35, 98, 101
    recognition of, 36
    rejection of, 51, 68, 233, 238, 249–50
    return of, 12, 50–51, 74–75, 236–37,
        238–39
    as salvation for humanity, 37–38, 232,
        236
    successor of, 134–35
    in the Temple, 99
Jewish people, 233–36
Jináb-i-Bahá. See Bahá'u'lláh
Job
    faithfulness of, 200
    glossary definition for, 275
John the Baptist, 235, 239
judgment, divine, 160
justice, 41–42, 117–19, 150, 184

K

Karbilá, glossary definition for, 275
Kázim, Siyyid
    glossary definition for, 275
    Promised One and, 12, 13
Kingdom of God, 103, 149, 236, 237, 247–
    49
kings. See rulers
Kitáb-i-Aqdas. See Most Holy Book
knowledge, 101, 176–77
Koran
    the Báb and, 22

contents of, 98
    glossary definition for, 276
Krishna, Immaculate Manifestation of, 246

L

language, international auxiliary
    adoption of, 179–80, 229
    glossary definition for, 275
Last Day, 103–4, 251
    See also Day of Judgment
laws of God, 42, 112–14, 157, 190–91,
    241
League of Nations, 184
lepers, Jesus heals, 242
Lesser Covenant. See Covenant of Bahá'u'lláh
Lesser Peace
    establishment of, 216, 217
    glossary definition for, 276
    See also peace
life, purpose of, 5, 95, 107, 114–15
Local Spiritual Assemblies, 219, 223
    glossary definition for, 276
London, 'Abdu'l-Bahá in, 147
love, 41, 95, 115–16, 149–50, 158, 213–14

M

Máh-Kú, 22
Mahmúd, Shaykh, 80
Maiden, 32
Maitreye, 246
Manifestations of God
    glossary definition for, 276
    See also Prophets
marriage, 161–62, 193–95
martyrdom, 101–2
Mary, Virgin, 232
Master, the
    'Abdu'l-Bahá as, 139
    glossary definition for, 276
    See also 'Abdu'l-Bahá
material civilization, 173–74
materialists, 173
    glossary definition for, 276
material world, 115–16, 188–90
Mecca, glossary definition for, 276

Medina, glossary definition for, 276
men, equality and, 162–73
Messiah
    glossary definition for, 276
    Jesus as, 51, 233–36, 238
Micah, 74
Mihdí, Mírzá
    death of, 78
    glossary definition for, 277
Miller, Reverend William
    glossary definition for, 277
    return of Christ and, 12
miracles, 54–55, 242
Mírzá, glossary definition for, 277
Mírzá Yahyá. See Azal
moderation, 189–90, 256
Modern Age, 3–4, 215
Mongol, 39
    glossary definition for, 277
monks, 116
"moon" in New Testament, 50–51
Moses
    glossary definition for, 277
    power of, 98
Most Great Branch
    'Abdu'l-Bahá as, 139
    See also 'Abdu'l-Bahá
Most Great Peace, 216, 217, 225
    See also peace
Most Great Prison. See 'Akká
Most Holy Book (Kitáb-i-Aqdas), 80–81,
    117–18, 136
Mount Carmel
    Bahá'u'lláh at, 82–83, 124
    Universal House of Justice on, 248
Muḥammad, Mullá, 44–45
Muḥammad-'Alí, 141–42, 214
Muḥammad-Taqí, Shaykh, 125
Muḥammad (the Prophet), 75
    glossary definition for, 277
    misunderstandings about, 98
    qualities of, 98, 99–100
    successor of, 135
Mullá, glossary definition for, 277
Murtaḍáy-i-Anṣárí, Shaykh, 244–45
music, 196–97
Muslims, the Bible and, 232–33

Mystery of God, the
    'Abdu'l-Bahá as, 139
    See also 'Abdu'l-Bahá

N

Nabíl, 43–44
Najaf, glossary definition for, 277
Napoleon III, 66–67, 102
Náṣiri'd-Dín Sháh, 31
    Bábís attempt to kill, 28
    Bahá'u'lláh writes to, 64–65
    glossary definition for, 277
Naṣṣár, Ibráhím, 208
National Association for the Advancement of
    Colored People, Conference of,
    159
National Spiritual Assemblies, 219
    glossary definition for, 277
nations, international governing body of,
    182–85
Navváb (Ásíyih Khánum)
    glossary definition for, 277
    the poor and, 165
nearness to God, 41, 42–43
    barriers to, 189
    happiness and, 150
    prayer and, 151
    tests and, 202
New Hampshire, 146
New Testament, symbolism of, 48–51
new world order
    Bahá'í vision for, 225–30
    birth of, 217–18
    glossary definition for, 277
Nicolas, A. L. M., 37–38
North America, 146

O

obedience to God's laws, 42, 112–14, 157
old world order
    destruction of, 217–18
    glossary definition for, 278
    See also new world order
oneness
    of God, 93, 97, 157
    of humanity, 158–62, 203–4, 227–30

original sin, 241
Ottoman empire
    glossary definition for, 278
    government of, corruption in, 142–43
    sultan of (See 'Abdu'l-'Azíz, Sulṭán)

P

Paris, 'Abdu'l-Bahá in, 173
peace, 174
    achieving, 69
    international auxiliary language and, 180
    international governing body and, 183
    oneness of humanity and, 158, 160
    See also Lesser Peace; Most Great Peace
Peary, Admiral, 146
Persia. See Iran
Persian, Hidden Words in, 40
Peter (the Rock), 68, 134–35, 200, 250
Phelps, Myron, 205–7
physical cleanliness, 195
physicians, 195–96
Pius IX, Pope, 68
Plato, 244
politics, participation in, 256
poor, the, 42, 154, 178, 206
poverty, extremes of, 178, 229
prayer, 151–52, 195–96, 243–44
prejudice, 158–62, 170
press, the, 229
priests, 116
profession, 191–93
Progressive Revelation, 96, 149
Promised One, 12
    the Báb as, 23
    Bahá'u'lláh as, 5, 249–50, 251
Promise of World Peace, The, 257–58
Prophets
    attributes of God in, 99, 104, 239–40
    conduct of, 127
    foresight of, 102
    future appearance of, 119
    glossary definition for, 278
    identifying true ones, 237, 239
    laws of, 245, 247
    natures of, 99–100, 104

persecution and rejection of, 48, 49, 105,
        176
    power of, 98
    purpose of, 48, 95–96, 97–98, 111–13
    recognition of, 112
    religious leaders and, 49–51
    station of, 104
prosperity, true, 175
punishment, 118–19

Q

Qurratu'l-'Ayn, 164

R

race, 160–62
rebirth, Bahá'í writings on, 241
Red Cross, 245
religion
    decline in, 169–70
    importance of, 169
    intolerance of, 170
    oneness of, 157
    science and, 171–74, 176, 229
    unity of, 155, 245–46
    Western leaders and, 4
religious leaders
    justice and, 117
    Prophets and, 49–51
repentance, Bahá'í writings on, 241
revelation of Bahá'u'lláh
    process of, 89–91
    receipt of, 32
    significance of, 102–4, 129
    spiritual forces released by, 215–16, 217–
        18
reward, 118–19
Roman Catholicism, 135
Roosevelt, Theodore, 146
rulers
    Bahá'u'lláh addresses, 63–70, 117–18,
        176, 181–82, 216–17
    of nineteenth century, 63
    the poor and, 42, 178

S

salvation, Bahá'í writings on, 241–42
Satan, symbol of, 242–43
science, 171–74, 176, 177, 229
Seal of the Prophets, 22
seeker, 188, 259
self-knowledge, 114, 158
service, 192–93
Seven Valleys, 188
shah, glossary definition for, 278
Sháh-Bahrám, 246
Shaykh, glossary definition for, 278
Shí'ih Islam
    glossary definition for, 278
    origin of, 135
Shiraz
    the Báb in, 21
    glossary definition for, 278
    Mullá Ḥusayn in, 13–14
Shoghi Effendi
    appointed Guardian, 214–15
    glossary definition for, 278
Shrine of Bahá'u'lláh, 126
Shrine of the Báb, 124
Sinai, glossary definition for, 278
Siyyid, glossary definition for, 279
social welfare, 178
Socrates, 244
soul, the, 95
    the afterlife and, 107–9, 243–45
    the body and, 195–96
    journey of, 188
    nature of, 107–9, 171
    of Prophets, 99
Spiritual Assemblies
    duties of, 223
    Local and National, 219, 276
spiritual civilization, 173–74, 217
spiritual growth
    character and, 150, 153–54
    as process, 187–89, 255
    Prophets aid in, 111–13
    self-knowledge and, 114
"stars" in New Testament, 51
suffering, purpose of, 199–202
Sulaymaniyyah, Bahá'u'lláh in, 40
"sun" in New Testament, 50–51

Sunní Islam
    glossary definition for, 279
    origin of, 135

T

Tablet of Carmel, 124
Tabriz, the Báb in, 23
Táhirih (Qurratu'l-'Ayn), 164
Tehran, glossary definition for, 279
Tenth Avatar, 246
tests, purpose of, 199–202
Titanic, 'Abdu'l-Bahá and, 200–201
Torah, 235
Trinity, the, 240–41
truth, investigation of, 105, 175–76, 256,
    259–60
Turks, Young, 143
    glossary definition for, 279
twentieth century, 182

U

United Nations, 184–85
United States
    'Abdu'l-Bahá in, 146
    role of, 217
unity
    in diversity, 225–26
    of family, 194
    of humanity, 182, 227–30, 253
    of religions, 155, 245–46
Universal House of Justice
    establishment of, 214, 218
    glossary definition for, 279
    as infallible, 219
    seat of, 218, 248

V

Vaḥíd, 21
    glossary definition for, 279
Victoria, Queen, 68–69
Virgin Mary, 232
von Goumoens, Captain, 30

W

war, holy, 256
Washington D.C., 'Abdu'l-Bahá in, 161
wealth, 178–79, 189, 229
weapons, 173, 174, 181, 183
weights and measures, universal, 180, 229
welfare, social, 178
Wilhelm I, Kaiser, 67–68
Will and Testament of 'Abdu'l-Bahá
    content of, 213–14
    glossary definition for, 279
wings of humanity, 162–63, 174
wisdom, essence of, 118
women, 162–67
Word of God
    power of, 100–102, 152, 153, 253
    as standard, 105
    symbolism in, 50–51
    understanding of, 51–52
    See also Bhagavad-Gita; Bible; Koran;
        writings of Bahá'u'lláh
words, deeds and, 160, 161
work as worship, 191–93
world commonwealth, 228–30
    See also international governing body

world order. *See* new world order; old world
    order
World War I, 204–5
writings of Bahá'u'lláh
    process of revelation of, 89–91
    as proof of Prophethood, 90
    study of, 153
    truths and principles in, 129
    See also Book of Certitude; Book of the
        Covenant; Epistle to the Son of
        the Wolf; Hidden Words; Seven
        Valleys; Tablet of Carmel

Y

Young Turks, 143
    glossary definition for, 279

Z

Zoroaster
    glossary definition for, 280
    Iran and, 9
    Sháh-Bahrám and, 246

For more information about the Bahá'í Faith,
or to contact the Bahá'ís near you, visit
http://www.us.bahai.org/
or call
1-800-22-UNITE

BAHÁ'Í PUBLISHING AND
THE BAHÁ'Í FAITH

Bahá'í Publishing produces books based on the teachings of the Bahá'í Faith. Founded nearly 160 years ago, the Bahá'í Faith has spread to some 235 nations and territories and is now accepted by more than five million people. The word "Bahá'í" means "follower of Bahá'u'lláh." Bahá'u'lláh, the Founder of the Bahá'í Faith, asserted that He is the Messenger of God for all of humanity in this day. The cornerstone of His teachings is the establishment of the spiritual unity of humankind, which will be achieved by personal transformation and the application of clearly identified spiritual principles. Bahá'ís also believe that there is but one religion and that all the Messengers of God—among them Abraham, Zoroaster, Moses, Krishna, Buddha, Jesus, and Muḥammad—have progressively revealed its nature. Together, the world's great religions are expressions of a single, unfolding divine plan. Human beings, not God's Messengers, are the source of religious divisions, prejudices, and hatreds.

The Bahá'í Faith is not a sect or denomination of another religion, nor is it a cult or a social movement. Rather, it is a globally recognized independent world religion founded on new books of scripture revealed by Bahá'u'lláh.

Bahá'í Publishing is an imprint of the National Spiritual Assembly of the Bahá'ís of the United States.

OTHER BOOKS AVAILABLE
FROM BAHÁ'Í PUBLISHING

The Hidden Words
by Bahá'u'lláh

A collection of lyrical, gem-like verses of scripture that convey timeless spiritual wisdom "clothed in the garment of brevity," the Hidden Words is one of the most important and cherished scriptural works of the Bahá'í Faith.

Revealed by Bahá'u'lláh, the founder of the religion, the verses are a perfect guidebook to walking a spiritual path and drawing closer to God. They address themes such as turning to God, humility, detachment, and love, to name but a few. These verses are among Bahá'u'lláh's earliest and best-known works, having been translated into more than seventy languages and read by millions worldwide. This edition will offer many American readers their first introduction to the vast collection of Bahá'í scripture.

The Kitáb-i-Íqán: The Book of Certitude
by Bahá'u'lláh

The Book of Certitude is one of the most important scriptural works in all of religious history. In it Bahá'u'lláh gives a sweeping overview of religious truth, explaining the underlying unity of the world's religions, describing the universality of the revelations humankind has received from the Prophets of God, illuminating their fundamental teachings, and elucidating allegorical passages from the New Testament and the Koran that have given rise to misunderstandings among religious leaders, practitioners, and the public. Revealed in the span of two days and two nights, the work is, in the words of its translator, Shoghi Effendi, "the most important book written on the spiritual significance" of the Bahá'í Faith.

Advancement of Women: A Bahá'í Perspective
by Janet A. Khan and Peter J. Khan

Advancement of Women presents the Bahá'í Faith's global perspective on the equality of the sexes, including:
- The meaning of equality
- The education of women and the need for their participation in the world at large
- The profound effects of equality on the family and family relationships
- The intimate relationship between equality of the sexes and global peace
- Chastity, modesty, sexual harassment, and rape

The equality of women and men is one of the basic tenets of the Bahá'í Faith, and much is said on the subject in Bahá'í writings. Until now, however, no single volume created for a general audience has provided comprehensive coverage of the Bahá'í teachings on this topic. In this broad survey, husband-and-wife team Janet and Peter Khan address even those aspects of equality of the sexes that are usually ignored or glossed over in the existing literature.

Tactfully treating a subject that often provokes argumentation, contention, polarization of attitudes, and accusations, the authors elevate the discussion to a new level that challenges all while offending none.

The Bahá'í Faith: The Emerging Global Religion
by William S. Hatcher and J. Douglas Martin
Explore the history, teachings, structure, and community life of the worldwide Bahá'í community—what may well be the most diverse organized body of people on earth—through this revised and updated comprehensive introduction (2002).

Named by the *Encylopaedia Britannica* as a book that has made "significant contributions to knowledge and understanding" of religious thought, *The Bahá'í Faith* covers the most recent developments in a Faith that, in just over 150 years, has grown to become the second most widespread of the independent world religions.

An excellent introduction. [*The Bahá'í Faith*] offers a clear analysis of the religious and ethical values on which Bahá'ism is based (such as all-embracing peace, world harmony, the important role of women, to mention only a few)."—Annemarie Schimmel, past president, International Association for the History of Religions

"Provide[s] non-Bahá'í readers with an excellent introduction to the history, beliefs, and sociopolitical structure of a religion that originated in Persia in the mid-1800s and has since blossomed into an international organization with . . . adherents from almost every country on earth."
—*Montreal Gazette*

It's Not Your Fault: How Healing Relationships Change Your Brain & Can Help You Overcome a Painful Past
by Patricia Romano McGraw
Simply put, you can't think your way to happiness if you're suffering the effects of trauma or abuse. Yet every day, millions receive this message from a multi-billion-dollar self-help industry. As a result, many think it's their fault when their efforts to heal themselves fail. Far too many sincere, intelligent, and highly motivated people who have followed popular advice for self-healing still feel depressed, anxious, unloved, and unlovable. Why is this? If popular pathways for self-healing don't work, what does? How can those who suffer begin to find relief, function better, and feel genuinely optimistic, relaxed, loved, and lovable? This engaging and highly readable book, based on the author's professional experience in treating those who suffer from the devastating effects of emotional trauma, offers hope for those who suffer and those who care about them. McGraw describes how trauma affects the brain and, therefore, one's ability to carry out "good advice"; explains the subtle and largely hidden processes of attunement and attachment that take place between parents and children, examining their impact on all future relationships; tells what is needed for healing to occur; discusses the profound health benefits of spirituality and a relationship with God in assisting and accelerating the healing process; and suggests how members of the helping professions can begin to tap the deepest, most authentic parts of themselves to touch the hearts of those they seek to help.

Marriage beyond Black and White: An Interracial Family Portrait
by David Douglas and Barbara Douglas

A powerful story about the marriage of a Black man and a White woman, *Marriage beyond Black and White* offers a poignant and sometimes painful look at what it was like to be an interracial couple in the United States from the early 1940s to the mid-1990s. Breaking one of the strongest taboos in American society at the time, Barbara Wilson Tinker and Carlyle Douglas met, fell in love, married, and began raising a family. At the time of their wedding, interracial marriage was outlawed in twenty-seven states and was regarded as an anathema in the rest.

Barbara began writing their story to record both the triumphs and hardships of interracial marriage. Her son David completed the family chronicle. The result will uplift and inspire any reader whose life is touched by injustice, offering an invaluable perspective on the roles of faith and spiritual transformation in combating prejudice and racism.

Refresh and Gladden My Spirit: Prayers and Meditations from Bahá'í Scripture
Introduction by Pamela Brode

Discover the Bahá'í approach to prayer with this uplifting collection of prayers and short, inspirational extracts from Bahá'í scripture. More than 120 prayers in *Refresh and Gladden My Spirit* offer solace and inspiration on themes including spiritual growth, nearness to God, comfort, contentment, happiness, difficult times, healing, material needs, praise and gratitude, and strength, to name only a few. An introduction by Pamela Brode examines the powerful effects of prayer and meditation in daily life, outlines the Bahá'í approach to prayer, and considers questions such as "What is prayer?" "Why pray?" "Are our prayers answered?" and "Does prayer benefit the world?"

Release the Sun
by William Sears

Millennial fervor gripped many people around the world in the early nineteenth century. While Christians anticipated the return of Jesus Christ, a wave of expectation swept through Islam that the "Lord of the Age" would soon appear. In Persia, this reached a dramatic climax on May 23, 1844, when a twenty-five-year-old merchant from S̲h̲íráz named Siyyid 'Alí-Muḥammad, later titled "the Báb," announced that he was the bearer of a divine Revelation destined to transform the spiritual life of the human race. Furthermore, he claimed that he was but the herald of another Messenger, who would soon bring a far greater Revelation that would usher in an age of universal peace. Against a backdrop of wide-scale moral decay in Persian society, this declaration aroused hope and excitement among all classes. The Báb quickly attracted tens of thousands of followers, including influential members of the clergy—and the brutal hand of a fearful government bent on destroying this movement that threatened to rock the established order.

Release the Sun tells the extraordinary story of the Báb, the Prophet-Herald of the Bahá'í Faith. Drawing on contemporary accounts, William Sears vividly describes one of the most significant but little-known periods in religious history since the rise of Christianity and Islam.

Seeking Faith: Is Religion Really What You Think It Is?
by Nathan Rutstein

What's your concept of religion? A 2001 Gallup Poll on religion in America found that while nearly two out of three Americans claim to be a member of a church or synagogue, more than half of those polled believe that religion is losing its influence on society. *Seeking Faith* examines today's concepts of religion and the various reasons why people are searching in new directions for hope and spiritual guidance. Author Nathan Rutstein explores the need for a sense of purpose, direction, and meaning in life, and the need for spiritual solutions to global problems in the social, economic, environmental, and political realms. Rutstein also discusses the concept of the Spiritual Guide, or Divine Educator, and introduces the teachings of Bahá'u'lláh and the beliefs of the Bahá'í Faith.

A Wayfarer's Guide to Bringing the Sacred Home
by Joseph Sheppherd
What's the spiritual connection between self, family, and community? Why is it so important that we understand and cultivate these key relationships? *A Wayfarer's Guide to Bringing the Sacred Home* offers a Bahá'í perspective on issues that shape our lives and the lives of those around us: the vital role of spirituality in personal transformation, the divine nature of child-rearing and unity in the family, and the importance of overcoming barriers to building strong communities—each offering joy, hope, and confidence to a challenged world. Inspiring extracts and prayers from Bahá'í scripture are included. This is an enlightening read for anyone seeking to bring spirituality into their daily lives.

Visit your favorite bookstore today to find or request these titles from Bahá'í Publishing.

Printed in the United States
200079BV00010B/1-93/A